THE SOVIET UNION AND THE ASIA-PACIFIC REGION

THE SOVIET UNION AND THE ASIA-PACIFIC REGION

Views from the Region

Edited by Pushpa Thambipillai
and
Daniel C. Matuszewski

PRAEGER

New York
Westport, Connecticut
London

Library of Congress Cataloging-in-Publication Data

The Soviet Union and the Asia-Pacific Region: view from the region / edited by
  Pushpa Thambipillai and Daniel C. Matuszewski.
        p.   cm.
    Includes bibliographies and index.
    ISBN 0–275–93212–5 (alk. paper)
    1. Asia—Foreign relations—Soviet Union. 2. Soviet Union—Foreign relations—Asia.
  3. Pacific Ocean Region—Foreign relations—Soviet Union. 4. Soviet Union—Foreign
  relations—Pacific Ocean Region. 5. Soviet Union—Foreign relations—1975–
  I. Thambipillai, Pushpa. II. Matuszewski, Daniel C.
  DS33.4.S65S686   1989
  327.47095—dc19   88–27506

Library of Congress Catalog Card Number: 88–27506
ISBN: 0–275–93212–5

First published in 1989

Praeger Publishers, One Madison Avenue, New York, NY 10010
A division of Greenwood Press, Inc.

Printed in the United States of America

The paper used in this book complies with the Permanent Paper Standard issued by the
National Information Standards Organization (Z39.48–1984).

10 9 8 7 6 5 4 3 2 1

Contents

Preface

In the countries of the Asia-Pacific region, there has been renewed interest in the Soviet Union. This interest is a consequence of Mikhail Gorbachev's ascent to Soviet leadership, his domestic reform programs, and his overtures for friendship and enhanced cooperation with the countries of the Asia-Pacific region. Although it was not called a "Gorbachev doctrine," the Soviet leader's major speech in the Soviet Far East city of Vladivostok on 28 July 1986 was widely read and commented upon throughout East and Southeast Asia. This speech was accompanied by a flurry of diplomatic activity in the region that has been chronicled in the chapters of this volume. Asia-Pacific peoples and leaders were asking: How much has the Soviet Union really changed? Is it genuine in seeking new relationships with our countries? Will China, the principal target of Soviet overtures, respond positively and, if so, what will the implications be for the rest of the region? What do the Soviets have to offer the region in practical terms?

The main driving force behind the unprecedented recent spate of Soviet economic and political overtures to the nations of the Asia-Pacific region is the crisis in the Soviet political economy that has been evolving over the past two decades. The crisis has resulted from the volatile combination of the increasing obsolescence of its internal economic and political mechanisms and the rapidly improving competitive economic posture of other major international actors.

There has been a slow and painful emergence of consensus among Soviet policy and technocratic elites that the costs of muddling through as usual will be higher and ultimately more corrosive to the stability of the system than will a series of sharp surgical steps designed to reshape and rationalize the structures of the outmoded command economy. Mikhail Gorbachev is engaged in a highly complex reform experiment intended to modernize the interface between Soviet politics and economics and permit the USSR to retain its place among the world's leading powers at the turn of the next century.

To accomplish this, the Soviet Union needs both a period of relative international peace and a benign set of relations with its major competitors in Asia, Europe, and North America. The dynamics of its position imply that it needs a *peredyshka*, a breathing space, in world affairs in order to concentrate on its own domestic transformation. It also needs a major shift of investment from the military to the civilian sphere and, in the most desirable of scenarios, financial and technological inputs from its more affluent and advanced global competitors. To a substantial degree, Moscow has been impelled into reform by the developmental examples of Japan and China and the striking economic dynamism of the smaller nations of the region, as well as by the real dangers of a fall from competitive grace.

Collectively, the chapters in this volume provide a broad portrait of the state of current Soviet relations with the countries of the region, perceptions of the Soviet role, and prospects for change. In examining Gorbachev's Soviet Union, the contributors evince a mixture of enthusiasm and apprehension about Moscow's new policy overtures. There is skepticism about the likelihood of truly fundamental shifts, either in domestic control structures in the USSR or in the traditional Soviet reliance on military instrumentalities in foreign policy behavior. Past experience with the Soviet Union has led to an almost universal "wait-and-see" attitude among scholars and the policymakers they quote. At the same time, there is intense curiosity to see whether the promising rhetoric can or will be matched by deeds.

The geometric pace of the new technological revolution, emerging as it has in good part in the dynamic countries of the Asia-Pacific region, has presented Moscow with the shock equivalent of a second Port Arthur. Coping with that challenge will entail economic, social, and political adjustments of unpredictable and intriguing dimensions for the Soviet system. Analysts from the area are watching this phenomenon closely.

This book would not have been possible without the support of various institutions and individuals. Principal funding came from the East-West Center, and we are particularly grateful for the sustained support of Victor Li, president, and Seiji Naya, director of the Resource Systems Institute. Charles E. Morrison, coordinator of the International Relations Program, was involved in initiating and organizing the project and assisted the editors in preparing this volume. The project was cosponsored by the Soviet Union in the Pacific-Asia Region (Supar) program of the University of Hawaii, headed by John Stephan. Stephan and Patricia Polansky, Russian bibliographer at the University's Hamilton library, generously gave of their time to help plan the project and participate in it. We are grateful to the International Research and Exchanges Board (IREX) at Princeton, New Jersey, for allowing Daniel Matuszewski the time to assist in editing this volume.

We also wish to thank those involved at the East-West Center in the preparation of the manuscript: Lynn Garrett, Faye Sotirakis, and David Puhlick, editors, Sheree Groves, International Relations Program Project Assistant, and Dorine McConnell and Dorothy Villasenor, secretaries, as well as the staff of Praeger Publishers.

The views expressed in this book are those of the individual authors. We are grateful to them for their enthusiasm and cooperation throughout the project.

THE SOVIET UNION AND THE ASIA-PACIFIC REGION

Soviet Reforms and the Asia-Pacific Challenge

Daniel C. Matuszewski

Over the past two years the new Soviet leadership has generated a series of striking and potentially far-reaching domestic reform programs. These reforms are linked both in their origins and potential effects to Moscow's intricate relations with the countries of East Asia and the Pacific. Mikhail Gorbachev and his technocrat lieutenants have begun to implement a number of innovative departures in the economic, social, and cultural spheres that could have substantial impact both on political structures within the USSR and on Soviet approaches to China, Japan, the countries of the Association of Southeast Asian Nations (ASEAN), and the island nations of the region.

STAGNATION: STIMULUS TO CHANGE

For at least the past decade the Soviet society and economy have been afflicted by a peculiar inertia and stagnation, a paralysis of economic mechanisms brought about by overreliance on central planning structures inadequate for the increasingly complicated tasks of a technotronic age. Contributing to this stagnation was overinvestment in military programs, which had virtually become Moscow's sole instrumentality in dealing with the outside developing world. These imbalances have brought about a societal crisis that Gorbachev has vigorously deplored in a variety of media and public affairs settings since his accession. A number of critical features have come to mark the Soviet economy and society over the past decade: Moscow's almost unidimensional reliance on forms of military behavior in the foreign policy arena; the overcommitment and overexpenditure entailed by such reliance; the decline in economic growth rates; the increasing apathy and nonproductivity of the Soviet worker; and, perhaps most important, the serious decline in public morale, especially among the economic, cultural, and political elites.

In the more simple, iron-and-steel industrial age of the 1930s or 1950s, it may have been possible for a great power to experience a protracted period of stall and malaise and still remain competitive globally. However, the geometric pace of technological innovation in the 1980s, and the significance and impact of semiconductors, microprocessing techniques, and supercomputers have changed the nature of economic and military competition so dramatically and irreversibly that the Soviet Union can ill afford such stagnation.

In the earlier, simpler age, Moscow could overcome growth problems with lavish investment strategies: massive infusions of human resources or capital designed to build a lagging area of its economy or to "catch up with and overtake the West." The decades of the 1970s and 1980s presented the Soviet Union with a far more complicated set of technological challenges. The information and communications revolution caught Soviet society and its leadership unaware and unprepared.

The Brezhnev leadership and its lack of imagination manifested that unpreparedness; during that period the Soviet economy began to lag badly in almost all sectors. The poor performance of Soviet agriculture was almost proverbial, and industrial growth also flagged as essential investments in machine tool replacement and upgrading were not made. Central planning structures hobbled local management initiative, leaving managers without incentives or the latitude to innovate or correct glaring production inefficiencies. The padding of output figures became the norm, and *pokazukha*, bureaucratic sham and whitewash, disguised the true state of production. Crippling both agriculture and industry alike was the horrendous condition of the transportation and shipping infrastructure.[1]

Complicating the economic picture has been the apathy of the working classes. The decades of the 1960s and 1970s had seen the evolution of something resembling a tacit social contract between the party and the working populace, whereby the latter exchanged civic obedience and political allegiance to the system for assured social welfare support, a basic standard of living, and minimum work guarantees. Such guaranteed employment spawned minimal work habits, and low pay and lack of incentives bred negligible interest and morale. Worker productivity remained correspondingly low.[2] Attitudes of lassitude and minimal commitment lay behind the popular expression, "The government pretends to pay us and we pretend to work." Under such conditions, absenteeism, alcoholism, poor work habits, and corruption proliferated, causing some Western economists to use the term "kleptocracy" to describe the Soviet economic system. It was clearly an unhealthy situation.

Gorbachev's current restructuring is a major effort to liberate the talents and creative energies of a people that has grown far too accustomed to the free lunch the state welfare system has provided. In the face of Japanese and Western development of advanced microcircuitry, data management wizardry, and computer-literate work forces, the Soviets can no longer make do with stubby pencils, abacuses, and stifling welfare structures. An acknowledgment of the implications of the extraordinary shifts in technology, information accumulation and utilization, and management techniques is the driving force behind current Soviet reforms.

INTERNAL OBSTACLES TO REFORM

Any analysis of this critical, potentially watershed, period in Soviet history should include a careful assessment of stable features of the system as well as those pressures for change that could generate important modifications in the system's structure. The systemic obstacles inhibiting fundamental reform are all too real. The reform approaches of the new leadership challenge a number of vested interests and incumbents whose present and potential resistance will affect the success or failure of the enterprise.

Radical reform measures immediately raise concerns about a potential challenge to the position and privileges of the Communist party in a centrally structured command economy and political system. Attempts to appoint key personnel on the basis of talent and merit fly in the face of the *nomenklatura* system, a system of approved appointments from a closed list drawn up at the center of the establishment. Reform initiatives intended to rationalize procedures threaten the positions of incumbents in the ministerial bureaucracies, who will put up determined resistance to any loss of office or diminution of their authority. In a somewhat different manner, reform initiatives threaten traditional managerial groups, which are inexperienced in new entrepreneurial settings. Even where their positions may not be obviously jeopardized, such managers are likely to carry on old, inefficient business practices as the safest and surest approach while initially chaotic and often contradictory new procedures are being introduced. Their expectation is likely to be that the innovations will be stillborn and that it may be best to await a return to business as usual. Middle managers are often faced with a special dilemma: Old levels of accountability remain at the same time that new standards of performance are demanded. New elements of insecurity are introduced into the system, important safety nets are removed, and the potential for bankruptcy and firings adds a threatening new dimension.

The reform initiatives of the Gorbachev regime also threaten the working class in some unexpected ways. The leadership has attempted to elaborate a new work ethic, asking people to work harder, drink less, and turn out higher-quality goods while offering little in the way of incentives, attractive salaries, or benefits. The relative predominance of sticks and absence of carrots is no more appreciated by workers than it is by managerial groups, and it is popularly perceived as a violation of the tacit social contract between the regime and the citizenry. Sociological surveys done by specialized Soviet institutes over the past two years have documented workers' lack of understanding and enthusiasm for the early reforms; continuing distrust would be a major obstacle to their successful implementation.

The reformers' attempts to eradicate corruption and the illegal second economy raise parallel threats to the traditional mores of the population. This campaign endangers the pervasive and time-sanctioned pattern of corruption that has marked all social and economic levels and jeopardizes habits of behavior that have permitted generations of Soviet citizens to evade and circumvent crippling regulations, notorious shortages, and inefficiencies. The vigorous crackdown on this tradition of genial corruption removes many of the treasured safety valves that had made the official system tolerable. These efforts are doubly mistrusted by the populace, which doubts that the safety valves will truly be replaced by any equitable supply of goods and resources at comparable levels of accessibility.

If moves against petty and pervasive corruption threaten the poor comforts of the populace as a whole, they also threaten the interests of the non-Russian minorities in the nationality republics even more directly and specifically. Over the past twenty years, during the Brezhnev period, the Muscovite center has handled the management of center-periphery relations with an approach resembling benign neglect. In return for implicit guarantees of ultimate political allegiance to the Soviet regime, Moscow has turned a blind eye to the republics' assumption of substantial local control over the social, cultural, and, to a certain extent, economic lives of their communities while also evolving indigenous patterns of corruption that permitted them to compensate for the more glaring systemic inefficiencies. Such habits are no longer acceptable to the internationalist Gorbachev and his rational technocratic lieutenants, and they have moved with a vengeance to crush corruption and inefficiency, pull the reins of economic and political control back into the hands of Moscow, and rationalize the performance of the all-Union system.

Whatever the merits of this effort, it exacerbates minority sensitivities by closing down the mechanisms of the illegal but cherished second economy, thereby crystallizing aspirations for more equitable socioeconomic roles in the official establishment and perhaps generating demands for a more truly federalist structure for the republics. The purges, riots, and demonstrations seen in Kazakhstan, Armenia, and Azerbaijan since late 1986 have only been the most overt symptom of these trends. Managing minority aspirations while imposing new rational controls over the all-Union economy will be not the least of Gorbachev's dilemmas.

GLASNOST: ENLISTING THE ELITE

The parallel campaign of *glasnost*—the newly permissible criticism of economic, social, and cultural inefficiencies and shortcomings—has as its primary function the exposure and removal of obstacles that might hinder the rational restructuring of the state economy. As a secondary function, it is intended to enlist the support for reform of the cultural intelligentsia, historically skeptical of the regime. It is in this aspect of the reform strategy that the Gorbachev regime has taken some of its more daring departures. Sensing an urgent social need to break with the more paralyzing forms of official hypocrisy from the past, the leadership has eased censorship and allowed an extraordinary burst of creativity in literature, theater, cinema, television, the news media as a whole, and professional and specialized journals.

The refreshing and often startling flood of cultural activity has indeed served to co-opt and commit a substantial portion of the intelligentsia, firmly enlisting them in the reform enterprise. Nevertheless, the very success of this phenomenon risks its ultimate reversal. The problem is that there are no natural limits to this new "openness" to review the mistakes of the present and the crimes of the past. The perpetrators or beneficiaries of the Stalinist crimes and abuses remain entrenched throughout the establishment, and the energetic efforts of the cultural intelligentsia and the technocratic elites, each with its own reasons, to unmask these individuals introduce the possibility of some explosive scenarios. The ferocious verbal battles currently being fought on the cultural scene give only the slightest indication of the potential for confrontation between these social forces.

An open-ended process of social criticism carries obvious seeds of political confrontation as well and clearly threatens the coercive apparatus of the state—the security agencies and other repressive organs that have been closely associated with the crimes of the past and the continuing injustices of the present. The centrifugal force created by a squaring of accounts will slow and deflect the reform process.

INTERNAL AND EXTERNAL PRESSURES FOR REFORM

In spite of these imposing and possibly crushing structural obstacles, the pressures, indeed imperatives, for change and reform impale the Soviet leadership and the system on the horns of a dilemma. The stagnation of the Soviet economy and crisis of morale within the leadership contrasted with continued innovation or growth outside the Soviet Union may make the costs of maintaining the status quo much higher than those engendered by the introduction of radical reforms. Many in the Soviet intellectual, cultural, technocratic, and managerial elites have long been persuaded of the need to repair and restore the prestige and image of Soviet society. The proud Soviet, and especially Russian, elites have been intensely embarrassed by the gross inefficiencies of the system and have become enthusiastic supporters and participants in the reform process. It is less clear that they have an effective understanding of the structural nature of the problem and can devise an adequate set of systemic responses.

The fragility of the reform phenomenon—and the ultimate costs of its potential failure—are only too obvious to its proponents and practitioners. Given the imposing internal obstacles and opposition to reform, the reformers are all the more intent on reducing the external pressures on such transformation and on establishing new international links that will support their economic and social restructuring. Given the dynamics of the international economy, the Soviet Union's position in relation to the nations of the Asia-Pacific region may be the most promising source of stimulus for change.

A prime example of this is the technological advances of Japan, especially in the computer and electronics fields. If Japan's position at the cutting edge of high technology were not enough to catch Moscow's attention, its recent leap past the Soviet Union to become the world's second largest producer of goods and services (as measured by the gross national product) definitely played that role. To fall behind Japan, a country with less than half the Soviet Union's population, was a terrible shock to Moscow. The impact of this phenomenon has been as dramatic as the impact of Japan's military victory over tsarist Russia in 1904—an event that played a central role in the genesis of the 1905 Russian Revolution. The geometric pace of Tokyo's economic and technological advances has compounded Moscow's internal anxieties and helped jolt the Soviet system out of its lethargy.

The broad-ranging and unexpectedly successful economic reforms introduced in the late 1970s and early 1980s by the Chinese under Deng Xiaoping have had a similarly catalytic effect on Soviet thinking and practice. Deng had declared that it does not matter whether a cat is black or white as long as it catches mice, and through a coherent and intelligently staged set of reform measures, the Chinese leadership had begun to make significant economic and technological advances.

The specter of a technology- and capital-rich Japan somehow melding its resources with the increasingly inventive and energetic China— a melding further backed by a protective and, in Soviet eyes, potentially aggressive U.S. military presence—has not only triggered anxiety in Moscow, but has served to stimulate and shape Gorbachev's intense new drive for economic and social reform in the Soviet Union. As he has said repeatedly and with increasing urgency, whether the USSR enters the twenty-first century as a first-rate power or not depends directly on the success or failure of the Soviet response to this challenge, that is, the success or failure of his own reform movement.

Gorbachev's perception of these issues and their clear linkage in his mind to Soviet overtures toward the countries of the Asia-Pacific region was expressed in his Vladivostok speech of July 1986.[3] Addressing worker and party groups in the Soviet Far East, Gorbachev not only underlined his sense of the economic and social deficiencies of the system in those regions of the Soviet Union, but made it clear that those shortcomings were characteristic of the Soviet system as a whole. Problems of poor planning, inadequate or inappropriate investment, inept or inert management, an insufficient and at times apathetic labor force, a miserable transportation network and infrastructure, and unimaginative policy guidance from Moscow—all were crippling the region and the country as a whole and preventing the Soviet Union from taking advantage of the enormous natural resources and economic opportunities available to build productive relations with the rapidly advancing nations of the dynamic Asia-Pacific area.[4]

Gorbachev emphasized both the sheer size of this area and the extraordinarily rich and complex cultural heritage of the great countries that share in the drama and challenge of its development: China, Japan, the ASEAN nations, Australia and New Zealand, and the United States. Stressing this region's importance in the future, he did not hesitate to point to its advantages in comparison to a heavily militarized and politically fragmented Europe. By contrast, in spite of the existence of some obvious hot spots, in the Asia-Pacific region the pattern of conventional and strategic weapons deployment and the corresponding network of political alignments are much less dense. This provides enormous opportunities for positive economic development and cultural interaction. His speeches in Vladivostok and throughout the week of his visit to the Soviet Far East were marked by a series of overtures to the individual nations of the area for the development of productive bilateral relations and an enhanced pattern of multilateral regional cooperation.

NEW SOVIET RELATIONS WITH CHINA

China occupies a special position in Gorbachev's concerns and projections. In the Vladivostok presentation, he made clear that after almost two decades of verbal and often considerably more deadly jousting between the two socialist giants, Moscow is seriously ready to explore the establishment of normal relations with Beijing. Aside from specific overtures—a token withdrawal of Soviet troops from the Mongolian People's Republic, a compromise on demarcation of the Amur River border, and an agreement on joint construction of the Xinjiang-Kazakhstan rail link—Gorbachev depicted a context for cooperation even more intriguing.

It is Gorbachev's view that history itself has set out a common, extraordinarily weighty, mission for China and the Soviet Union. Critical trends in the increasingly interdependent world economy depend on the performance of these two great socialist powers. Beijing and Moscow share an identical goal: acceleration of their domestic socioeconomic development. There is a historic fit between the priorities and the purposes of the two states. Under these circumstances, there is excellent reason for them to be mutually supportive, to cooperate and share experience and resources in the attainment of common goals. Most important, there is an immediate reason for coordination in the unusual and highly promising complementarity of their two economies. In Gorbachev's words, enormous opportunities were literally knocking at the door.[5]

These are dramatic rhetorical steps away from the confrontational stance Moscow had taken toward Beijing for more than two decades. Two patterns coalesced in the late 1970s to begin to moderate the Soviet perception of China: (1) faltering Soviet economic performance, compounded in good part by an overinvestment in expensive weapons programs and opportunistic military meddling in regional conflicts and (2) China's initiation of a program of reforms that promised to transform it into a major and very different economic power than might earlier have been anticipated. Soviet analysts had been looking closely at the Chinese experience throughout the 1960s and 1970s and had evolved an interesting framework for analysis and interpretation. In reading that extensive and intricate literature, one could not escape the conclusion—especially at the nadir of Russian-Chinese relations that occurred during the atrocities of the Cultural

Revolution at the peak of Mao's political machinations—that many Soviet specialists were wielding their thinking and writing about China as a two-edged sword, both as a way of understanding and interpreting the Chinese phenomenon and as a way of obliquely commenting on and criticizing Soviet political and economic realities. China became a prism through which Soviet structural flaws could be attacked in Aesopian terms.[6]

Having thus closely studied and utilized the Chinese experiment during the worst of times in the late 1960s and early 1970s, these Soviet analysts-cum-policymakers were in a position to use the positive innovations in Chinese economic and political approaches in the early 1980s in much the same way. It is important to understand these parallels as well as the background and profile of the Soviet analysis establishment, which helped to shape the shifts in policy toward China and Asia.[7]

PERSONNEL CHANGES AND REFORM

Since mid-1985 there have been widespread personnel changes not only in the Soviet Foreign Ministry and Central Committee departments responsible for China and Asia, but also in the directorships and personnel of the key institutes of the Academy of Sciences. Furthermore, something resembling a consensus seems to have emerged within the Soviet China studies and policymaking community. The view is that China may be on the verge of some important reform breakthroughs. The China watchers believe it would be very much in the interests of the USSR not only to follow that process closely and sympathetically, but to attempt to normalize Sino-Soviet relations, find some common socialist ground on which to expand economic and political cooperation, and gain some breathing space for essential Soviet reform programs. Personnel shifts at upper diplomatic and political levels have helped to redesign and redirect the Soviet foreign policy apparatus and have created a new institutional environment conducive to the possible improvement of relations not only between Moscow and Beijing, but also between Moscow and other major countries of the Asia-Pacific region.

Eduard Shevardnadze has replaced Andrei Gromyko as minister of foreign affairs, thereby removing a long-entrenched incumbent and supplanting him with a party and police functionary from a small Caucasian republic. This clearly placed the reins of foreign policy control more directly in Gorbachev's hands. Similarly, the senior diplomat from the Soviet career service, Anatoly Dobrynin, was put in charge of the International Department of the Central Committee of the Party and that department was strengthened by a number of other senior appointments, substantially enhancing its foreign policy role vis-à-vis the Foreign Ministry and making it more responsive to Gorbachev's intentions and programs. Gorbachev and his subordinates in these positions have repeatedly made it clear that, in spite of the significance of arms control issues with the United States, the Soviet Union would seek to deemphasize relations with the United States in its diplomacy and would undertake more active efforts to create linkages with other important world areas.

Within the first year and a half of Gorbachev's incumbency, the new foreign policy apparatus composed some impressive rhetorical flourishes addressed to the countries of the Asia-Pacific region, of which the Vladivostok speech of July 1986 was only the most prominent. The Ministry of Foreign Affairs itself was further restructured with the creation of new departments of South Asian, Pacific Ocean, and international economic affairs. New ambassadors were appointed to China and Japan, and there were changes in the leadership of key research institutes and policy publications.[8] The significance of these personnel and organizational changes for individual countries and subregions is noted in many of the subsequent chapters in this volume.

THE NEW SOVIET IMPERATIVE

The real significance of Gorbachev's 1986 speech in Vladivostok lay not so much in his political gestures toward China or his nuclear proposals designed to contain U.S. strategic deployments in the region—although these approaches too have their importance for Moscow—but in his expressed fears about maintaining Soviet economic competitiveness, his perceptions of the commercial and technological dynamism of the Asia-Pacific region, and his clearly articulated intention to expand Soviet trade and access to advanced technology in order to stimulate innovation in the sluggish Soviet economy. Whether or not Gorbachev's new diplomatic and commercial establishments are equal to the task and can go beyond their initial rhetorical flourishes, the domestic stimuli for such a courtship are immediate and urgent.[9]

NOTES

1. Seweryn Bialer, *The Soviet Paradox* (New York: Alfred A. Knopf, 1986), 57–80.
2. Mikhail Heller and Aleksandr Nekrich, *Utopiia u vlasti: Istoriia Sovetskogo Soiuza s 1917 goda do nashikh dnei (Utopia and Power: History of the Soviet Union from 1917 up to our Days)*, second revised edition (London: Overseas Publi-

cations Interchange Ltd., 1986). See also Blair A. Ruble, "The Social Dimensions of Perestroyka," *Soviet Economy* 3 (April–June 1987): 171–183. The latter work cites useful analysis from Peter Hauslohner, "The Gorbachev Regime as a 'Yuppie' Administration." Unpublished paper presented at the conference, "Gorbachev's First Year," University of California at Berkeley, 21–23 March 1986.

3. Daniel C. Matuszewski, "Nationalities in the Soviet Future: Trends under Gorbachev," in Lawrence W. Lerner and Donald W. Treadgold, *Gorbachev and the Soviet Future* (Boulder, Colo.: Westview Press, forthcoming).

4. *Perestroika neotlozhna, ona kasaetsia vsekh i vo vsem. Sbornik materialov o poezdke M.S. Gorbacheva na Dal'nii Vostok, 25–31 iiulia 1986 goda* (*Restructuring Is Urgent, It Concerns Everyone and Everything. A Collection of Materials on the Trip of M. S. Gorbachev to the Far East Region, 25–32 July 1986*) (Moscow: Political Literature Publishing House, 1986).

5. For a more extended and reflective description of these systemic difficulties, see the English-language version of Gorbachev's recent book, *Perestroika: New Thinking for Our Country and for the World* (New York: Harper & Row, 1987).

6. Bialer's chapter on the Sino-Soviet conflict in *Soviet Paradox*, 232–256; see also Kenneth G. Lieberthal, "Sino-Soviet Conflict in the 1970s: Its Evolution and Implications for the Strategic Triangle," R-2342–NA (Santa Monica, Calif.: Rand Corporation, July 1978); William G. Hyland, "The Sino-Soviet Conflict: A Search for New Security Strategies," in Richard H. Solomon, ed., *Asian Security in the 1980s* (Cambridge, Mass.: Oelgeschlager, Gunn and Hain, 1982). For a recent Chinese look at these patterns that takes a cautious view of Soviet post-Vladivostok overtures on Vietnam, Afghanistan, and Mongolia, see Han Nianlong, "Views on the Current Situation in the Asia-Pacific Region," *Journal of the Chinese People's Institute of Foreign Affairs*, No. 4 (June 1987): 1–9.

7. See Gilbert Rozman, *A Mirror for Socialism: Soviet Criticisms of China* (Princeton, N.J.: Princeton University Press, 1985); Gretchen Ann Sandles, "Soviet Images of the People's Republic of China, 1949–1979," (doctoral diss., University of Michigan, 1981); Morris Rothenberg, *Whither China: The View from the Kremlin* (Miami, Fla.: University of Miami, Center for Advanced International Studies, 1977); F. M. Burlatskii, *Mao Tszedun i ego nasledniki (Mao Zedong and His Heirs)* (Moscow: International Relations, 1979); and for a specialized, especially polemical view, see Victor Louis, *The Coming Decline of the Chinese Empire* (New York: New York Times Books, 1979).

Also see, for example, *Obshchestvo i gosudarstvo v Kitae: Tezisy i doklady (Society and State in China: Theses and Reports)*, three volumes (Moscow: Academy of Sciences of the USSR, Institute of Oriental Studies, 1976); G. D. Sukharchuk, ed., *Kitai: obshchestvo i gosudarstvo (China: Society and State)* (Moscow: Nauka Publishing House, 1973); and L. P. Deliusin, ed., *Kitai: traditsii i sovremennost (China: Traditions and Modernity)*, (Moscow: Nauka Publishing House, 1976). By contrast, see the much harsher series of volumes that continued to appear throughout the 1970s criticizing Chinese politics,

"A Dangerous Course," *Opasnyi kurs. Pekin: kurs, vrazhdebnyi miru, demokratii i sotsializmu (A Dangerous Course. Peking: A Course Hostile to Peace, Democracy, and Societies)* (Moscow: Politizdat Publishing House, 1974).

8. Arnold L. Horelick, "Soviet Foreign Policy under Gorbachev," in Murray Feshbach, ed., *National Security Issues of the USSR* (Dordrecht: Martinus Nijhoff Publishers, 1987); Gail Warshofsky Lapidus, "The USSR and Asia in 1986: Gorbachev's New Initiatives," *Asian Survey*, January 1987.

The Russians have had a long and distinguished tradition of analysis of the languages, cultures, and economies of the countries on their southern and eastern peripheries. Within their ideological framework, the Soviets have continued that tradition and invested even more dramatically in this impressive research establishment. Over the past two decades, this analytical and scholarly community has become increasingly sophisticated and has reached out for accurate readings for the use of Soviet decision makers. The ideological tone of their work has been modified considerably, and a new, at times almost naive, emphasis has been placed on the need for scientific predictability. In any event, Soviet scholarship on the countries of the Asia-Pacific region has expanded in volume and improved appreciably in quality, and it is clear that new investments in and commitments to this research establishment have been made in the past few years.

Academy institutes in Moscow and the outlying republics have been restructured, restaffed, and strengthened; new centers for Asia-Pacific studies have been established in Vladivostok and Khabarovsk; and professional journals and publications have been expanded and given fresh mandates to minimize polemics and cant and provide more sophisticated assessments of major economic, social, and cultural trends in the region. The emphasis of such work reflects the increased fascination with China, the lesser but still impressive interest in Japan, and the growing interest in the region as a whole.

A profile of recent articles in the major journal *Problemy dal'nego Vostoka* is instructive in this regard. For the pertinent three-year period 1985–1987, this key publication carried over 170 substantive contributions on China, over 60 on Japan, approximately 20 on Korea, and 15 on the United States. ASEAN as a whole was covered in only 9 articles. Vietnam was the major subject of 7 articles, compared to 12 contributions on the Mongolian People's Republic. Australia and New Zealand provided the focus for only one major article over the three years. This journal was expanded in 1987 from four to six issues annually.

9. *Perestroika neotlozhna*, 9–14; see also *Perestroika*, 180–186; Gail Warshofsky Lapidus, "Gorbachev's Agenda: Domestic Reforms and Foreign Policy," in Peter Juviler and Hiroshi Kimura, eds., *Gorbachev's Reforms: Progress and Prospects* (Boulder, Colo.: Westview Press, forthcoming). For other useful contextual perceptions of these issues, see Tao Dayong, "Sino-U.S. Economic Relations in the Asia-Pacific Context," *Journal of the Chinese People's Institute of Foreign Affairs*, no. 5 (September 1987): 16–24; Saburo Okita, "The Outlook for Pacific Cooperation and the Role of Japan," *Japan Review of International Affairs* 1, no. 1 (Spring/Summer 1987), 2–16.

2

Gorbachev's Policy Toward the Asia-Pacific Region

Ni Xiaoquan

CURRENT SOVIET FOREIGN POLICY ISSUES

Gorbachev's general foreign policy includes relations with the Asia-Pacific region. Therefore, to clearly understand Gorbachev's policy toward the Asia-Pacific region, it is necessary first to understand the strategic objective of his general foreign policy.

Gorbachev inherited not only a seriously deficient economy but also a rigid and obsolete foreign policy. Consequently, today the Soviet Union is in a very unfavorable position in its competition with the United States for global superiority. It is even faced with the possibility of losing its present superpower status and being reduced to an economically second-class state in the next century or even by the end of this century. Gorbachev views this grim situation confronting the Soviet Union very soberly. To reverse this trend, it is imperative for him to make major economic and political reforms and to use new approaches in Soviet foreign policy. Gorbachev stated that "it is necessary to take new attitudes and use new methods to solve international problems."[1]

Then what is the general objective of Gorbachev's foreign policy? In his report to the 27th Congress of the Communist Party of the Soviet Union (CPSU), Gorbachev stated that the CPSU's main objective was "to provide the Soviet people with the possibility of working under conditions of lasting peace and freedom." He expressed himself more clearly at the International Conference for a Nonnuclear World in Moscow on 16 February 1987: "I want to say frankly to our own people, to you all and to the whole world that our international policy depends more than any time in the past on our domestic policy and on our desire to concentrate our efforts on perfecting our country's work of construction. It is precisely because of this that we need a lasting peace and a predictable and constructive direction in international relations." Gorbachev further emphasized the need to have "a high degree of accuracy in assessing one's own possibilities, restraint, and an exceptionally high sense of responsibility when decisions are made." He also stressed the need for "tactical flexibility, a readiness for mutually acceptable compromises, and an orientation on dialogue and mutual understanding rather than on confrontation."[2] Gorbachev and other Soviet spokesmen have described this as "new political thinking."

As we can see, Gorbachev's foreign policy objective differs significantly from that pursued by the Soviet leaders in the 1970s who were "constantly expanding the position of socialism." Soviet foreign policy in the second half of the 1970s was characterized by global offensiveness. Today Gorbachev hopes to create a peaceful international environment that would accelerate social and economic development in the Soviet Union, which he feels is most important to his country. To achieve this aim, Gorbachev has constantly stressed the necessity to "reduce the level of military confrontation," "relax international tension," and "strengthen cooperation on a worldwide scale."

Although Gorbachev's remarks should be welcomed, his actions are more revealing. People have raised some questions following his actions in dealing with external affairs. Has there been a fundamental change in the long-range objective of Soviet foreign policy? Does Soviet foreign policy still contain elements of hegemony and power politics? While stressing "tactical flexibility," Gorbachev has also emphasized "firmness in upholding principles and stands."[3] What are these "principles and stands"? Is Gorbachev taking a conciliatory posture to gain momentum so that the Soviet Union can eventually gain a more favorable position in its future competition for global superiority with the United States? Understandably, people should raise these questions because they all interrelate with one main issue: What is the general strategic objective of Gorbachev's foreign policy? The key to understanding his policy toward the Asia-Pacific region is to study Gorbachev's actions.

IMPORTANCE OF THE ASIA-PACIFIC REGION TO THE SOVIETS

Since the beginning of 1986 Gorbachev has paid unprecedented attention to the Asia-Pacific region. In January 1986 he sent Eduard Shevardnadze, the Soviet foreign minister, to Japan for an official visit—the first visit by a Soviet foreign minister in more than a decade. In April 1986 the Soviet government issued a statement concerning

Soviet policy in the Asia-Pacific region. In July Gorbachev deliberately flew to Vladivostok, a Far Eastern city on the Sino-Soviet border, to deliver an important speech that elaborated on his Asia-Pacific policy. In November he visited India, his first visit to an Asian country. In December 1986, when new leaders were replacing the old in the ruling party of Vietnam, Yegor Ligachev, the second in command of the CPSU, led a high-level CPSU delegation to the 6th Party Congress of Vietnam. In early 1987 Soviet Foreign Minister Shevardnadze visited a number of countries in the Asia-Pacific region, including Australia, Indonesia, Vietnam, Laos, and Kampuchea. During this period, Gorbachev also sent other senior government officials to visit the capitals of many Asia-Pacific countries in an effort to improve relations. Since 1986 the Soviet Union has also established ties with a number of South Pacific nations.

Gorbachev has paid particular attention to the Asia-Pacific region primarily for the following reasons. First, great economic, political, and military changes are taking place in this region, making its strategic position in the world increasingly important. The Asia-Pacific region covers almost half of the earth's total area, and its population accounts for over half of the world's total. The thirty-four Asia-Pacific countries account for almost half of the world's total wealth. Over the last twenty-five years, East Asia's share of the world's total gross national product has increased threefold and its share in the total international trade has increased twofold. Its total trade volume presently constitutes almost one-fifth of the world's total. By the year 2000 the gross national product of East Asia alone will make up one-fourth of the world's total. The Asia-Pacific region, especially its western areas, is presently one of the new, important driving forces of the world's economy. This region contains major powers and major power interests. Both the United States and the Soviet Union have established powerful economic and strategic interests in the Asia-Pacific region. Japan is already an economic and technological giant and also has great military potential. China, a developing socialist country, has a vast territory, tremendous natural resources, and a huge population, even though its economy and culture are still relatively backward. It is not difficult to imagine that relations among these countries have significant impact upon the general international situation.

Although the importance of the Asia-Pacific region to the United States will not surpass that of Western Europe in the near future, the United States has already begun to shift its economic, political, and military priorities from Western Europe to Asia and the Pacific. United States trade with Asia was $116 billion in 1980, surpassing for the first time the combined value of exports and imports to Europe. In 1985

United States trade with this region reached $187 billion, which was 25 percent more than its trade with the European Economic Community (EEC). From the late 1970s the United States increasingly involved itself in Asian affairs both politically and militarily, making Soviet leaders anxious. They claimed that the Pacific Ocean "is turning into an arena of military-political confrontation" and that the United States, with the help of Japan, "is attempting" to turn this region into "the second front" or "the eastern front" against the Soviet Union. Gorbachev, in his July 1986 speech in Vladivostok, stated that "a militarized Washington-Tokyo-Seoul 'triangle' is taking shape."

In contrast, apart from the military sphere, the Soviet influence in the Asia-Pacific region up to now has been insignificant. The rigid economic model of the Soviet Union has little attraction in this region. Gorbachev admitted recently that "the growth rates of the national income in the past three five-year plan periods dropped by more than half. From the early 1970s most plan targets were not met. The economy as a whole became cumbersome and little responsive to innovation. The quality of a considerable part of the output no longer met the current requirements, and imbalances in production were aggravated."[4] The slow growth of the Soviet economy since the 1970s has contrasted to a certain extent with the economic development in some of the Asia-Pacific countries. With the exception of a few countries, the Soviet economic ties with this region are also weak. Despite a "striking" growth as compared with 1984, Soviet trade with Asia reached only 16.3 billion rubles in 1985, which constituted 11.5 percent of its total foreign trade of that year. Soviet trade with Japan, which is roughly half of its total trade with the countries in the western rim of the Pacific region, is only a little over US$4 billion a year. Such small trade volume cannot compare with the United States trade volume with this region, nor does it suit the superpower status of the Soviet Union.

On the other hand, the Soviet military presence in the Asia-Pacific region is very impressive. According to Western sources, over one-fourth of all the Soviet armed forces are now deployed to the Far East. It is equipped with 162 SS-20 missiles and 2,390 warplanes, including about 85 TN-20 supersonic Backfire bombers. The Soviet ground forces stationed in this region have been increased to more than 400,000 soldiers, armed with T-72 tanks. The Soviet Pacific fleet is now the largest of its four fleets, with more than 800 ships, including 2 aircraft carriers (the Soviet Union has 4 aircraft carriers in all), and 115 submarines, of which 31 are equipped with nuclear missiles. However, this huge military strength has not increased the prestige of the Soviet Union among the Asia-Pacific nations. On the contrary, these nations distrust the Soviet Union and feel threatened by its show of force of the last two decades, including stationing a large number of troops along the Sino-Soviet and Sino-Mongolian borders, its rigid attitude on the issue of Japan's northern territories, and, especially, its invasion and occupation of Afghanistan and its support for the Vietnamese occupation of Kampuchea. Gorbachev seems aware of the Soviet Union's present position in the Asia-Pacific region. To gain the diplomatic initiative and improve the Soviet Union's strategic position in this region as well as in the world, he is now trying hard to reverse this trend.

Gorbachev attaches much economic importance to the Asia-Pacific region. About 90 percent of the proven energy resources, three-fourths of the forest reserves, and 65 percent of the proven mineral resources of the USSR are concentrated in Siberia east of the Ural Mountains. The Soviet Far East also has very rich natural resources. Since fuel and raw materials production is being developed predominantly in the eastern part of the Soviet Union, the future development of the Soviet economy will depend to a great extent on the development of Siberia and the Soviet Far East. The significance of these areas is emphasized in the plan formulated at the 27th Party Congress and reaffirmed by Gorbachev: "On the whole, our country's economy has already been developing toward the direction of the Pacific Ocean in a broad way."[5] To accelerate the development of Siberia and the Soviet Far East, it is necessary for the Soviet Union to use the great economic and technological potentials of the Asia-Pacific region and strengthen economic, trade, and technological cooperation with it. The Soviet Union can import urgently needed capital and advanced technologies from Japan. Its economy and the Chinese economy can complement each other. The Soviet Union and these countries could provide reciprocal markets for each other's products. However, the Soviet Union must ease regional tension in the Asia-Pacific region and improve relations with the countries in this region if it intends to develop economic and technological agreements with them.

The impasse of Soviet-American relations has also caused Gorbachev to attach greater importance to the Asia-Pacific region. Although Gorbachev and President Reagan met in Reykjavik in October 1986, there has been no substantial progress in the arms control talks on space and nuclear weapons nor is it likely that there will be a major breakthrough soon on the issue of Strategic Defense Initiative (SDI), the main Soviet concern. Because of the stalemated Soviet-American relations and other factors, it is also difficult for the Soviets to develop their Western European relations, making it all the more important for the Soviet Union to improve its relations with the Asia-Pacific countries. Gorbachev hopes to develop Soviet-American relations by improving the Soviet relations with the Asia-Pacific countries.

The Soviet Union holds that because of the problems the United States is currently struggling with in the Asia-Pacific region, now is the time for it to expand its influence and take the diplomatic initiative in the region. For instance, the United States needs to resolve the issue of Taiwan with China, economic frictions with Japan, trade protection issues with other Asia-Pacific countries, and fishing rights with some South Pacific nations. Furthermore, the United States and New Zealand are squabbling with each other over port calls in New Zealand by nuclear-powered or nuclear-armed naval vessels.

In summary, the strategic position of the Asia-Pacific region is becoming increasingly important, and the region is quickly becoming a new political and economic center in the world. President Reagan has termed the twenty-first century "the Pacific era," which shows that the United States is aware of the strategic importance of the Asia-Pacific region in the coming decades and will try to strengthen further its political, economic, and military ties with many countries in the region. To improve the Soviet position in this region and realize its long-term strategic interests, Gorbachev needs to use "new attitudes" and "new methods" in the Soviet Asia-Pacific policy.

GORBACHEV'S ASIA-PACIFIC POLICY

Gorbachev abandoned the characteristic practices of his predecessors, which emphasized using military strength to expand Soviet influence in the Asia-Pacific region, and began using "charming diplomacy" to cultivate as many allies as possible in the region. In his Vladivostok speech of July 1986, Gorbachev emphasized that the Soviet Union is also "an Asian and Pacific country." He said that the Soviet interest is "not a claim to some sort of privileges or special status, it is not selfish attempts to strengthen our own security at others' expense, it is not a search for advantage to the detriment of others" and that the Soviet Union is in favor of "jointly building new and fair relations" in Asia and the Pacific. Obviously, Gorbachev's intent was to eliminate the apprehensions that many of the Asia-Pacific countries felt toward the Soviet Union and to gain their trust in his new policies.

Gorbachev feels that improving relations with China would result in a number of benefits to the Soviet Union. First, it would give the Soviet Union more time and strength to concentrate on its contention with the United States, its main adversary. Second, it would improve Soviet diplomatic relations with the other Asia-Pacific countries. Third, it would further develop Soviet economic and trade relations with China, which would promote and accelerate development of the Soviet domestic economy.

To improve Sino-Soviet relations, Gorbachev has made positive proposals. In his July 1986 speech in Vladivostok, he suggested for the first time that the Sino-Soviet border could be demarcated officially along the main navigation channel; whereas in the past, Soviet leaders always had insisted that the common border should run along the Chinese side of the Amur River. Furthermore, after an eight-year lapse, the Sino-Soviet negotiations on border issues resumed in February 1987. Gorbachev also indicated that the Soviet government would provide assistance in the construction of a railroad that would link China's Xinjiang-Uygur Autonomous Region and the Soviet Kazakhstan. In September 1986 during their visit to China, the Soviet first vice-chairman of the Council of Ministers and chairman of the State Planning Commission indicated that the Soviet Union would help China modernize over one hundred factories and enterprises. Since Gorbachev took office, trade has increased between the Soviet Union and China; in 1986 trade reached about $2.6 billion, a 30 percent increase over the previous year. According to their present trade agreement, it is expected to increase to $5 or $6 billion by 1990. Gorbachev has also taken an attitude that appears to be a little more flexible than before. In the past the Soviets had refused to discuss the Vietnamese aggression against Kampuchea and the Soviet troops in Afghanistan and on the Chinese border and in Mongolia, major obstacles to Sino-Soviet relations. Now Gorbachev has expressed willingness to discuss with China "any questions in which the two sides are interested."

Although Gorbachev has shown more flexibility in Sino-Soviet relations than his predecessors, he has not taken any effective measures to remove these major obstacles, especially its support of the Vietnamese aggression against Kampuchea, which China regards as crucial to improving Sino-Soviet relations. He and the other Soviet leaders will not seek to improve bilateral relations with anyone "at the expense or to the detriment of" their relations with other countries. Basically this is why no substantial progress has been made in developing political relations between the Soviet Union and China.

Gorbachev regards Japan as "a power of paramount importance." In his view, Japan not only possesses tremendous capital and advanced technologies but also is strengthening its military strategic cooperation with the United States. Therefore, Gorbachev hopes to develop Japanese-Soviet relations both to accelerate Soviet economic development, especially in Siberia and the Soviet Far East, and to ensure its security. Since 1986 Gorbachev's policy toward Japan has been more flexible. For instance, he has resumed regular consultations between the foreign ministers of both countries, which had been suspended for about eight years; once again permitted Japanese citizens to visit family graves on the Kuril Islands; and for the first time revealed a willingness to listen to Japan's arguments on the issue of the northern territories. Nevertheless, like his predecessors, Gorbachev also insists that the territorial issue between the Soviet Union and Japan "has already been solved" and that cooperation between the two countries should be extended "in an atmosphere of tranquility unburdened by the problems of the past." Undoubtedly, this territorial issue will continue to be an obstacle in developing Soviet-Japanese relations.

In his Asia-Pacific policy, Gorbachev has been more attentive to the countries of the Association of Southeast Asian Nations (ASEAN). In his Vladivostok speech, he first admitted that there were a good many "positive elements" in the ASEAN activities and in bilateral ties. Shortly before that the Deputy Foreign Minister M. S. Kapitsa of the Soviet Union during his visit to some ASEAN countries indicated that the Soviet Union acknowledged that ASEAN is "really" a political, economic, and cultural association and hopes to cooperate with the ASEAN countries. Since 1986 the Soviet Union has actively pursued diplomatic and trade activities in many ASEAN countries by offering to provide them with economic aid and promote trade with them under favorable conditions. Nevertheless, the Soviet support of Vietnamese aggression against Kampuchea continues to exert a negative impact upon the relations between the Soviet Union and the ASEAN countries.

Since 1986, through economic diplomacy, the Soviet Union has also developed relations with a number of island nations in the South Pacific, such as Kiribati, Vanuatu, and Fiji. This interest has aroused attention since this area is near the transpacific shipping lanes between the United States and the western Pacific rim and there is a U.S. missile range at Kwajalein in the Marshall Islands, which is considered to be very important to the development of President Reagan's antiballistic missile defensive systems.

Gorbachev's policy toward the Asia-Pacific region also reflects a willingness to "cooperate" with the United States in the region. In his Vladivostok speech, Gorbachev explicitly acknowledged that the United States was "a great Pacific power," which had "important economic and political interests in the region" and that "without the United States, without its participation, it is impossible to solve the problem of security and cooperation in the Pacific zone in a manner satisfactory to all." He also mentioned that there were considerable opportunities both in the Far East and in the Pacific for mutually advantageous cooperation between the Soviet Union and the United States. This indicates that Gorbachev hopes to reach a certain understanding with the United States that is advantageous to the interests of both countries in the Asia-Pacific region and ease the increasing tension. He proposed in his speech the "inclusion of the Asia-Pacific region in the overall process of the creation of a comprehensive system of international security" that includes disbanding military alliances and abandoning foreign bases in Asia and the Pacific. Yet, despite Gorbachev's remarks, the strength of the Soviet Pacific fleet has continued to increase. In August 1986 this fleet carried out in a vast area of the Sea of Okhotsk and the Sea of Japan an exercise that was reported to be of the largest scale in the last few years.

ASSESSMENT OF GORBACHEV'S POLICY

What conclusions can be drawn from Gorbachev's policy toward the Asia-Pacific region? There are three major differences between Gorbachev's Asia-Pacific policy and those of his predecessors. First, Gorbachev has attached much greater importance to this region than his predecessors. Previous Soviet leaders neglected the importance of the Asia-Pacific region and only paid attention to the United States and Europe. Recently Gorbachev made a speech in India in which he said that "peace in Europe and peace in Asia are of equal significance in our policy."[6] Gorbachev and other Soviet spokesmen have repeatedly emphasized in recent times that the Soviet Union is not going to communicate "only with the United States." This directive indicates that the Soviet Union wants more of an international balance in its diplomatic relations by developing relations with Western Europe and the Asia-Pacific region. Second, whereas the Asia-Pacific policies of past Soviet leaders were both tough and rigid, Gorbachev's policy toward this region is much more flexible and has been described as "charming diplomacy." Furthermore, he has constantly pursued "peace offensives" and emphasized "cooperation" and "dialogue." During disputes, he has been willing to "listen to" others' arguments. Third, past Soviet leaders used their military forces to expand Soviet influence, whereas Gorbachev has complemented political diplomacy with economic diplomacy. The Soviet government stated on 23 April 1986 that it would "take a more active part in the international division of labor and trade, economic, scientific and technological cooperation among the Asia-Pacific countries." Anatoly Dobrynin, secretary of the Central Committee of the CPSU, also wrote that "essentially, the conception of the comprehensive system of international security also includes [the] economic sphere."[7] Therefore, it is expected that the Soviet Union will more actively develop economic and trade relations with countries in the Asia-Pacific region.

Gorbachev's Asia-Pacific policy and those of his predecessors have three main similarities. First, Gorbachev also regards the United States as his main adversary to superiority in this region.[8] Second, until now Gorbachev has failed to remove the major obstacles to improving Sino-Soviet and Japanese-Soviet relations. He is still supporting Vietnam's aggression toward Kampuchea; Soviet troops are still in Afghanistan, on the Chinese border, and in Mongolia;[9] and he still insists that the territorial issue with Japan "does not exist." Third, although Gorbachev has emphasized economic diplomacy in the Asia-Pacific region, he still relies heavily on military strength to support the Soviet policy in this region.

To accelerate the Soviet Union's economic development so that it can compete more effectively with the United States in the future, Gorbachev obviously needs to improve relations with the Asia-Pacific countries and develop further economic and trade alliances with them. However, Soviet policy toward this region remains essentially unchanged; it will be difficult for the Soviet Union to improve and develop relations with the Asia-Pacific countries.

Presently, the Soviet Union is experiencing spectacular changes. However, the extent to which these changes may affect its foreign policy, including its policy toward the Asia-Pacific region, remains to be seen. To maintain peace and stability in the Asia-Pacific region, the Soviet leaders must first take effective measures to remove the "hot spots" and obstacles in this region.

NOTES

1. See Gorbachev's speech at the International Conference for a Nonnuclear World held in Moscow on 16 February 1987.
2. See Gorbachev's political report to the 27th Congress of the CPSU held in February 1986.
3. Ibid. See also Anatoly Dobrynin, "For a Nonnuclear World, Toward the 21st Century," *Kommunist*, no. 9 (1986).
4. See Mikhail Gorbachev's report at the Plenary Meeting of the CPSU Central Committee on 27 January 1987.
5. See Gorbachev's speech at the Ceremonial Meeting Devoted to the Presentation of the Order of Lenin to Vladivostok on 28 July 1986.
6. See Gorbachev's speech to the Indian Parliament on 27 November 1986.
7. See Dobrynin, "For a Nonnuclear World."
8. There was a short period in the past when Soviet leaders attempted to cooperate with the United States in an effort to oppose China.
9. When visiting Moscow on 31 January 1987, the foreign minister of the Mongolian People's Republic announced that whether the Soviet troops would be totally withdrawn would depend on the improvement of Mongolia's political relations with its neighbors, particularly with China.

3

Japanese Perceptions and Policies Toward the Soviet Union:
Changes and Prospects Under the Gorbachev Era

Tsuyoshi Hasegawa

Postwar Japanese perceptions of the outside world have undergone various changes, but at least one thing has not changed—the extreme unpopularity of the Soviet Union among Japanese.[1] One public opinion survey after another indicates that the Soviet Union is the most unpopular country among Japanese. This does not simply mean passive indifference; it denotes a more active negative meaning: the Soviet Union provokes Japanese suspicions, if not outright hatred. I have examined elsewhere in detail the many historical, political, cultural, and military reasons for the negative image of the Soviet Union.[2]

The unpopularity of the Soviet Union is not uniquely Japanese.[3] What is unique are the policy implications of this unpopularity. In the United States, the Soviet Union, despite its unpopularity, is recognized as one of the most important countries with which the United States must reach some accord.[4] Hence, one of the top priorities of any U.S. administration is to construct a comprehensive strategy toward the Soviet Union. Furthermore, the United States has developed an intricate network of official and unofficial communications with the Soviet Union, and the importance of these channels is not questioned. In contrast, the Japanese limited interactions between the two countries. The Soviet Union shares this lack of interest in improving the relationship as well. Thus Japanese-Soviet relations in the postwar years are characterized above all by a mutual disinterest in improving relations beyond minimal contact.

This chapter examines why such unusual relations have developed, the changes since Gorbachev's accession to power, and the prospects for change in relations in the near future.

THE LOW PRIORITY OF THE SOVIET UNION IN JAPANESE POLICY

Japan's foreign policy goals are (1) protection of its economic interests, (2) protection of its national security, and (3) promotion of a stable international environment.[5] The Soviet Union plays only a minimal role in Japan's pursuit of economic security. Japan's total volume of trade with the Soviet Union was only 1.5 percent of its total trade in 1986.[6] The oil shock of 1973 necessitated Japan to diversify its energy sources, temporarily raising hopes for increased trade activities with the Soviet Union. But the successful structural change in Japan's economy in subsequent years diminished such hopes, and the oil glut in the world market in the 1980s suppressed the earlier enthusiasm. As the Soviet economy began to falter in the latter half of the 1970s, Siberian development was postponed, and the Japanese involvement in projects there was substantially reduced. Soviet spokesmen argue that Japanese-Soviet trade declined because of the Japanese government's political decisions, but even without politics, it was destined to decline.[7] Japanese-Soviet economic relations are based on unequal needs: Japan does not need the Soviet Union as much as the Soviet Union needs Japan's technology and financial assistance.

Japanese security interests are diametrically opposed to those of the Soviet Union. Japan and Russia have been principal military opponents in northeast Asia since the nineteenth century and have fought four wars in this century. This adversarial relationship has resulted partially from conflicting interests in the region and partially from the geopolitical situation. Japanese-Russian cooperation existed only during the brief periods of 1906–1916 and 1941–1945.[8] As the Soviet Union achieved the status of a global military superpower, the bow-shaped Japanese archipelago became an even more irksome obstacle because it controlled the three crucial straits that gave the Soviet Pacific fleet access to the Pacific. The Soviet military buildup in the 1970s provoked the fear of a Soviet military threat among Japanese. Particularly, the deployment of a division in the northern islands in the late 1970s alarmed many Japanese, prompting Japan to increase its security ties with the United States.

Japan's military power is, of course, minuscule compared with the colossal destructive power of the Soviet Union. But Japan's security is assured by her alliance with the United States. This security arrangement has inevitably caused the Soviet Union to treat its relations with

Japan in terms of U.S.-Soviet relations. For the Japanese, too, the Japanese-U.S. security arrangement has a profound consequence for Japanese-Soviet relations. In security matters, Japan does not have to deal with the Soviet Union directly, since such direct dealing with the Soviet Union can be left to the United States. Hence, while the Soviet emergence as a global superpower has necessitated the United States and Western Europe to increase their contact with the Soviet Union, Japan has been shielded from such necessity.

Japan and the Soviet Union have not found much in common pertaining to the third goal of Japanese foreign policy—to create a stable international environment. The Japanese have considered Soviet proposals for Asian collective security and a bilateral treaty of good neighborliness self-serving and designed to further Soviet interests at the expense of others. Moreover, the rapid Soviet military buildup in the Far East, when the United States showed signs of withdrawal from Asia, was regarded as an important destabilizing factor in the region.

The deterioration of Japanese-Soviet relations in the 1970s coincided with the Sino-Japanese rapprochement. Unquestionably, this rapprochement greatly contributed to regional stability. But there are some doubts whether Japan could have achieved this rapprochement without alienating the Soviet Union, and whether it was wise for Japan to tilt so heavily toward China even to the point of subscribing to the Chinese-sponsored antihegemony clause aimed against the USSR.[9]

Japan's disinterest in improving its relations with the Soviet Union is further reinforced by the peculiar status that Soviet affairs occupy in the Japanese foreign policy decision-making mechanism. While various actors (bureaucratic organizations, Liberal Democratic Party (LDP) politicians, business communities) influence the decision-making process in formulating policies toward other countries, the Foreign Ministry dominates the formulation of Japan's Soviet policy. Within the Foreign Ministry, the Soviet Desk, which has the reputation of having a hawkish outlook toward the Soviet Union, plays a decisive role. Therefore, it cannot be expected that initiatives to improve relations with the Soviet Union would come from the government.

THE LOW PRIORITY OF JAPAN IN SOVIET POLICY

Among the Soviet Union's relations with major industrialized countries, Japanese-Soviet relations occupy an unusual place. Although four Japanese prime ministers have visited Moscow—Ichiro Hatoyama in 1956, Kakuei Tanaka in 1973, Zenko Suzuki in 1982 (at Leonid Brezhnev's funeral), and Yasuhiro Nakasone in 1985 (at Konstantin Chernenko's funeral)—no general secretaries of the Communist Party of the Soviet Union (CPSU) nor chairmen of the Council of Ministers have ever set foot in Japan. Even more humiliating for the Japanese, from January 1976 until January 1986, no Soviet foreign ministers bothered to visit Japan. This clear one-sidedness in visitations has more than symbolic significance; it underscores the low priority that the Soviet Union has accorded to Japan in its foreign policy.

It is puzzling why Japan has retained such an insignificant position in Soviet foreign policy, particularly when one considers Japan's emergence as a global economic power. In contrast, Western Europe occupies a high place in Soviet priorities for at least two reasons. First, the Soviets seek to weaken the Western alliance by decoupling Western Europe from the United States. Second, the Soviet Union is interested in acquiring technology needed for the modernization of its economy. For these reasons, the Soviet leadership has pursued a rather sophisticated, moderately successful policy toward Western Europe. One would assume that for the same reasons Japan should play an analogous position in Soviet global strategy in Asia, but this is not the case. One wonders if this neglect is part of a carefully thought-out global master plan that we have yet to decipher, or simply a result of error.

The low priority accorded to Soviet policy toward Japan is even more puzzling when one considers that Japan is one of the most popular countries among the Soviets. It is known that Japanese culture has fascinated the Soviets for many years. But, because the Soviet political elite are not identical to the cultured intelligentsia and culture basically is irrelevant to Soviet foreign policy, the high cultural esteem for Japan held by the Soviets has not found equivalent respect for Japan among the Soviet foreign policy decision makers.

Japan's emergence as one of the most powerful economic powers in the world has been problematic for Soviet foreign policy. Capitalistic Japan now has a gross national product larger than that of the Soviet Union. Japan is now a leader in the most advanced technology, whereas the Soviet Union has lagged far behind. If the Soviet Union has not caught up with the Western capitalistic nations, there is an excuse that it is still in the process of catching up with them. But to lag behind Japan simply does not conform to their sense of *zakonomernost*, their sense of the natural order of things. Japan's success has compounded the Soviet Union's embarrassment over its mediocre economic performance. One of the easiest things that ideologues could do in such a case is to ignore Japan's economic achievements. Of course, Japan's economic achievements were not completely ignored. Specialists on Japan began in the 1970s to study Japan's economic development and particularly its economic management. Their research has provided an important precondition for according Japan an important place in Soviet foreign policy.

Japan's economic development also raised a practical question on the Soviet Union's own strategy for economic development. If the détente policy pursued by Leonid Brezhnev was partly designed to modernize the Soviet economy by borrowing Western technology, Japanese technology could not be ignored. Thus from an economic standpoint, it was necessary to reevaluate Japan's position in Soviet policy, as the contradiction between the political-ideological downgrading of Japan and its practical economic significance became glaringly apparent.

Under Brezhnev, it was impossible to resolve this contradiction by fundamentally reevaluating Japan's position in Soviet global strategy. During the Brezhnev period, the most important factor in the Soviet concept of the correlation of forces was military power. The primacy of military power was reflected in its Asian policy in the sense that the Soviet primary targets were, first, the United States and, second, China. Japan, as a lesser military power, was not worth considering on the same level. Thus, Japanese-Soviet relations were only a function of U.S.-Soviet and Sino-Soviet relations. This view was most forcefully championed by Gromyko, who not only perceived international politics through this bipolar vision but also reportedly simply disliked Japan.[10]

The downgrading of Japan's significance may have been reinforced by the generational prejudice of the Soviet leadership. The old men who wielded power in the Politburo such as Brezhnev and Gromyko belonged to the generation who grew up watching Japanese militarism threaten their security and subsequently watching their victorious Red Army defeat the Japanese in Manchuria, Sakhalin Island, and the Kuriles. They must have had a hard time reconciling their image of a humiliated Japan reduced to a second-class nation with that of an economic giant that can produce better and more than the victorious Soviet Union. Certainly, their image of Japan was significantly different from that of the younger generation who grew up watching Japanese economic achievements.

THE NORTHERN TERRITORIAL ISSUE

The northern territorial issue remains a major obstacle to the improvement of Japanese-Soviet relations. Although competing Japanese and Russian interests in the area date back to the seventeenth century, only three bilateral treaties were concluded before the Second World War. The Shimoda Treaty in 1855 drew the border in the Kuriles between Uruppu and Etorofu, giving four of the islands to Japan. With the St. Petersburg Treaty in 1875, Japan gave up its claim on Sakhalin in return for exclusive territorial rights in the Kuriles. With the Portsmouth Peace Treaty in 1905 at the end of the Russo-Japanese War, Japan claimed South Sakhalin. It should be pointed out that the territory that Japan acquired through "unlawful military aggression," as described in the Yalta Agreement, could be applied only to South Sakhalin.

The Yalta Secret Agreement stipulated that the Kurile Islands were to be "handed over" to the Soviet Union after Japan's surrender. (In contrast, South Sakhalin was to be returned to the Soviet Union.) The Soviet Union claims that when Japan accepted the Potsdam Declaration, it also accepted the Yalta Secret Agreement; hence Japan abandoned its claim to all the contested islands. Japan, however, has argued that since it was not party to the Yalta Agreement and the Secret Agreement remained secret until February 1946, Japan should not be bound by a treaty it never signed and that it did not know existed. In any case, the four southern islands claimed by Japan were occupied by the Soviet Union along with the rest of the Kurile Islands. About 17,000 Japanese residents were evacuated by 1948.

A history of the territorial dispute between Japan and the Soviet Union shows that the Soviet position has not been uniform and has shifted depending upon the results it wanted to gain from Japan. Despite the range of options offered by the Soviets, they have never allowed the possibility of returning the two bigger islands. Thus far, its hinted maximum concessions have been the return of the small islands, Shikoitan and Habomais.

The Japanese government equates the northern territorial issue with the entire Japanese policy toward the Soviet Union. Japanese attitudes toward the northern territorial issue can be divided into two groups: The *iriguchi-ron* (entry theory) group believes that the solution of the territorial issue must be a precondition for improvement of bilateral relations, while the *deguchi-ron* (exit theory) group argues that marked improvement of bilateral relations will eventually lead to a solution of the territorial issue satisfactory to Japan's interests. The Japanese government, particularly the Foreign Ministry, takes an adamant *iriguchi-ron* view.

CHANGES IN SOVIET POLICY TOWARD JAPAN UNDER GORBACHEV

Since Gorbachev's accession to power, Soviet policy toward Japan has shown numerous signs of change. When Prime Minister Zenko Suzuki went to Moscow for Brezhnev's funeral in 1983, he was not among the privileged heads of state who were received by Yuri

Andropov. But at Konstantin Chernenko's funeral in March 1985, Gorbachev met with Yasuhiro Nakasone and indicated that his regime would take a different view of Japan.

One of the most significant changes under Gorbachev's regime is his personnel policy. In July 1985 Foreign Minister Gromyko was replaced by Eduard Shevardnadze. This and other changes were accompanied by "new thinking" in the Soviet approach to international relations, such as downgrading the diplomatic value of military power and emphasizing economic interdependency despite differences in economic systems. This approach necessitates reevaluation of Soviet policy toward Japan.[11]

One of the most important personnel changes directly related to Soviet policy toward Japan was the replacement of Ambassador Petr Abrasimov by Nikolai Soloviev in May 1987. Unlike his predecessors, Soloviev is a career diplomat without membership in the Central Committee. Yet he served as head of the Second Far Eastern Department in the Foreign Ministry for ten years and has a wide range of acquaintances in Japan. Fluent in Japanese and knowledgeable in Japanese culture and society, he is expected to be more effective than his "influential" predecessors.[12] This change in the ambassadorial post might signal a change in the Soviet approach to Japan from the previous high-handed manner to a more businesslike manner with emphasis on economic and technological cooperation.

One of the most obvious changes that the Soviet Union could make to indicate to Japan the seriousness of its intention to shift its approach would be to fire Ivan Kovalenko, deputy chief of the International Department of the Central Committee, who is said to have been the most influential person in Soviet policy toward Japan. Kovalenko's initial contact with Japan was to interrogate Japanese prisoners of war in Siberia. This experience is reported to have formed his basic perception of Japan, including a firm belief that the Japanese should be bullied to subjection from the position of strength. Kovalenko reportedly greatly influenced Gromyko's views on these questions. Last year, *Mainichi* reported that Kovalenko's influence was being undercut and that a Soviet source revealed the possibility of an imminent replacement of Kovalenko, but as of early Fall 1988 Kovalenko retains his post.[13]

The Foreign Ministry's organizational change is also significant for Soviet policy toward Japan. In June 1986 the Asian section of the ministry was streamlined to correspond to the reality of the Asia-Pacific region. The Japanese section was elevated to a higher department, indicating a changed Soviet perception of Japan.[14]

The first concrete sign of change was Shevardnadze's visit to Japan in January 1986. It was the first time since 1976 that a Soviet foreign minister visited Japan. (The last time a Japanese foreign minister had visited the Soviet Union was in 1978.) Shevardnadze agreed to resume regular ministerial visits, thus ending this abnormal condition.

The most important issue discussed during the foreign ministers' conference was the territorial issue. The Japanese side succeeded in having Shevardnadze accept the expression, "to negotiate the unresolved questions," in a joint statement, although Shevardnadze himself repeated the Soviet position that the territorial question had been resolved. That the question was raised at all and that the expression indicating the existence of "unresolved questions" was included in the joint statement demonstrated a softening of the Soviets' previous intransigence.[15]

Foreign Minister Shintaro Abe's visit to Moscow in May 1986 and the subsequent follow-up negotiations produced a cultural agreement for the first time. Another result was the reestablishment of the Committee for Cooperation on Science and Technology, which had been suspended since Japan joined the sanctions against Poland and the Soviet Union. The Soviets were vitally interested in the reestablishment of this committee. But the Japanese made this conditional on the Soviet acceptance of visits without visas by the Japanese to their relatives' graves in Sakhalin and the northern islands—a practice that had been suspended by the Soviets since 1976. The Soviet Union accepted this condition, although it limited the Japanese access only to two islands, Shikotan and Habomais.

In Gorbachev's speech to the 27th Party Congress, he referred to the imperialist world divided by the United States, Western Europe, and Japan. This was the first time in a general secretary's speech before a Party Congress that Japan was mentioned as an independent power comparable with the United States and Western Europe. More importantly, Gorbachev concluded that, although the mutual interests among the imperialists would not be destroyed, the United States could no longer expect either Western Europe or Japan to obey its orders obediently at the sacrifice of their own interests.[16] This passage may indicate Gorbachev's intention to elevate Japan to an equal position with Western Europe in his attempts to decouple other imperialist powers from the United States.

Gorbachev's Vladivostok Speech

Gorbachev's Vladivostok speech in July 1986 signified a major departure from the traditional Soviet foreign policy orientation. First, it marked the beginning of an active Soviet Asia-Pacific policy. Second, the Vladivostok speech repudiated previous Soviet policy characterized by the primacy of military power and affirmed the redirection of Soviet efforts to develop political and economic ties with the region.[17]

Although the Vladivostok speech referred to specific measures to improve relations with China, no concrete measures regarding Japanese relations were included. Gorbachev referred to Japan as a power of prime significance that accomplished in a short span of time incredible achievements in industry, trade, education, science, and technology. He also praised Japan's nonnuclear policy. According to Gorbachev, Japan was the first victim of atomic weapons and officially adopts three nonnuclear principles on which it conducts foreign policy, although these principles and the peace-oriented constitution have tended to be ignored in recent years. Gorbachev mentioned that Japanese-Soviet relations showed signs of developing in a better direction and stated: "The objective situation of the two countries . . . requires more cooperation on a healthy, realistic basis in a quiet atmosphere, not burdened by the problems of the past. We have set the beginning in this direction this year."[18]

The Japanese public had three different interpretations of the Vladivostok speech. The first was the enthusiastic endorsement of the speech as the beginning of a Soviet Asian policy with a totally different orientation. Mineo Nakajima, the leading proponent of this interpretation, argued that Japan should respond with flexibility to Gorbachev's call for improved relations. At the opposite pole, Shinkichi Hogan, Akira Sono, and other hawkish critics of the Soviet Union saw nothing new in the Vladivostok speech; they argued that Gorbachev's speech represented nothing but a standard Soviet tactic to obtain Japanese economic cooperation without paying anything in return. The third interpretation offered by Hiroshi Kimura was that although the Vladivostok speech contained the seeds of a new Soviet Asian policy, it also was hampered by the persistence of themes from the Soviets' traditional Asian policy.[19]

Some of Kimura's arguments that sought continuity between traditional Soviet policy and the Vladivostok speech are not convincing.[20] He also overlooked the importance of what was not mentioned in the speech: the usual denunciation of Japan's security arrangement with the United States and the warning of revival of Japanese militarism. These omissions may have indicated Soviet willingness to improve bilateral relations while acknowledging the Japanese-U.S. security arrangements as a reality. Nevertheless, Kimura is correct to conclude that the Vladivostok speech cannot be taken as a completely new departure from the traditional policy.

Gorbachev did not offer anything new and specific regarding the territorial question, a position that could not be expected to elicit a positive Japanese reaction. The expression, "cooperation on a healthy, realistic basis in a quiet atmosphere, not burdened by the problems of the past," could mean that the Soviet Union would be realistic enough to accept Japan's security arrangements and that the Soviet Union was willing to solve the territorial question, irrespective of its past positions, as Nakajima argued. But it was bound to be interpreted by many as an attempt to gain economic cooperation without paying the necessary price of solving the territorial issue. If the Vladivostok speech was an attempt to create momentum in Japan for improvement of bilateral relations, it fell short of this objective precisely because it did not express Soviet willingness, if any, to talk about the northern territorial issue or to accept Japan's claims. Although the Vladivostok speech did not bring about specific changes, it symbolized the new thinking in Asian policy.[21]

Gorbachev's Unrealized Visit to Japan

When Foreign Minister Abe visited Moscow, he formally invited Gorbachev to come to Japan. After the foreign ministers' conference in May 1986, Gorbachev's visit to Japan seemed as if it would finally materialize. Such a visit would have been a big step toward the improvement of Japanese-Soviet relations, since no general secretaries had ever visited Japan. Gorbachev himself suggested in his Vladivostok speech "the exchange of mutual visits at a higher level" than the foreign ministerial level.[22] At his press conference on 29 September 1986, Ambassador Soloviev mentioned that the general secretary's visit to Japan had been decided on in principle, but that the specific date was still indefinite.[23] In October a Japanese Foreign Ministry source revealed that both countries were negotiating on scheduling Gorbachev's visit to Japan around 15 January 1987.

However, the momentum that was building toward Gorbachev's visit to Japan was suddenly dampened. On 24 October Gorbachev attacked "the military alliance among the United States, Japan, and South Korea" at the reception of Kim Il-sung.[24] Furthermore, in November the then deputy foreign minister, Kapista, criticized Japan's participation in the Strategic Defense Initiative (SDI) and Japan's and the United States' joint military exercise.[25] Soviet criticism of Japan's military role, which had been muted at least since Shevardnadze's visit to Japan, was renewed. Finally, on 14 November in Moscow, Shevardnadze told Deputy Foreign Minister Shinichi Yanai that since Gorbachev's schedule for the next year was still being adjusted, it would be impossible to visit Japan in January.[26] This virtually ended the idea of an early visit by Gorbachev to Japan.

Why did the Soviets cancel Gorbachev's visit in November? The failure of the Reykjavik presummit and the marked decline of Nakasone's political prestige are not plausible explanations. Japanese-Soviet relations do not necessarily correspond to the rise and fall of U.S.-Soviet relations. If anything, the "failure" of Reykjavik dampened Japanese enthusiasm to court Gorbachev's visit.

The Japanese domestic factor may have been a supplementary factor, if not the decisive one. It should be pointed out that the moderate improvement of Japanese-Soviet relations in 1986 was also motivated by the Japanese desire for improvement. This desire can be explained partly by Nakasone's personal philosophy that without the solution of the territorial question it would be impossible to end Japan's "postwar era" (*sengo no sokessan*). Nakasone took on this mission himself partly because he needed a diplomatic victory in his bid for reelection beyond the limit allowed by the LDP party statutes. But Nakasone's prestige showed some signs of eroding by the fall of 1986. The Soviets may well have considered it wise to wait and see what would happen to Nakasone's power.

There might also have been a Soviet domestic factor. The plenum of the Central Committee, which was scheduled to open in December 1986, was postponed until January. In December Kunaev was dismissed from the Politburo, which resulted in a street riot in Alma Ata. As it turned out, the January plenum, which dealt with the cadre question, was a crucial meeting for Gorbachev's *perestroika*. It may have been that at this crucial juncture it was impossible for Gorbachev to leave the country.[27]

The reasons just cited do not seem decisive, however. A more important reason seems to be the Soviet assessment that the Japanese were not forthcoming with the concessions appropriate for Gorbachev's visit. The Soviets may have hoped to begin negotiations with Japan on economic cooperation and security questions in Asia, while shelving the territorial issue as an unsolved question. It became clear from October to November that the Japanese government had not changed its adamant *iriguchi-ron* as a precondition for entering into negotiations on other matters. The Soviet government must have concluded that a premature visit by Gorbachev to Japan without his being prepared to meet Japan's high expectations would be counterproductive.[28]

Japanese-Soviet Relations Deteriorate

The most serious crisis facing Japan in the 1980s was the increase in Japanese-U.S. economic friction. In 1987 this crisis reached the dangerous point where economic and security issues tend to be merged into one emotional issue. After the Japanese metropolitan police indicted Toshiba Machine Co. on 30 April for a possible Coordinating Committee for Export Controls (COCOM) violation, four Japanese were arrested on 20 May for suspicion of selling classified U.S. Air Force information taken from Yokota Air Base to Soviet agents. On 20 July there was another espionage case involving an executive of Tokyo Instruments for Aeronautics, who confessed that he had sold classified defense information to a Soviet agent. The Japanese Ministry of Trade and Industry (MITI), which was lenient in the past in enforcing the COCOM rules, has now toughened its export regulations because of mounting pressure from the United States.

Another issue involving the United States and the Soviet Union indirectly affected Japan in the spring of 1987 exactly when the Toshiba incident surfaced. At the end of February, Gorbachev made a new proposal on Intermediate-Range Nuclear Forces (INF), one that would accept the zero option in Europe. Differences between the United States and the Soviet Union suddenly narrowed and made an accord on INF realistic for the first time. But the Soviet insistence on retaining 100 SS-20 warheads in Asia, which Reagan had accepted at Reykjavik, displeased both Japan and China, prompting Nakasone to comment that the United States should consider deploying INF in Alaska.

The Soviet government watched these developments apprehensively and protested rather lamely that these spy cases and the Toshiba incident were consciously concocted by the Japanese government to poison the relationship between Japan and the Soviet Union. The Japanese government reacted with cool detachment to Gorbachev's INF announcement that the Soviet Union would eliminate the SS-20 warheads from Asia without requiring reciprocal reduction of any nuclear forces of its adversaries. (His accompanying statement intentionally excluded Japan from the countries armed with U.S. nuclear weapons.) Following Gorbachev's announcement, to add insult to injury, Japan decided to join the U.S.-sponsored SDI. On 20 August Moscow expelled a military attaché and a deputy director of Mitsubishi Trading Company's Moscow office on trumped-up charges. This was the first time in postwar history that a Japanese diplomat had been expelled from the Soviet Union.[29] The apparent thaw in Japanese-Soviet relations in 1986 began quickly to deteriorate again only one year after the Vladivostok speech. Nevertheless, the Soviet government seems careful not to destroy the framework of normalized relations with Japan, which it had labored to create since Shevardnadze's visit. Nakasone, in turn, expressed his regret for the Soviet action but reaffirmed his hope that both countries would preserve the normalized bilateral relations.

FUTURE PROSPECTS

It is not likely that Japanese-Soviet relations will drastically improve in the near future. Neither side is willing to change its position on the northern territorial issue. Why is the Soviet Union so intransigent on this question? First, the four islands are militarily significant in controlling the sea, land, and air in and around the Sea of Okhotsk.[30] Second, these islands are practically the only viable leverage available to the Soviet Union.

The arms race in Asia and the Pacific is being stepped up. The complexity of Asian international politics will make it extremely difficult to achieve an arms control agreement in this region. But if Japan continues to insist on a solution to the territorial question as a precondition of any agreement with the Soviet Union, Japan might miss the chance to conclude a valuable arms control agreement or a crisis management agreement with the Soviet Union. The resulting instability in the region will not serve the best interests of Japan.

Japan could afford to ignore the task of improving relations with the Soviet Union in the past because she enjoyed stable relations with the United States and China. Although the stability of Japan's relations with these countries is unlikely to be destroyed in the near future, there are already clear signs of visible strains. Japanese-U.S. relations are facing difficult trade frictions. China is critical of the Japanese government's decision to remove the self-imposed limit of 1 percent of GNP for defense spending. It is likely that China would continue to oppose Japan's increased military role in the region. To ensure stability in the region, it might become necessary to develop some kind of arms control regime acceptable to Japan, the United States, and China, as well as to the Soviet Union.

Japan has not presented a comprehensive picture of the role of the Soviet Union in Asian stability. Does Japan take the view that there is no role the Soviet Union can play in Asian politics? If not, what positive role can Japan expect from the Soviet Union? If Japan is threatened by the Soviet military presence, how far does Japan expect the Soviet Union to scale it down, and what price will it pay to reduce its own military presence and that of its allies? What specific arms control proposal does Japan propose to reduce military tension in Asia?

It is important for Japanese foreign policy to integrate the Soviet Union in Asian international relations and not to exclude it. It is imperative, therefore, for the Japanese government and Japan's opinion leaders to begin calm and careful discussions on how this could be done without compromising Japan's national interests.

NOTES

1. See Tsuyoshi Hasegawa, "Japanese Perceptions of the Soviet Union: 1960–1985," *Acta Slavica Iaponica* 5 (1987): 37–70.
2. For detailed discussions on this subject, see ibid.
3. See William Watts, "American Views of the Soviet Union" (Paper presented at the conference entitled "U.S.-Japan Relations and the Soviet Union," Tokyo, 20–22 May 1987).
4. Ibid., 18–21.
5. Gaimusho, *Wagagaikono kinkyo: gaikoi seisho, showa 60 nenban* (*New Developments of Our Foreign Policy: Blue Book of Japanese Foreign Policy for 1985*) (Tokyo: 1986), 3–4.
6. Sotobo, *Ekonomikku torendo* (*Economic Trends*) 2–4 (1986): 111.
7. Leslie Dienes, "Regional Development and National Policy Choices: the Asian USSR," *Acta Slavic Iaponica* 4 (1986): 49–52; Kazuyuki Kimbara, "Development of Siberia and Japan," *Acta Slavica Iaponica* 4 (1986): 66–78; Gordon B. Smith, "Recent Trends in Japanese-Soviet Trades," *Acta Slavica Iaponica* 5 (1987): 111–123.
8. Kimura Hiroshi, "Basic Determinants of Soviet-Japanese Relations: Background, Framework, Perceptions, and Issues," *Acta Slavica Iaponica* 5 (1987): 75.
9. For instance, Nakajima Mineo, *Gorubachofu sorenno yomikata: shinsenryakuno shiniwa nanika* (*How to Read Gorbachev's Soviet Union: What Is the Real Meaning of the New Strategy?*) (Tokyo: Daiichikikakusha, 1987), 179–180.
10. Kimura, 77–78.
11. See Tsuyoshi Hasegawa, "The New Thinking and Gorbachev's Foreign and Military Policy" (Paper submitted to the conference entitled "U.S.-Soviet Relations and the Soviet Union," Tokyo, May 1987); also Tsuyoshi Hasegawa, "Gaiko-gunji seisakuni miru Gorubachofuno 'shinshiso'" ("Gorbachev's 'New Thinking' in Soviet Foreign and Military Policy"), *Chuokoron* (August 1987): 216–228.
12. "Soren kitteno nihontsu shokugyogaikoukann—Nikorai Sorobiyofu" ("Nikolai Soloviev—A Professional Diplomat Regarded as One of the Best Japanese Specialists"), *Sekaishuho*, 20 May 1986, 29.
13. *Mainichi*, 15 July 1986.
14. Kimura Hiroshi, "Soron: soren no Ajia taiheiyo seisaku no tenkai" ("An Overview: New Development of Soviet Policy toward Asia-Pacific"), *Soren Kenkyu* 3 (1986): 23.
15. "Nisso aratana shuppatsu" ("New Start of Japanese-Soviet Relations"), *Nihonkeizai Shimbun*, 19 January 1986.
16. Soren Taishikan Kohobu, *Soren kyosanto dai27kaiaikai shiryosh* (Soviet Embassy Public Relations Office, *Materials on the 27th Congress of the Communist Party of the Soviet Union*) (Tokyo: Ariesu Kshobo, 1986), 23.
17. Nakajima, *Gorubachofu sorenn no yomikata*, 132–170.
18. *Izvestiia*, 29 July 1986.
19. Kimura, *Soron*, 22–23.
20. For detailed discussion on this point, see Tsuyoshi Hasegawa, "Japan-Soviet Relations under Gorbachev" (Paper presented to a conference on the Soviet

Union and the Asia-Pacific Region, East-West Center, Honolulu, March 1987).

21. See Hasegawa, "The New Thinking and Gorbachev's Foreign and Military Policy."

22. *Izvestiia*, 29 July 1986.

23. *Hokkaido Shimbun*, 30 September 1986.

24. *Hokkaido Shimbun*, 25 October 1986.

25. *Hokkaido Shimbun*, 15 November 1986.

26. *Mainichi*, 15 November 1986; *Hokkaido Shimbun*, 15 November 1986.

27. See Marc Zlotnik's analysis on the power struggle within the CPSU as reported in *Japan Times*, 1 May 1987.

28. Kimura Hiroshi, "Go shokicho ichigatsu honichi naze kieta; sono neraiwo reiseini kangaenaose" ("Why Gorbachev's Visit in January to Japan Was Cancelled: We Must Rethink His Goals Soberly"), *Sankei*, 24 December 1986.

29. *Asahi*, 21 August 1987; *Hokkaido Shimbun*, 21 August 1987.

30. Boeicho, *Nihonno boei* (Japanese Self-Defense Agency, *Japanese Defense*) (Tokyo: Boeicho, 1986), 35–36.

4

South Korean Perceptions of the Soviet Union

Hakjoon Kim

SOUTH KOREAN PERCEPTIONS IN HISTORICAL PERSPECTIVE

Don't be deceived by the Soviets,
Don't count on the Americans,
The Japanese will soon rise again,
So, Koreans, look out for yourselves!

These are the warnings of a Korean rhyme popular in the middle of 1946 when the U.S.-Soviet negotiations on unifying Korea were almost stalemated. This rhyme reflects the Koreans' distrust and suspicion of the Soviet Union, one of the major powers competing for influence in Korea.[1]

The continuing negative attitude of the South Koreans toward the Soviet Union was confirmed by several opinion polls. In an opinion survey conducted by Professor Chong-u So of Yonsei University in 1980, the Soviet Union was the third most disliked country by South Koreans. Another opinion survey conducted by *Dong-A Ilbo (East Asia Daily)* in collaboration with the Statistical Research Institute of Korea University in 1982 indicated the same: North Korea was the most disliked country; Japan was the second; the Soviet Union was the third; and the People's Republic of China was the fourth.[2]

The Korean perception of the Soviet Union was not necessarily negative in the pre-Korean liberation period. In the late Korean Kingdom period, some Korean leaders wanted to enlist Russian aid to preserve Korea's independence. Yet other groups likened the Soviet Union to "a wolf," claiming that "the Russians are prone to pick quarrels with us and swoop down upon us by force of arms."[3] The new policy of liberating captive nations proposed by the Soviet government after the end of the First World War caused many Koreans to expect Soviet assistance in their struggle for independence. Korean communists believed that Korea's independence would be achieved with the Soviet Union's help.

Factors Contributing to South Korean Perceptions

However, in the postliberation period, the South Korean perception of the Soviet Union became almost totally negative. A number of factors explain the South Koreans' generally unfavorable attitude toward the Soviet Union.

First, the South Koreans are taught from elementary school that Korea was very important for tsarist Russia and that the Soviet policy toward Korea was aggressive. The Soviet Union's policy toward Korea was regarded as an extension of tsarist Russia. Therefore, it is not unusual for the South Koreans to regard the Soviet Union as "a big Red Bear" coveting an ice-free port in Korea. Even the Korean War of 1950 was once interpreted as a Soviet effort to secure ice-free ports in the southern part of Korea. However, a number of authorities contend that Korea was insignificant to Russia.[4] The Russian policy toward Korea was less planned and coherent than Western historians generally claim it to be. Russia did not attempt to seize Korea in the 1880s because it did not wish to jeopardize relations with China. In the 1890s and early twentieth century, Russia could not seize Korea because this would have provoked a war with Japan. Therefore, for Russia, Korea was not worth risking war with China or Japan.

Second, the South Koreans generally believe that the tragic decision to divide Korea at the 38th parallel was made at the Yalta Conference held in February 1945 in Yalta, a Crimean city of the Soviet Union.[5] Therefore, they associate their fatherland's tragedy with the "aggressive Red Bear," even though many authorities dispute this contention.[6]

Third, the three-year Soviet occupation of North Korea following the Korean division in August 1945 and the Soviet misconduct during that period instilled an unforgettable negative image of the Soviets. The Soviet misconduct in the North was so rampant in some areas that women had to disguise themselves as men to avoid rape, and wholesale looting of both Japanese and Korean property was commonplace. This raping and pillaging increased the Koreans' anti-Soviet feeling so sharply that according to Edwin W. Pauley, a member of the United States Reparations Commission for China and Korea, "two or three [Soviets] are killed every night by Koreans who have no weapons other than a rock."[7] Moreover, the Soviets blatantly manipulated the Korean economy for their own purposes during this period. In December 1947, the Soviets suddenly withdrew all money from circulation without announcing details on a new currency. Soviet occupational personnel had rid themselves of the old money beforehand and profited greatly from the new devalued currency. From late 1945 through 1948 the Soviets removed almost without any compensation 2 billion bushels of rice, 150,000 tons of sea products, and one complete steel refinery.[8]

Fourth, by 1948 the Soviets had implanted a communist regime in one of the most conservative societies in East Asia. As Robert Scalapino and Chong-sik Lee indicated, "North Korea came to communism not via an indigenous revolution, not through a union of communism and nationalism, but on the backs of the Red Army. The result was an extensive use of coercion, even more than might have been a sizable domestic base for the communist movement. North Korea, especially after the beginning of 1946, became a police state."[9] Some 800,000 individuals fled to the South between August 1945 and September 1948, when the communist state was officially inaugurated. These refugees were not "reactionaries" by any means, but they did become a strong anti-Soviet force in South Korea. The South Koreans felt that the Soviet Union had been responsible for the establishment of a hostile communist regime in the North that hindered the Korean unification.

Fifth, South Koreans generally believe that the Soviet Union began the Korean War in June 1950, even though recent Western research hesitates in blaming Stalin for its initiation, and the revisionists even contend that Stalin was not directly responsible for the outbreak of the Korean War.[10] In South Korea, Stalin has been portrayed as the instigator of the Korean War, and revisionist works are alien to the general public and viewed as "pro-Moscow."

Sixth, "the Korean War syndrome and the hysteria of anticommunism in the post–Korean War period" was an important factor in shaping the negative attitudes of the South Koreans toward the Soviet Union.[11] Syngman Rhee, the three-term president of the First Republic (1948–1960), played a particularly important role in this regard. As a staunch anticommunist and a pro-U.S. politician, he openly described the Soviet Union as the leader of communist dictatorships that should be "destroyed" by a Western crusade. South Koreans were told that the Soviet leaders have a grand design for world conquest and are attempting to add Korea to its "large bag of captive states." Therefore, South Korea should be a stronghold for the Western camp to thwart their "wicked design." He thus rejected even the idea of peaceful coexistence between the East and the West.[12] His successors from 1960 to 1972, John M. Chang, premier of the Second Republic (1960–1961), and Chung-Hee Park, the leader of the military government (1961–

1963) and the two-term president of the Third Republic (1963–1972), held identical attitudes toward the Soviet Union.

Seventh, the South Koreans believed that the Soviet Union was responsible for Korea's failure to be admitted to the United Nations. Indeed, the Soviet Union is the only member of the United Nations Security Council to veto South Korea's application for admission four times.

South Korean Images of the Soviet Union

The South Korean perception of the Soviet Union was extremely negative particularly before the 1970s. In this period, at least six prevailing images of the Soviet Union evolved. First, the Soviet Union was a totalitarian state supported by an official ideology, one mass party led by one man, a terroristic police, a communications monopoly, and a centrally directed economy. Images of the "blood-thirsty dictator" and the "secret police agent knocking at the home of a private citizen at midnight" were prevalent. These types of images were used often in social science textbooks and in political cartoons. It may be safe to surmise that if an average South Korean citizen with a high-school education was asked what he knew about the Soviet Union, the answer would have been Stalin, Beria, and the KGB.

Second, the Soviet Union was ruled by using continuous purges without fair and public trials and maintained by countless labor camps. Alexander Solzhenitsyn's *One Day in the Life of Ivan Denisovich*, a chilling portrayal of life in the labor camps, contributed to shaping the very gloomy and negative image of the Soviet Union among South Koreans.

Third, the Soviet Union was obsessed with secrecy—the Kremlin image. To the South Koreans the Soviet Union was a state full of intrigue and conspiracy. Even now, South Koreans describe a man who is secretive as "a Kremlin-like man."

Fourth, the Soviet Union was an anti-intellectual Orwellian state as described in *1984* and therefore produced many dissident intellectuals. Boris Pasternak, Alexander Solzhenitsyn, Andrei Amalrik, the Medvedev brothers, and Andrei Sakharov are well known to South Koreans with college educations.

Fifth, the Soviet Union was the merciless and monolithic oppressor of East European countries that longed for their independence from the Soviet empire. The Polish Revolt and the Hungarian Uprising in 1956 and the "Prague Spring" in 1968 symbolized to the South Koreans the small nations' fight for freedom against an oppressive super-power.

Sixth, the Soviet Union was aggressive, warlike, and risk taking. The South Korean mass media perceived almost every major international conflict as a direct or indirect result of aggressive Soviet behavior. The Soviet invasion of Hungary in 1956, the Cuban missile crisis in 1962, and the Soviet invasion of Czechoslovakia in 1968, among other events, confirmed the Soviet bellicose image perceived by the South Koreans.

In response to the South Koreans' distrust, the Soviets virulently and frequently denounced South Korea's actions. For instance, the Soviets denounced the South Korean–Japanese amity agreement of 1965 as the beginning of a U.S.-inspired Northeast Asian version of NATO. When the Asian and Pacific Council (ASPAC) was founded in June 1966 under the aegis of South Korea, Moscow condemned it as an attempt to form an anticommunist military alliance under U.S. sponsorship.[13] The Soviet Union also vehemently denounced South Korea's participation in the Vietnam War.

Changes in South Korean Perception

The South Korean perception of the Soviet Union shaped during the Cold War began to change slightly in the early 1970s. When the Nixon administration came to power in 1969, South Korea started rethinking the premises of its Cold War policy. The new U.S. foreign policy concentrated on developing a balance of power in an atmosphere of détente with the Soviet Union and the People's Republic of China. Under these circumstances, it was doubtful whether South Korea could sustain its anticommunist and anti-Soviet perception and policy. South Korea had no choice but to change its policy toward the Soviet Union. Also, the United States encouraged the South Korean leaders to modify their perception of communist states. Morton Abramowitz's policy paper, "Moving the Glacier: The Two Koreas and the Powers," had a considerable impact on reshaping the outlook of the South Korean decision makers.[14] Although he wrote this paper as a research associate at the International Institute for Strategic Studies in London while on leave from the United States State Department, the South Korean decision makers considered his views as largely representative of the United States government. Abramowitz suggested a "South Korean *Nordpolitik*" under which South Korea would "begin an active diplomacy toward communist nations, particularly the Soviet Union and East European countries." It is not known if the

United States officially recommended that the South Korean government take the measure proposed by Abramowitz. However, as Sungjoo Han indicated, the South Korean leaders concluded that Washington would not object if they took a more flexible approach toward communist nations including the Soviet Union. Accordingly, since 1971 the South Korean government has attempted to establish a working relationship with the Soviet Union.[15]

Considering that the Soviet Union had been portrayed as a feared enemy that should be opposed, it was remarkable how little public opposition there was to the government's new conciliatory approach. Despite the sudden turnaround by the government in 1971, the press unanimously supported the new "realistic" policy. Even when President Park declared on 23 June 1973 his government's willingness to establish official contact with the communist states including the Soviet Union, the reactions were generally positive, ranging from enthusiastic support by his Democratic Republican Party to a guarded acceptance by the opposition politicians.[16] An opinion survey conducted by Young-ho Lee, a political scientist, revealed that 53 percent of the respondents supported the establishment of diplomatic relations with communist states including the Soviet Union, while 23 percent opposed it.[17]

The South Korean perception of the Soviet Union, however, did not substantially change, particularly at the mass level. They still tended to perceive the Soviet Union as a totalitarian and oppressive communist police state seeking aggressive and imperialistic goals. Yet they accepted the governmental policy shift because they recognized that accommodating the Soviet Union and other communist countries would be necessary to the survival of South Korea.

The Soviet's attitude toward the South Korean proposals for mutual contact was somewhat positive. The Soviet Union indicated that it was willing to allow itself and other East European nations to have limited contacts with Seoul. In April 1978 the Soviet Union quickly returned the passengers and crew of a Korean Airlines jet that had strayed over Soviet territory and made a forced landing on a frozen lake about 280 miles south of Murmansk. The South Koreans were impressed with the cooperative and businesslike manner in which the Soviets handled the situation. Most of them viewed this episode as evidence of Soviet goodwill toward South Korea.[18] Ho-jeh Lee of Korea University commented in the *Choson Ilbo* (*Korea Daily*) on 2 May 1978 that the Soviet handling of the case "successfully contributed to converting the anti-Soviet sentiment among the South Koreans to a friendly one."

However, the South Korean perception of the Soviet Union has become negative again since the late 1970s because of the Soviet

Union's support for the Vietnamese invasion of Kampuchea in 1978, and its military intervention in Afghanistan in 1979. A South Korean historian wrote the following:

> While watching the development of the Afghanistan crisis, I, more than ever, have become convinced that the Russians, in spite of the multifaceted changes since the Bolshevik revolution, have not changed. The age old Russian imperialism characterized by Peter the Great and Catherine the Great has remained immutable as seen in the expansion of the Red Army in the Balkans and in Eastern Europe and is now seen again in Afghanistan. If the World cannot stop the Red Army in Afghanistan today, the Russians will not stop there. . . . I believe that the source of the Soviet invasion in Afghanistan has come from two seemingly antithetical sources: the traditional Russian imperialism and the communist contempt of human lives.[19]

SOUTH KOREAN PERCEPTIONS IN THE 1980s

Since the world situation in the 1980s has gradually developed into a "Second Cold War" era, the Cold War mentality against the Soviet Union has become evident again in South Korea. Moreover, the Soviet military buildup in the Far East has made the South Koreans anxious about their national security. Sang-woo Rhee, a South Korean authority on military affairs in East Asia, warned that "the shift of American military superiority to the Soviet Union undermines the South Korean sense of security. They are concerned about the unusual military build-up of North Korea. They are concerned about any move by the Soviet Union."[20] He also stated that the "South Koreans believe that the superpower balance is tilting toward Soviet superiority."[21]

The case of the ill-fated Korean Airlines passenger jetliner that was shot down by a Soviet fighter on 1 September 1983 solidified the South Korean negative perception of the Soviet Union. The *Korea Herald's* editorial on 3 September reflected the South Korean anti-Soviet sentiments aptly. "The wanton assault can never be excused for any reason. It must be denounced in the name of peace loving peoples everywhere. The Kremlin should come out with the truth of its crime, apologize to the world, and acknowledge the obligation to assume all consequences arising from shooting down the civilian aircraft." Byung-joon Ahn, a leading North Korea specialist in Seoul, warns, "Now that Kim Il Sung is willing to ask for Moscow's help in his struggle against Seoul and Washington, there is a danger that Moscow will be tempted to take advantage of this opportunity. Should it decide to supply

Pyongyang with new weapons, for example, tensions will again be heightened on the divided peninsula."[22]

The South Koreans perceive the Soviets "less as a direct threat than as the likely agent behind a North Korean offensive."[23] Because only the Soviets are "considered capable of sustaining a significant war effort from the North, the South Koreans do not quibble when the United States emphasizes the USSR as the principal problem for Asian security."[24] On the other hand, some South Korean experts are concerned that if U.S. policy is too anti-Soviet, South Korea might be the first to suffer.[25]

The advent of the Gorbachev regime in March 1985 was perceived as an indication of a possible change, albeit partial, in the domestic politics and foreign policies of the Soviet Union. Kyung-won Kim, the South Korean ambassador to the United Nations, commented that "the emergence of Gorbachev could be viewed as a process of modernization in Russia, which would require more emphasis on reality, pragmatic management of the society as a whole, and technology development."

While admitting that "we should not jump to the hasty conclusion that Gorbachev is a man of moderation and pragmatism," he expected that "under the young leader the Soviet Union will pursue a less rigid and more dynamic diplomacy."[26]

Although the South Korean public's image of the Soviets could have improved at this point, the Chernobyl nuclear accident in April 1986 further strengthened its negative perception of the Soviet Union. Most South Korean newspapers carried the story as a lead article. Describing the accident as "catastrophic" and "having far-reaching impact far beyond the Soviet border," the local press sharply criticized the Soviets for not disclosing exact information. Clearly, the Soviet handling of this accident solidified the South Korean general belief that the Kremlin leadership sacrifices humanism in the interest of its closed communist policy.

Gorbachev's speech on Asia and the Pacific made on 28 July 1986 at Vladivostok tended to strengthen the South Korean perception that the Soviet Union posed a threat to their security. A major theme of Gorbachev's Vladivostok speech was rapprochement with Asian countries, particularly with China, after a quarter century of verbal and physical sniping. At a closed session of the National Unification Board on 1 August 1986, a few political scientists in South Korea argued that Gorbachev's stress on bilateral relations between the Soviet Union and every Asian country and on the necessity of reducing tensions between the two Koreas indicated some willingness to improve Soviet relations with South Korea. It was noted that Gorbachev's call for an Asian version of the Helsinki Agreement would favor the status quo situation, recognizing a divided Korea. However, the press generally perceived the Vladivostok speech as a Soviet declaration of advancement into Asia and the Pacific, "driving a wedge between China and Western powers in its attempt to isolate Beijing and, furthermore, to undermine U.S. influence in the region."[27] The *Choson Ilbo* ran a series of six articles each titled "The Soviet Union Is Coming" that claimed the Soviets were attempting to influence the Asia-Pacific region. Russophobia was clear in these widely read articles.

Soon most South Korean newspapers became very attentive to the Soviet–North Korean military collaboration. Quoting "informed American government sources" and Japanese newspapers, they expressed grave misgivings and concerns about the Soviet military buildup in the East Sea (Sea of Japan) and the western Pacific. They also claimed that the Soviet Union had begun to develop North Korea's Wonsan harbor into a second Cam Ranh Bay by sending its Pacific fleet frequently to this vital North Korean port.

Kim Il-sung's visit to Moscow in October 1986 heightened South Korea's suspicion of the Soviet Union's military ties with North Korea. Although most Western analysts observed that Kim failed to secure any substantial Soviet assistance for his country's flagging economy,[28] the South Korean newspapers contended that his visit strengthened the Soviet–North Korean "military alignments."

President Chun of South Korea on 12 August 1986 reported at a news conference that "I am watching, with particular concern, the current moves of North Korea to rapidly expand its military links with the Soviet Union." Noting a high Soviet military officer's alleged press remarks that "the Soviet Pacific Navy is ready to wage joint operations with North Korea," he argued that "this indicates a possibility of Soviet ground forces intervening on behalf of North Korea."[29] Again, while presiding over a National Security Council meeting, he warned that intensifying military ties between the Soviet Union and North Korea posed "a great threat to the nation."[30] A month later, South Korea agreed with Japan at the fourteenth regular South Korea–Japan ministerial conference that "growing military cooperation between Pyongyang and Moscow is posing a threat to the maintenance of stability in Northeast Asia."[31] Recently Ki-tak Lee of Yonsei University, a noted Sovietologist in South Korea, asserted that "by closely allying itself with North Korea, the Soviet Union has the intention of taking aggressive initiatives to shake the strategic balance in Northeast Asia, including the Korean peninsula."[32]

Against this backdrop it is no surprise that the survey conducted by Han-sik Nam of Kwangju Education College in late 1986 showed that the Soviet Union had replaced Japan as the least favored country among South Korean primary school students. In the survey 50 percent considered the Soviet Union the least favored, 21 percent Japan, 9 percent China, 3 percent the United States, and 2.5 percent Iran. The same survey conducted in 1976 had indicated that 76.7 percent did not like Japan, 10.9 percent the Soviet Union, and 9 percent North Korea.[33]

How are Gorbachev's recent "reform measures" perceived in South Korea? The answer is a mixed one. While the return of Andrei Sakharov to Moscow and releases of political dissidents have received much attention and increased expectation for greater liberalization in the Soviet Union, the South Korean press speculated that its political and economic reforms "will be inevitably much more limited than those in Hungary and China."[34]

CONCLUSIONS

The South Korean perception of the Soviet Union is negative. South Korea is mindful of the history of Soviet belligerency and views the Soviet Union as a relentlessly opportunistic power. However, South Korea is determined to continue its open-door policy toward the Soviet Union. In view of the importance of the approaching Seoul Olympiad, the South Korean government, despite its persistent anger over the Korean Airlines incident, explored cautiously the possibilities of improving its frozen relations with the Soviet Union and of averting another Soviet-led Olympic boycott in 1988.[35] Moscow appeared to have reconciled itself to the Seoul Olympic Games in 1988, if only to prevent a clash with its East European allies, which a second successive boycott would inevitably provoke.[36] Under these common circumstances, the two countries resumed limited nonpolitical contacts. In August 1984 two South Korean representatives attended an international geological meeting in Moscow.[37] In September 1985 the Soviet judoists joined the 14th World Judo Championships for Men held in Seoul. This Soviet judo team is the first official sports team to ever visit South Korea.[38] In April 1986 the chairman of the USSR Sports Committee, Marat Gramov, attended the Seoul conference of the Association of National Olympic Committees (ANOC).

Soviet participation in the recently concluded 1988 Olympics in Seoul most likely had an important effect on South Korean perceptions of the Soviet Union. However, it is too soon to judge. As South Korea's foreign minister stressed earlier, Soviet participation would provide impetus for improving relations between Seoul and Moscow.[39] The coming months will bear witness to this expectation.

NOTES

1. K. Hwang, *The Neutralized Unification of Korea in Perspective* (Cambridge, Mass.: Schenkman, 1980), 1. For further analysis on Korean-Soviet relations see Hakjoon Kim, *Korea in Soviet East Asian Policy* (Seoul: Institute of International Peace Studies, 1987).

2. So's survey results were reported in *Chosun Ilbo*, 5 March 1980. The Dong-A Ilbo survey results were reported in its 13 January 1982 issue. For details, see Pyong-choon Hahm, "The Korean Perception of the United States," in Young-nok Koo and Dae-sook Suh, eds., *Korea and the United States: A Century of Cooperation* (Honolulu: University of Hawaii Press, 1984), 45.

3. Ho-jeh Lee, "Changes in the Perception of Foreign Affairs since the Years of the Opening of Korea," *Korea Journal* 18, no. 8 (August 1978): 24–25.

4. See Seung Kwong Synn, *The Russo-Japanese Rivalry Over Korea, 1876–1904* (Seoul: Yuk Phub Sa, 1981).

5. Syngman Rhee popularized this contention, and this thesis is common in writings by South Korean politicians and diplomats. See Pyong-jik Yim (Ben C. Limb), *Imjongeso Indokaji: Yim Pyong-jik Oekyo-hoekorok (From the Korean Provisional Government to India: Ben C. Limb's Diplomatic Memoirs)* (Seoul: Yowonsa, 1964), 261–263.

6. See Soon Sung Cho, *Korea in World Politics, 1940–1950: An Evaluation of American Responsibility* (Berkeley: University of California Press, 1967), 53–56.

7. Robert R. Simmons, *The Strained Alliance: Peking, Pyongyang, Moscow and the Politics of the Korean Civil War* (New York: The Free Press, 1975), 21–22.

8. Ibid., 22.

9. Robert A. Scalapino and Chong-sik Lee, *Communism in Korea* (Berkeley: University of California Press, 1972), 380.

10. See Bruce Cumings, *The Origins of the Korean War*, 2 vols. (Princeton, N.J.: Princeton University Press, 1981), vol. 1, *Liberation and the Emergence of Separate Regimes, 1945–1947*.

11. Ilpyong J. Kim, "Policies Toward China and the Soviet Union," in Young-nok Koo and Sungjoo Han, eds., *The Foreign Policy of the Republic of Korea* (New York: Columbia University Press, 1985), 198.

12. Foreign Broadcasts Information Service, *Daily Report* (South Korea: 2 June 1959).

13. Ibid.

14. Morton Abramowitz, "Moving the Glacier: The Two Koreas and the Powers," *Adelphi Papers*, no. 80 (London: International Institute for Strategic Studies, August 1971), 23.

15. Sungjoo Han, "South Korean Policy Toward the Soviet Union," in Sungjoo Han, ed., *Soviet Policy in Asia: Expansion or Accommodation?* (Seoul: Panmun Book Co., 1980), 322.

16. Ibid.

17. Young-ho Lee, *Han'gukinui Kach'ikwan (Koreans' Value Perceptions)* (Seoul: Iljisa, 1975), 77–78.

18. Han, 327.

19. Won-sul Lee, "Soviet Behavior," *Korea Herald*, 15 March 1980.

20. Sang-woo Rhee, "The Roots of South Korean Anxiety About National Security," in Sang-woo Rhee, ed., *Security and Unification of Korea,* 2d ed. (Seoul: Sogang University Press, 1984), 240.
21. Sang-woo Rhee, "Implications of Eroding Super-Power Balance in East Asia," in ibid., 410.
22. Byung-joon Ahn, "The Soviet Union and the Korean Peninsula," *Asian Affairs* 2, no. 5 (Winter 1985): 18–19.
23. Bernard K. Gordon, "Asian Angst," *Foreign Policy,* 47 (Summer 1982): 53.
24. Ibid.
25. Ibid.
26. *Korea Times,* 14 March 1985.
27. Ibid., 30 July 1986.
28. Ibid., 1 November 1986.
29. *Korea Herald,* 12 August 1986.
30. Ibid., 5 November 1986.
31. Ibid., 6 December 1986.
32. Ibid., 7 January 1987.
33. *Korea Times,* 25 February 1987.
34. *Korea Herald,* 14 November 1986. See also *Korea Times,* 8 February 1987.
35. Chae-jin Lee, "South Korea in 1984: Seeking Peace and Prosperity," *Asian Survey* 25, no. 1 (January 1985): 85.
36. *Far Eastern Economic Review,* 29 August 1985: 22.
37. Lee, 85.
38. *Korea Herald,* 21 September 1985.
39. Kwang-soo Choi, "The Situation on the Korean Peninsula and in the Surrounding Region and Korea's Foreign Policy Direction," *Korea & World Affairs* 11, no. 2 (Summer 1987): 229.

5

Reprise or Transformation?
Some Thoughts on Sino-Soviet Relations in the 1990s

Steven I. Levine

INTRODUCTION

The time has come to compose an epitaph for the Sino-Soviet conflict. From the 1960s into the 1980s this conflict was an apparently permanent landmark amidst the shifting terrain of international politics. However, over the past five years or so, significant changes in the relationship between the People's Republic of China (PRC) and the Soviet Union have accumulated to the point where we can now begin to speak of this conflict in the past tense. The scholars and analysts whose stock-in-trade has been exegesis of the Sino-Soviet conflict must recognize this reality and commence the difficult task of revamping their vocabulary and devising new approaches to analyze the relations between Moscow and Beijing.

Of course, many observers may consider it premature at best to issue a death certificate for the Sino-Soviet conflict. The current Sino-Soviet relationship is by no means free of important conflicts of interests, particularly regarding regional political issues such as Kampuchea and Afghanistan. Roughly one million Soviet and Chinese troops still face each other across a lengthy and, in part, disputed border, while their commanders continue to perceive each other as potential adversaries. Moreover, Chinese leaders still affirm that there can be no normalization of Chinese-Soviet relations until what they term the Three Obstacles are removed: Soviet support for the Vietnamese occupation of Kampuchea, the Soviet invasion of Afghanistan, and the large-scale Soviet military deployments along the Sino-Soviet border.

Nevertheless, the trend is clear. In political as well as economic terms, bilateral relations between Moscow and Beijing have improved significantly since 1982. Enhanced prospects now exist for resolving the regional political issues as well. Moreover, it seems likely that if the parallel reform programs now underway in China and the Soviet Union remain on course, they will provide a further impetus for improved relations in the 1990s. The amelioration of Sino-Soviet relations has taken place in a step-by-step manner without the high drama of the Sino-U.S. breakthrough in 1971–1972. Moreover, the Chinese have taken great care to minimize the importance of what has transpired. Thus it has been difficult for many observers to note the transformation that has in fact occurred by now.

Thomas G. Hart proposes that the most recent phase of Sino-Soviet relations be viewed as a "cold war termination process."[1] His analysis convincingly demonstrates that most of the specific issues that caused the original Sino-Soviet conflict as well as those that emerged in subsequent years have been resolved or rendered dormant.[2] What remains for leaders on both sides is to muster the will to resolve remaining points of conflict or at least not to allow contentious issues to dominate the relationship. Such political will now exists both in Moscow and Beijing.

This chapter will (1) briefly reconsider the history of Sino-Soviet relations since 1949; (2) analyze the changes that have occurred over the past five years; and (3) assess the prospects for the relationship in the 1990s.

DEALING WITH HISTORY

In October 1987 Deng Xiaoping, referring to China's troubled relations with the socialist bloc during the late Maoist era, said, "Let the past be blown away by the wind."[3] However, an understanding of history is essential for grasping the current state of affairs in Sino-Soviet relations. Here a few basic points must suffice.

First, the Sino-Soviet alliance of the 1950s was neither a mistake nor a disaster. Although the alliance eventually failed to satisfy the expectations of either partner, it represented a rational policy choice for both Moscow and Beijing within the strategic and political environment of 1950. For the leaders of the Chinese Communist Party (CCP) in particular, an alliance with the Soviet Union was a preferred choice, not a second-best alternative to the so-called lost chance of a relationship with the United States.

Second, the alliance with Moscow, while never ideal or trouble free, served Chinese foreign policy and domestic development goals reasonably well until the late 1950s. As Moscow's junior partner, Beijing was able to play an increasingly active role in international politics while Chinese development strategy, based on a late Stalinist model, scored significant successes, particularly in creating an industrial infrastructure.

Third, the collapse of the alliance was due less to irreconcilable Sino-Soviet differences over symbolic and substantive issues than to (1) the absence of intra-alliance conflict resolution mechanisms and procedures and (2) Mao Zedong's and Khrushchev's insistence on forcing issues to the point of rupture. In fact, during what might be called the *acceleration* stage of the Sino-Soviet conflict (1959–1963), the arbitrary and idiosyncratic leadership of Mao and Khrushchev, two leaders brought up in the rough-and-tumble Stalin-era school of communist politics, was largely responsible for the failure to achieve and sustain compromise. Thereafter, during the *inertial* stage of the conflict (1964–1976), both Mao and Leonid Brezhnev precluded the possibility of Sino-Soviet détente by making a hard-line position on Sino-Soviet relations a test of loyalty to their personal leadership.

The *deceleration* stage of the Sino-Soviet conflict (1977–1984) was characterized by Soviet initiative and Chinese delayed response. Leonid Brezhnev himself, as well as other Soviet leaders, verbally indicated a desire for improved relations with China. However, Chinese leaders focused on normalizing relations with the United States. One way to accomplish this was by accentuating the threat of Soviet expansionism that both the PRC and the United States supposedly confronted, and by pursuing a united front policy to contain the USSR.

The strategy of securing a U.S. connection was a great success. In fact, so rapidly did Sino-U.S. relations develop after 1979 that soon Beijing could afford to refocus its attention on Soviet relations. It is not saying too much to suggest that Sino-U.S. normalization made Sino-Soviet détente possible.

By this time, a strategic shift, from the Maoist focus on class struggle to the Dengist goal of modernization and development, had taken place at the Third Plenum of the 11th Central Committee in December 1978. This reorientation provided the Chinese with both the environment and the rationale for improving Sino-Soviet relations. During the last fifteen years of the Maoist period (1961–1976), one contentious issue after another—ideological conflict, territorial disputes, revolutionary rivalries, foreign policy differences—had piled up in the Sino-Soviet relationship forming an indissoluble mass like the coagulum in a clogged drain. Now political developments in China—particularly the restoration of political realism and the beginnings of the reform program—produced pressures for change that slowly began to break up the mass of "insoluble" issues.[4]

China's renewed focus on a long-term program of domestic modernization suggested the need for a stable and peaceful international environment.[5] At the very least, the renewal of a Sino-Soviet dialogue and the resumption of contacts could provide a less risky way of managing the perceived Soviet threat than the shrill polemical stance of the anti-Soviet coalition approach. More positively through economic cooperation, the Soviet Union and its East European allies could contribute to the strengthening of China's national economy—the fundamental goal of the Four Modernizations Program. Thus, at the threshold of the 1980s, China joined the Soviet Union in recognizing the dysfunctional impact of the Sino-Soviet conflict upon their national interests. Both states were now ready to embark upon a process of dialogue and contact.

SINO-SOVIET DÉTENTE

The improvement in Sino-Soviet relations has been a process of accretion without any breakthrough events. Throughout, the Soviets have maintained the initiative while the Chinese, for reasons suggested below, have been slow to admit that any fundamental change has occurred in their relations with the USSR.

Economics rather than politics have been the primary instrument for bridging the gap. In this area, an exchange of visits between the vice-premiers, Ivan Arkhipov and Yao Yilin, in December 1984 and July 1985 respectively, played an important role. These visits resulted in the signing of a long-term trade agreement (1986–1990) envisioning a $14 billion turnover in that period; the establishment of a Sino-Soviet Commission on Economic, Trade, Scientific, and Technological Cooperation, to promote the resumption of scientific and technical exchanges; and the signing of an agreement providing for Soviet assistance in the modernization of Soviet-designed industrial plans from the 1950s.[6] Regular meetings of the joint Sino-Soviet Commission contribute to the institutionalization of the economic relationship.

From a virtual absence of trade in the early 1970s, the Soviet Union has regained its position as one of China's major trading partners, rising to fifth place in 1986. Trade turnover increased from US$1.2 billion in 1984 to $2.64 billion in 1986.[7] However, this is still only a small percent of China's total foreign trade and about a third of the U.S.-China trade turnover. This is a far cry from the 1950s when the USSR and Eastern Europe accounted for some two-thirds of China's total trade.

The Soviet Union ships machinery, steel, electrical generating equipment, transportation equipment, fertilizer, and other industrial products to the PRC in exchange for light industrial products including textiles, processed foodstuffs, handicrafts, minerals, and livestock.[8] China's exports to the Soviet Union benefit from the absence of the protectionist barriers encountered in Western markets, and commodity-starved Soviet consumers are not particularly finicky about quality.

As a socialist country, the Soviet Union does not take part in the foreign investment side in China or in the development of the coastal cities. Its still modest role focuses on the revitalization of the "rust belt" enterprises of the northeast and of China's interior. If central planning in China is reduced over the next several years, as is presently envisaged, the scope for the traditional sort of Sino-Soviet economic exchanges may diminish accordingly. However, in a growing economy this still provides ample room for the expansion of Sino-Soviet trade. Moreover, the decentralization of economic decision making has facilitated the revival of border trade between the contiguous Chinese provinces and Soviet republics. After a break of twenty years, Heilongjiang, Inner Mongolia, and Xinjiang are linked economically once again with eastern Siberia and Soviet Central Asia. Maritime shipping and river transport along the Amur and Sungari rivers in northeast China resumed in 1986. Although the value of the border trade is still only a tiny percentage of Sino-Soviet total trade, it is important because it contributes to and reflects a more relaxed atmosphere along the border.[9]

The Sino-Soviet links in culture, education, science and technology, sports, and theater that were severed during the 1960s also have been reforged. In the area of education, for example, the number of exchange students increased from a mere twenty in 1983–1984 to several hundred currently. Of course, this is still only a small fraction of the nearly 20,000 Chinese students presently in the United States.

The essence of Sino-Soviet relations lies in the political and security arenas, where serious conflicts of interests persist. Chinese defense planners continue to view the USSR as their primary potential adversary; however, their actions bespeak no fear of imminent conflict. The reduction in force of the People's Liberation Army (by some 1 million troops), the conversion of many defense industries to civilian production, and the reduction in the percentage of the national budget allocated to defense all indicate this.

In recent years, political relations between China and the Soviet Union have multiplied, even though they have not yet culminated in the summit meeting that Soviet General Secretary Gorbachev has proposed on more than one occasion. The Chinese have maintained a rigid and artificial separation between state-to-state relations, where they acknowledge significant improvement, and party-to-party relations, where they have remained unbending thus far.

Several channels, in addition to the embassies, now exist for Soviet and Chinese officials to exchange views and discuss problems. Talks at the deputy foreign minister level, begun in the fall of 1979 and suspended after the Soviet invasion of Afghanistan in December, resumed in October 1982. These talks, which by the fall of 1987 had gone through eleven rounds, alternate between Moscow and Beijing every six months and provide a secure channel for discussion on a wide variety of subjects. It was from these talks that the initial agreements on the resumption of economic and cultural ties developed.

In February 1987 negotiations to resolve the Sino-Soviet boundary disputes resumed after a nine-year hiatus. By the end of the second round in August 1987, these talks had progressed to the point where working groups of technical experts were tasked with examining in detail the eastern sector of the boundary.[10] The Soviet and Chinese foreign ministers meet annually during the United Nations General Assembly session to exchange views. In December 1987 shortly after the signing of the INF treaty, Moscow dispatched Deputy Foreign Minister Igor Rogachev to Beijing to brief Chinese officials.[11] The exchange of visits by high-level officials transpire in an increasingly cordial atmosphere.

Upon assuming leadership in March 1985, Mikhail Gorbachev intensified efforts to improve relations with the PRC. In his report to the 27th Congress of the CPSU in February 1986, he expressed satisfaction with the improvement of Soviet relations with China and asserted that "the reserves for cooperation between the USSR and China are enormous."[12] On 28 July 1986 in his Vladivostok speech, Gorbachev undertook a major initiative toward the Chinese. He reiterated Soviet acceptance of the median-line principle for the disputed river boundary in the Far East, outlined expanded prospects for Soviet-Chinese economic cooperation, offered to consider a drawdown of Soviet troops along the Sino-Soviet and Sino-Mongolian borders, and announced a token withdrawal of Soviet forces from Afghanistan. Shortly thereafter, he expressed an interest in a summit meeting with Chinese leaders, an interest he has repeated.

Chinese leaders have reacted cautiously to these Soviet initiatives. On the one hand, they have welcomed the substantive changes in Sino-Soviet relations and expressed satisfaction with the increasing level of trade, cultural exchanges, and opportunities for discussion of vital issues. On the other hand, they have resisted the suggestion that Sino-Soviet relations can be normalized until the Soviets remove the

Three Obstacles from the relationship. Deng Xiaoping and other senior Chinese leaders have made it clear that movement on Kampuchea, in particular, is the indispensable precondition for any Sino-Soviet summit. This is the most difficult of the issues for the Soviets and has been singled out by the Chinese for precisely that reason.

While important Chinese officials meet regularly with their Soviet counterparts, the Chinese have thus far refused to resume party-to-party relations with the CPSU. For example, the CCP refrained from sending a delegation to the 70th anniversary celebration of the Bolshevik Revolution in November 1987, although a former high-ranking Chinese diplomat, Zhang Wenjin, attended in his capacity as head of the Chinese People's Association for Friendship with Foreign Countries.[13] By withholding party ties (which by now have been reestablished with all of Moscow's East European partners), the CCP maintains its symbolic disapproval of "hegemonic" Soviet behavior in the international communist movement without jeopardizing any concrete Chinese interests. Some Western observers, it seems to me, have made too much of China's refusal to reestablish party links with the CPSU.

What explanation may be offered for China's behavior? First, under the rubric of their "independent foreign policy" enunciated in 1982, the Chinese are concerned about maintaining a certain balance in their relations with the two superpowers, a balance that presently inclines toward the United States for both strategic and economic reasons. Chinese leaders have been at pains to assure the United States that the Three Obstacles constitute a kind of built-in limit to Sino-Soviet rapprochement. This is important partly to ensure the flow of U.S. high technology and investment capital to China and to maintain equilibrium in the strategic triangle.

Second, China's insistence on removal of the Three Obstacles functions as a kind of psychological device to reassure the Chinese themselves that they can maintain a truly independent foreign policy and not lean too far into the embrace of one or the other of the superpowers.[14] It provides some distance between China and the Soviet Union functioning very much like the Taiwan issue in U.S.-China relations.

Paradoxically, perhaps the Three Obstacles, rather than being a barrier to Sino-Soviet normalization, have actually been the framework within which that normalization has occurred. Furthermore, by now normal relations between the Soviet Union and China have basically been restored notwithstanding the absence of party-to-party ties and the lack of a summit meeting. These will come in due course. The framework of the Three Obstacles may now be dismantled without jeopardizing the structure of Sino-Soviet relations.

REFORMING SOCIALISM AND SINO-SOVIET RELATIONS

In the late 1980s both China and the Soviet Union have set themselves on a difficult and long-term course of reform that involves major restructuring of their economic, political, and social systems. What are the effects of the reform programs on the relations between the two countries?[15]

As Sino-Soviet relations continue to improve in the late 1980s, the pursuit of reform programs in both countries forges an additional link between them. Reform leaders in both China and the Soviet Union recognize a set of similar structural, attitudinal, and cultural problems that they must tackle if reform is to succeed.

Recognition of the imperative of reform has restored a tentative measure of solidarity to the fractured world of communism. There are undoubtedly leaders in Moscow as in Beijing who look anxiously at the reform program of their neighbor from the perspective of national power rivalry and security concerns. But there is also an acknowledgment in both countries that to a certain degree the fate of their reform programs is linked. The lines between "revisionists" and "dogmatists" no longer run along national boundaries as they appeared to during the era of Sino-Soviet ideological polemics. And those polemics themselves have long since outlived their usefulness. Within the communist world, reform-minded leaders draw sustenance from a common reservoir of ideas, techniques, practices, and innovations and in turn contribute to this same reservoir.

Gorbachev and his associates have acknowledged China's lead in the process of socialist reform and indicated an interest in borrowing suitable elements of the Chinese experience. This smooths the path for further Sino-Soviet accord. It is also a far cry from the early 1950s when it was China that borrowed massively and uncritically from the Soviet experience of building socialism. Perhaps the elder brother–younger brother metaphor that was used to depict the Soviet-Chinese relationship in the 1950s may now be replaced by the notion of first cousins within the extended family of socialist countries, first cousins who have restored civility to their relations after a prolonged period of conflict. The mutual interest that Moscow and Beijing display in each other's reform is a form of external legitimation, but still within the socialist system and therefore much more useful, from an ideological perspective at least, than the plaudits of the capitalist heathen.

What would be the consequence if reform should falter or fail in either China or the Soviet Union? A "restorationist" leadership that came to power in one of the countries, but not in the other, might attempt to reimpose some version of an old orthodoxy.[16] In that case, it would be tempted to pick up the ideological cudgels once again and attack its reforming neighbor in the name of ideological purity. On the other hand, if both reform programs collapse more or less simultaneously, it seems doubtful that this would lead to enhanced Sino-Soviet cooperation. A reversion to rival nationalisms seems more probable.

PROSPECTS FOR THE 1990s

The Sino-Soviet relationship that has developed within the past several years is anchored in two new realities. The first is the existence of a much stronger and internationally recognized Chinese state that enjoys a broad network of relationships within the global political system. Second is the painfully acquired Soviet awareness that the limits of power apply even to states with superpower status. The days of simple Soviet *diktat* within the communist world are a thing of the past even with respect to lesser allies.

Compared to the 1950s, there is a much-diminished sense of expectation in both Moscow and Beijing as to the benefits of the Sino-Soviet relationship. But from the intervening decades of unproductive conflict, there is also a sense of the inutility of strife between the two countries.

Too much attention is paid, in my judgment, to the short-term impediments to greater Sino-Soviet cooperation and interchange. The famous Three Obstacles may never have really been serious obstacles at all and in any case, they are increasingly irrelevant.

Are there any limits to Sino-Soviet accord? As two historic empires and as contiguous modern states concerned with ensuring their security and their welfare, China and the Soviet Union possess divergent national interests. As they strive to project their power, they are very likely to find themselves competing for influence in Asia and, as China acquires accoutrements of a global actor, in other regions as well. In a world of nuclear weapons and missile technology, these two nuclear powers will long remain wary of each other's capacity for destruction and prepare accordingly. The ideology of socialism, which is badly in need of revitalization, may eventually form a strong bond between them, but only if national differences are respected by leaders on both sides. Both the Soviet Union and the PRC will need to pay continuing attention to their relations with the United States, Japan, Western Europe, and the emerging major powers of coming decades. Their interests, expectations, and strategies for dealing with these states will diverge at many points. These are a few of the major reasons for supposing that Soviet and Chinese differences will persist and conflicts of interest intrude from time to time.

However, what has just been suggested is normal in international relations. Within limits set by geopolitical, historical, cultural, and other factors, the prospects for enhanced and accelerated Soviet-Chinese cooperation and exchanges in many fields are very good. This is the new reality that has taken shape in the past half-decade and that commands the attention of scholars, analysts, and policymakers.

NOTES

1. Thomas G. Hart, *Sino-Soviet Relations: The Prospects for Normalization* (Aldershot, Hampshire, England: Gower, 1987), 113.
2. Hart, 69–91.
3. Deng said this upon meeting Hungarian leader Janos Kadar during Kadar's visit to the PRC. *China Daily*, 14 October 1987, 1.
4. For a complete catalogue of the disputed issues, see Hart; for a view that emphasizes continuing conflicts, see Alfred D. Low, The *Sino-Soviet Confrontation Since Mao Zedong: Dispute, Detente, or Conflict?* (Boulder, Colo.: Social Science Monographs, Distributed by Columbia University Press, New York, 1987).
5. For a cautiously optimistic prognostication of Sino-Soviet relations from the vantage point of the late 1970s, see Steven I. Levine, "Some Thoughts on Sino-Soviet Relations in the 1980s," *International Journal* 34, no. 4 (Autumn 1979), 649–667.
6. *Pravda*, 28 July 1985, 4.
7. *The China Business Review* 14, no. 3 (May–June 1987): 20.
8. *China Daily*, 30 December 1987, 2; on Sino-Soviet economic relations, see the several articles in *The China Business Review* 14, no. 3 (May–June 1987): 12–25.
9. See, for example, *New York Times*, 28 September 1987, 1–2.
10. *Washington Post*, 9 February 1987, A13, A17; *China Daily*, 22 August 1987, 1.
11. *FBIS-China* 87–244 (21 December 1987): 4.
12. *Pravda*, 25 February 1986, 11.
13. *New York Times*, 27 October 1985, 5; *China Daily*, 24 December 1987, 1.
14. See Steven I. Levine, "The End of Sino-Soviet Estrangement," *Current History* 85, no. 512 (September 1986): 279–280.
15. The following section is taken from Steven I. Levine, "The Internal Dynamics of Sino-Soviet Relations: Ideology and Reform," part of an Occasional Paper published by the Wilson Center of the Smithsonian Institution.
16. I borrow the term "restorationist" from Harry Harding's usage in *China's Second Revolution* (Washington, D.C.: The Brookings Institution, 1987), 40–69.

6

Soviet Policy in Southeast Asia in the Gorbachev Era: Change or Continuity?

Robert C. Horn

The Soviet Union has been heavily involved in Southeast Asia virtually from the beginning of Khrushchev's mid-1950s "offensive" into the Third World, marked in this region by Indonesian president Sukarno's highly publicized visit to Moscow in 1956 and by increasing Soviet support for North Vietnam. Into this context of more than thirty years of Soviet efforts in the region has stepped the new Soviet leader, Mikhail Gorbachev, with a variety of proposals for peace and security in Asia.[1] Perhaps the most significant of his approaches to the region was described in his speech delivered in late July 1986 in the Soviet Far Eastern city of Vladivostok.[2] Among a host of proposals for "integrating the Asia-Pacific region into the general process of establishing a comprehensive system of international security," Gorbachev also called for expanded ties with ASEAN states, a resolution of the Kampuchea issue, and normalization of Sino-Vietnamese relations. These and other foreign policy initiatives raised anew the issue of the Soviet policies in the region.

CHINA AND SOVIET POLICY IN INDOCHINA

The events of 1978 in Indochina combined to forge a far closer Soviet-Vietnamese relationship than had existed previously, one that was much closer than most analysts could have imagined. Moscow has made extensive use of its available economic, military, and diplomatic resources to maintain its alliance with Vietnam and to bolster Hanoi's position in the region during the 1980s. Although reliable figures are impossible to obtain, there is no question that Soviet assistance to Vietnam's economy has been both substantial and critical. The USSR pledged approximately $2.5 billion to Vietnam's

Second Five-Year Plan (1976–1980).[3] Most estimates of Soviet funding for Hanoi's third plan (1981–1985) were in the $5–6 billion range, translating to $900 million to $1.3 billion per year.[4] These last figures support the commonly held conception that Soviet assistance for Vietnam has been running at approximately $3 million per day through the first half of the 1980s, more than double the previous rate. The Vietnamese reported in mid-1985 that the USSR would double its economic assistance to Vietnam again in the fourth plan period (1986–1990). Soviet leader Yegor Ligachev was reported to have corroborated this at the 6th Congress of the Vietnamese Communist Party (CPV) at the end of 1986: Moscow's planned economic aid for the new plan was between $12 and $13 billion, which would amount to approximately $2–2.5 billion per year or some $6 million per day.[5]

From Moscow's standpoint, this assistance is very substantial, representing some 35 percent of the USSR's total assistance to Third World countries.[6] Indeed, the Kremlin has reminded Vietnam that "the Soviet people have to share with you even things they are also needing."[7] For the Vietnamese, Soviet support is the main prop of the country's economy. Moscow furnishes between 80 to 100 percent of the country's oil, fertilizer, and metallurgy. Soviet aid is estimated at between one-fifth and one-half of the budget. Agreements signed in 1981 further integrated the Vietnamese economy into the socialist world system by more closely meshing the Soviet and Vietnamese planning cycles, formulating plans for Soviet involvement in some 40 new projects (in addition to 100 ongoing ones), and sending tens of thousands of Vietnamese "guest workers" to the USSR and Eastern Europe reportedly to help repay Hanoi's debts to the Soviet bloc.[8]

Vietnam's growing economic dependency on the USSR is also reflected in figures on Hanoi's indebtedness and trade flows. Vietnam's foreign debt has been rising dramatically, from $3.5 billion in 1981 to $6 billion in 1984; Moscow's share of this debt has also risen, from 50 percent in 1978 to 63 percent in 1981 and 67 percent in 1984. Trade flows reveal a similar pattern. The Soviet share of Vietnam's total trade turnover in 1976 was 38.7 percent, while in 1984 Moscow accounted for 60 percent of the country's imports and exports.

Such a tightening of the economic relationship has undoubtedly created some degree of discomfiture for both partners. Moscow has indicated concern with the "efficiency" with which its funds are used, while the Vietnamese have expressed their sensitivity over the control exercised by their powerful benefactor. These underlying tensions in the relationship were clearly illustrated in the negotiations regarding the level of Soviet support for Vietnam's Third Five-Year Plan. Moscow selected CPSU secretary and Politburo member Mikhail Gorbachev, known for his economic expertise, to make his first visit to

Asia at the head of the Soviet delegation to the CPV's 5th Congress in March 1982. Gorbachev concentrated on the Vietnamese economy and economic ties between the two countries. The key passage (which was published in *Pravda* but not in the Vietnam News Agency [*VNA*] text of his speech)[9] in his address to the congress asserted that the two were obliged "to be constantly concerned to increase the efficiency of cooperation and ensure its 100 percent yield. . . ." He continued: "With you we can cope fully with the precise fulfillment of all mutual pledges. You may be confident, comrades, that for our part we will do everything necessary for this. And we do not doubt that you too will act in the same way."

Reading between the lines, which the Vietnamese leaders undoubtedly did not find necessary after their private talks with the Soviet leader, we can assume that Gorbachev was complaining that Hanoi was not fulfilling its part of the economic bargain and that Moscow was far from confident about Vietnam's reliability to do so in the future.

Continuing Soviet assistance coupled with the continuing tension over Vietnam's economic performance have marked the economic relationship into 1987. During Le Duan's Moscow visit in mid-1985, Gorbachev, now the CPSU general secretary, made a number of significant gestures. He specifically agreed to increase the deliveries to Vietnam of critical items such as petroleum products, fertilizers, rolled metals, and cotton. Most importantly, the Soviets offered to extend a new credit on preferential terms (believed to carry a thirty-year maturity, a ten-year grace period, and an interest rate of only 2 percent) for the 1986–1990 plan and to defer Vietnam's repayments on earlier credits.

This generous, quickly concluded, and apparently painless agreement—in stark contrast to Soviet assistance for the previous plan—was followed, however, by increasingly explicit recognition of Vietnam's economic shortcomings both by Moscow and, particularly, by Hanoi. In the run-up to the CPV Congress and the expected leadership changes to be announced there at the end of 1986, Vietnamese politics were dominated by criticism and self-criticism by party leaders and branches regarding mishandling of the economy. The Soviets reportedly got directly in on the act in August when Truong Chinh was "scolded" for "mismanagement of the economy and mishandling of Soviet aid."[10] The Vietnamese leader himself admitted that "we have committed serious shortcomings and mistakes in economic leadership." Significantly, Chinh specifically admitted the misuse of Soviet aid: "The country's latent potentials as well as the great assistance of the Soviet Union and other fraternal socialist countries, far from being brought into full play, have been seriously squandered and face *the danger of gradually becoming exhausted.*"[11] The last part of this statement may refer to thinly veiled threats that Moscow had made in order to get its way on reforms in Vietnam's economic system.

In the military sphere, Moscow's assistance declined after 1975, but increased again after the Vietnamese invasion of Kampuchea in 1978 and the Chinese response in 1979. Most sources estimate that Soviet military aid during the 1980s has been running close to the level of the 1960s and early 1970s. This has added to Hanoi's already impressive armory, the largest and most sophisticated in Southeast Asia. Aside from weapons, Moscow's military support for Vietnam has been expressed in a number of other forms. The 1978 treaty contains a clause stating that if "one of the parties becomes the object of attack or of a threat of attack," the two will "immediately begin mutual consultation" to remove the threat and take "appropriate effective measures. . . ." This qualified Soviet support provided the crucial security umbrella under which Hanoi was able to invade Kampuchea and has been cited by both sides since as being a main foundation of their bilateral relationship. Moreover, in April 1984, during a time of recurrent Sino-Vietnamese tension and conflict along their mutual border, the Soviets took the unprecedented step of holding—and publicizing—joint amphibious exercises with the Vietnamese in the Gulf of Tonkin. Moscow assembled a large part of its Pacific fleet (now the largest of the four fleets in the Soviet navy), including the aircraft carrier *Minsk* and the amphibious assault ship *Ivan Rogov* as well as some 400 troops for the maneuvers that concluded with a landing on Vietnamese beaches.[12]

The most significant "return" on this investment is in the granting by Vietnam of base rights to the Soviets. Moscow's increasing use since 1979 of the former U.S. bases in South Vietnam, Cam Ranh Bay and Da Nang, as well as other sites in the country, has led to repeated charges that the Soviets now have full base facilities in Vietnam. The growth of the Soviet presence is undeniable. While in 1980–1981, for instance, there were somewhere between seven to ten Soviet ships in Cam Ranh Bay at any one time, this number increased to ten to fifteen in 1982, twenty-two in 1983, the mid-twenties in 1984, and twenty-five to thirty (including four to six submarines) in 1985. Moreover, the Soviets deployed offensive aircraft, TU-16 bombers, at Cam Ranh for the first time in late 1983. By late the next year, the nine original TU-16s had been supplemented by seven more in addition to four TU-95 reconnaissance aircraft, four TU-95 ASQ aircraft, and most significantly, at least fourteen MIG-23s.[13] During the 1980s, the Soviets have sought to improve the facilities, particularly at Cam Ranh. They have enlarged the petroleum storage capacity, installed docking facilities to service ships, and built new communications and intelligence facilities. A Thai report in late 1985 asserted that Cam Ranh Bay was now the USSR's largest overseas base.[14]

These facilities being developed at Cam Ranh Bay are obviously of great significance to the Soviets. They have given Moscow a warm-water port some 2,200 miles south of Vladivostok, one that increases the Soviet Union's capability of rapid deployment in the Indian Ocean and Persian Gulf regions as well as in Southeast Asia. Clearly, it enhances the potential for Soviet influence over strategic shipping lanes. The aircraft deployed by the Soviets have given them intelligence-gathering and combat capability over the entire ASEAN area. The communications and electronic surveillance facilities enable Moscow to monitor Chinese and American military activities and to communicate with the headquarters of the Pacific fleet in Vladivostok.[15]

The Soviets have gone to some lengths to deny that Cam Ranh Bay or any other facility in Vietnam, is a Soviet base. The Vietnamese have also been vocal in denying that Moscow has bases, contrasting the U.S. control and use of Subic Bay naval base in the Philippines for aggression against Southeast Asian targets with the limited Soviet facilities in Cam Ranh Bay. In a May 1984 interview, Hanoi's prime minister Pham Van Dong stated that the Soviets have "facilities" not "bases" in Vietnam, adding that "we would never. . .grant any country the right to have bases in Vietnam."[16]

Given Vietnam's historic sensitivity to infringements on its independence and sovereignty, such a base would seem to represent a substantial exercise of leverage by Moscow over Vietnamese policy. Thus, although we have no evidence of friction on this issue, we ought not to assume that there is none, for it seems likely that Hanoi is uncomfortable with the current arrangement.

Diplomatically, too, the Soviet Union has extended substantial support to Vietnam, particularly in backing its occupation of Kampuchea. Vietnam's involvement in Kampuchea is clearly in Hanoi's own interests, and it is difficult to see that the original Vietnamese invasion involved the Soviet Union's interests in any significant way, other than in the removal of a pro-Chinese regime in Phnom Penh and, of course, to support its Vietnamese ally. To the extent that Soviet support for Vietnam's war in Kampuchea is a trade-off for the Soviet base facilities, then the direct Soviet stake in the conflict has become substantially greater. In any case, Vietnam has been largely successful in influencing Soviet policy to endorse Vietnam's objectives. Hanoi has turned away Soviet attempts to establish its own influence in Indochina—as in the Pen Sovan affair in Phnom Penh in 1981.[17] There have also been rumors that the Soviets have been dissatisfied with Vietnam's inflexible stand regarding negotiations with ASEAN over

Kampuchea, yet the Kremlin has continued to support Vietnam in the United Nations and vis-à-vis the Nonaligned Movement and ASEAN.

The interrelationships among Vietnam, the Soviet Union, and China have provided for almost thirty years the fundamental framework for Vietnamese behavior as well as for the regional policies of both the USSR and PRC. For Hanoi the close relationship with the Soviet Union was essential in the face of China's hostility. Into the early 1980s, the Vietnamese leaders seemed secure in the knowledge of the dependability of Soviet support as the Sino-Soviet dispute showed no signs of abating.

Beginning early in 1981, however, the Soviets began repeated, if erratic, attempts to obtain Vietnamese endorsement of their first tentative efforts at a Sino-Soviet rapprochement. These efforts intensified in the fall of 1984. Gorbachev's positive references to China at Chernenko's funeral in March 1985 gave official confirmation to trends that had emerged in Soviet-Vietnamese meetings the previous October and had been symbolized by the successful Arkhipov visit to China in December.[18] Perhaps the clearest indication of the new direction of Soviet policy was the lack of a response from the Kremlin to the border fighting between China and Vietnam that reached its peak in April 1985. This fighting, said to be the heaviest since 1979, did not lead to a downward turn in Soviet-Chinese relations as had the fighting in April 1984. Le Duan's mid-year pilgrimage to Moscow provided further evidence: there were no attacks on China and both sides endorsed efforts at normalization with Beijing.[19]

Gorbachev's mid-1986 address in Vladivostok has its greatest significance for Soviet-Vietnamese relations in the context of this "China factor" and the connection between it and Kampuchea. Among the various things Gorbachev said, his focus on extending the olive branch to China had to be particularly disquieting to the Vietnamese. Not only did he speak in quite conciliatory terms about Sino-Soviet relations, but he also used a substantial portion of his speech to call for "additional measures for creating an atmosphere of good-neighborliness." Moreover, he seemed to offer concessions in two of the three obstacles to improved relations that China has cited.

Nevertheless, the Vietnamese received some assurances on the obstacle that directly involved them, Kampuchea. No Soviet concessions were even hinted at here, and Gorbachev explicitly endorsed Hanoi's stance that "it is impermissible" to try to reverse the current political situation in Kampuchea. He also indicated that the Kremlin was not going to pressure Vietnam on China's behalf or vice versa because this was basically a Sino-Vietnamese conflict. While Hanoi was pleased with Gorbachev's refusal to sacrifice Vietnamese interests in his quest for improved relations with China, both his implied recognition that China had a stake in Kampuchea (which the Socialist Republic of Vietnam leaders admitted only privately) *and* the neutral stance he took as to the source of conflict in the region caused friction in Soviet-Vietnamese relations.

The 6th Congress of the Communist Party of Vietnam, held in December 1986, provided a further opportunity to examine the China factor in Soviet-Vietnamese relations. Hanoi's lack of enthusiasm for the Soviet efforts at normalization was clear from the terse reference to them in the Central Committee's lengthy report to the congress: "We support the Soviet Union's policy of normalizing relations with China. . . ."[20] This support, albeit grudging, from the Vietnamese side was perhaps the quid pro quo for Moscow's explicit assurance that it would not develop relations with China "at the expense of any other countries' interests and *not at Socialist Vietnam's expense.*"[21]

The ninth round of Sino-Soviet normalization talks in October had also seemed to indicate a further step in Soviet-Vietnamese strains. The new Soviet negotiator, Igor Rogachev, who was deputy foreign minister and head of the ministry's department of Far Eastern and Asian affairs, arrived in Beijing declaring that he was ready to discuss *any* question of interest to both sides. This was never confirmed, however, and there was no reported discussion of the Kampuchea issue, other than Rogachev's rejection of Deng Xiaoping's proposal for a summit with Gorbachev anywhere in the USSR if Moscow agreed to press Vietnam to withdraw its troops from Kampuchea.[22] Rogachev was reported to have told the Chinese that China should hold direct negotiations with Vietnam on the matter, instead of asking the Soviet Union to press the Vietnamese. However, in the tenth round in Moscow in April 1987, the two sides did indeed have "detailed discussions" on a number of topics including "regional conflicts." Chinese commentary made it clear that the major focus of these discussions was Kampuchea, as well as Afghanistan. The talks were described as "beneficial" but also "frank" and there was no reported or evident progress on Kampuchea.[23] Nevertheless, the Chinese negotiator, Qian Qichen, enthusiastically emphasized that "we welcome the fact that the Soviet Union does not refuse now to discuss the Cambodian and Afghanistan questions with us."[24]

It seems clear that Hanoi was under pressure from both sides of the Moscow-Hanoi-Beijing triangle. For one, the Vietnamese were candid about their worry that "China really seeks to exert pressure on Vietnam through the improvement of Soviet-Chinese relations."[25] On the other hand, the Soviets had also increased the pressure somewhat on the Vietnamese, particularly since Gorbachev came into power. Vietnamese spokesmen are far less candid about this aspect, but one source was cited as pointedly remembering back to the war against the United States when Vietnam "could not be pressured by its aid donors to change its policy."[26] It is also clear that Hanoi was still succeeding in deflecting such pressures and, particularly, in maintaining Soviet support.

MOSCOW AND THE ASEAN STATES

The Soviet Union has sought with varying degrees of intensity over the past three decades to extend its presence in the rest of Southeast Asia beyond Indochina. Moscow's primary objective has been to gain recognition as a superpower and an Asian power, a power who would be a natural participant in all regional decisions. Second, the Soviets have sought to reduce the role and influence of its already regionally entrenched adversary, the United States. Third, the USSR has worked to "contain"—a term chosen intentionally because of the similarity it suggests to U.S. policy toward the Soviet Union—a newer rival and perceived threat, China. Finally, the Kremlin has sought to spread its own influence in Southeast Asia, as part of its growing global role and capabilities, particularly in the naval sphere.

Indonesia was Moscow's initial object of interest and attention when the Soviet Union first entered the region in the mid-1950s, but as Indonesia turned increasingly toward the West after 1966, the Soviet Union's interest in Indonesia and the region generally diminished. Changing major power relationships in Southeast Asia, beginning in 1969, resulted in a new "offensive" toward the region. This new Soviet effort was considerably broader than before, being directed not only at Indonesia but also Thailand, the new states of Malaysia and Singapore with whom Moscow had established diplomatic relations in the late 1960s, and the Philippines with whom the Soviets finally formalized ties only in 1976.[27] This Soviet offensive broadened further after 1975 with the communist victories in Indochina. The very slow enhancement of the Soviet Union's regional role, however, was interrupted by its support of Vietnam's invasion of Kampuchea in 1978. The polarization of Southeast Asia placed the USSR in opposition to the ASEAN states.

In their attempts to overcome the effects of this polarization in the 1980s, Kremlin policymakers have had a number of advantages or opportunities available to them. One has been widely shared regional concern about the PRC's role and future ambitions. The significance of this concern varies among the ASEAN members with the crux of the issue being whether the long-range threat to Southeast Asia emanates from Vietnam (Bangkok and Singapore's perception) or from China (Jakarta and Kuala Lumpur's fear). The Kremlin has long sought to exploit this difference. Soviet representatives have sought to reinforce Indonesia's and Malaysia's apprehensions and, at the same time, to reassure the Thai of the Soviet desire for normalized relations with Beijing.[28]

A second major opportunity for Moscow has been the broadly shared, if differentiated in substance and degree, concerns about the U.S. role in the region.[29] These have ranged from ideological and cultural concerns to economic problems, global issues such as the nuclear arms race and "Star Wars," and regional policies. A primary aspect of this Soviet effort has been to warn of the risk of ASEAN involvement in a U.S.-sponsored Pacific Community that would be developed by Washington "into a NATO-type military pact under the protective U.S. umbrella."[30] U.S. militarism—ranging from its support for the "Pol Pot clique" to "Star Wars," deploying nuclear weapons at U.S. bases in the Philippines, bombing Libya, and creating an arms stockpile in Thailand—is cited as evidence of Washington's insincerity.[31] The tour through several of the ASEAN states in May–June 1986 by a Soviet delegation led by A. U. Salimov, vice-president of the Presidium of the Supreme Soviet, had these warnings as its main motif.[32]

The other major theme of Moscow's effort to take advantage of strains in U.S. relations with ASEAN is in the economic realm. Normal long-term trade friction has lately been substantially exacerbated by growing protectionism in U.S. policy. In response to Thailand's criticism of Washington's rice subsidy program and its sale of sugar to China at a price below that of the world market, for example, the USSR eagerly expressed its interest in expanding trade and entering joint ventures with Bangkok.[33] Moscow offered a loan to Indonesia, held trade and industrial exhibitions in the region, and urged local states to send trade missions and hold exhibitions in the USSR. Indeed, in all of the visits of major Soviet officials to the region in the past two years, the theme of the opportunity for expanded economic cooperation was prominently displayed.

Finally, Moscow has sought to build its case for closer ties with the ASEAN states on its greater role in the region's affairs due to its ties in Vietnam. The Soviet Union's participation in the exchange of visits of political officials is predicated on the assumption that Moscow is unavoidably a regional player. Indeed, General Secretary Gorbachev in his Vladivostok speech cited Soviet friendship and "multiform relations" with Vietnam, as well as Laos and Kampuchea, as being "an integral part of overall Asian and Pacific security."

The Soviets have also faced several significant obstacles in their efforts to expand the USSR's regional ties, however. By far the most substantial of these has been Moscow's support for Vietnam's invasion and continuing occupation of Kampuchea. Repeatedly,

ASEAN states have told the Soviets that relations can only be improved if Moscow is able to help bring about a Vietnamese withdrawal.

There have been numerous rumors that the Soviets have been dissatisfied with Vietnam's inflexible stand regarding negotiations with ASEAN over Kampuchea. A resolution of the conflict would benefit Soviet interests by lessening U.S.-China-ASEAN solidarity and opening new opportunities to improve relations with the states of ASEAN and to further normalize relations with the PRC. The point is, however, that these and other objectives of Soviet policy have not been perceived to be significant enough to lead Moscow to pressure Hanoi for a settlement on anything other than Hanoi's own terms.

Another important obstacle in the way of Soviet efforts has been the positive perception many of the ASEAN elites hold of China. This has been particularly true in Thailand which, as a front-line state in the Kampuchean conflict, needs Chinese support. Over the last several years Sino-Thai relations have moved beyond merely a convergence of interests in opposition to the Vietnamese occupation of Kampuchea and have expanded into the military and economic fields. Of great significance for Soviet policy, too, were the positive developments in the PRC's relations with the most suspicious ASEAN states, Malaysia and Indonesia. Malaysian Prime Minister Mahathir made a successful visit to China in late 1985, and beginning in that year Jakarta also began to improve its ties with Beijing.

Third, Moscow has had difficulty in the economic aspects of its approach to the ASEAN states. The Soviet Union has had a long-running deficit in its trade with ASEAN states. Moscow's deficit in 1985 with Indonesia, for example, was $74.5 million (on a total trade turnover of $81.3 million) and with Malaysia was $175 million (on a total of $207 million). The Soviet trade deficit with Thailand for 1978–1985 was more than $1 billion. The fundamental issue was that Moscow was unable to provide sufficient items that these countries wanted to buy. As mentioned, the Soviets have pushed fairs and exhibitions in an effort to overcome reports that Soviet goods continued to be either inappropriate or of inferior quality. Even Soviet attempts at extending a loan were rebuffed: Jakarta rejected a 1985 Soviet offer of $180 million to build three hospitals because the repayment period was too short.

In addition, the USSR has been hampered by the very pervasive ties between many of the region's states and the United States. The ASEAN states have a wide range of relatively deep bonds with Washington— economic, military, political, and ideological. The Philippines is the most obvious example, but it is also true to a lesser extent of the others. For example, while Malaysia has encouraged the Kremlin recently with its interest in purchasing military helicopters from the USSR, it seems clear that this interest was only expressed as a means of getting greater U.S. attention.[34] In short, as countries in the region look for economic assistance and diplomatic support to offset either the Vietnamese or the Chinese, all follow these fundamental ties with the U.S. and look to Washington (and Tokyo) rather than to Moscow.

Finally and relatedly, the Kremlin is still struggling to overcome the common perception among ASEAN elites that the Soviet Union is an outsider in Southeast Asia. Regional suspicions of Moscow's motives and means continue to be high. This has ranged from apprehensions about Soviet espionage activities in Malaysia and ulterior motives behind offering scholarships to Thai students to Moscow's expanding military power in the region. Thailand has been the most vocal about the long-term dangers of increasing Soviet deployments at Cam Ranh Bay and other bases in Indochina.[35] While Indonesia's basic position is that this Soviet base does not respresent a threat to noncommunist Southeast Asia—other than in the sense of further "big power rivalry"—the Indonesian military (with U.S. assistance) has publicized the intrusion into Indonesia airspace of Soviet aircraft and into Indonesian waters of Soviet submarines.[36]

MOSCOW AND SOUTHEAST ASIA: VLADIVOSTOK AND BEYOND

Gorbachev's Vladivostok speech has thus far brought no substantive change in Soviet policy toward Southeast Asia. All the Soviet leader really said about the ASEAN states was that the USSR was "prepared to expand ties" with them.[37] In this sense, Gorbachev's new Asian "offensive" was no different from Brezhnev's of the late 1960s. Most of the goals in Soviet policy as well as the obstacles confronting Moscow appeared to be the same. The speech does seem to have signified a more vigorous Soviet effort, however. As we have seen, there has been an intensification of Soviet gestures toward the ASEAN states in the Gorbachev era, with more diplomatic visits, trade appeals, commercial negotiations, and the like.

A flurry of major diplomatic developments in the first half of 1987 provided new evidence of the nature of Gorbachev's Vladivostok approach. First, the new diplomatic activism that Gorbachev had signaled in that speech was confirmed when Foreign Minister Eduard Shevardnadze journeyed to the region—Thailand, Indonesia, the three Indochina states, and Australia—at the beginning of March. Despite hopeful expectations in Bangkok and Jakarta that Shevardnadze would be coming with significant new proposals for ending the impasse on Kampuchea, the Soviet spokesman indicated no change in Soviet policy. Shevardnadze did present a picture of reasonableness and openness, admitting that Moscow's Asian policy was at least in part an effort to reduce external pressures so it could concentrate on domestic issues as well as secure a place for the USSR as a "major, legitimate actor in the region with a political and economic—as well as its existing military—presence."[38] In mid-May Foreign Minister Siddhi Savetsila of Thailand visited Moscow to pursue the Kampuchea issue further, hoping to capitalize on the interest the USSR had shown in improving relations with Thailand and the rest of ASEAN since Gorbachev came to power and as illustrated by Shevardnadze's "smile diplomacy" two months earlier. Once again, however, the Soviets indicated no alteration in their support for Vietnam with Shevardnadze and merely reiterated that Moscow was still seeking a settlement of the conflict and that it did not believe the situation there was either deadlocked or insolvable.

The third significant visit in this period was that of the new general secretary of the Vietnamese Communist Party, Nguyen Van Linh, who arrived in Moscow on the heels of Siddhi's departure. On issues other than Kampuchea, Moscow and Hanoi seemed to hold virtually identical views, and one analyst observed that "the tension in Soviet-Vietnamese relations after . . . Gorbachev's Vladivostok speech . . . appears to have dissipated."[39] Nevertheless, the same analyst noted the continuation of subtle differences over Kampuchea. Undoubtedly Hanoi was uncomfortable about its patron's new willingness to discuss the Kampuchea issue with states opposed to Vietnam's role there: Shevardnadze had discussed it openly on his Asian trip, and Soviet negotiators had broached the subject with their Chinese counterparts for the first time during the just-concluded tenth round of Sino-Soviet talks. Moreover, Anatoly Zaitsev, director of the Southeast Asian Affairs Department of the Soviet Foreign Ministry, asserted in Bangkok in August that the USSR was ready "to include the Kampuchean conflict in the agenda of talks with officials from all concerned countries."[40] Moscow was thus walking a thin line. It was trying to convince both China and ASEAN of Soviet interest in ending the conflict while, in fact, not pressing the Vietnamese very hard on something so central to Hanoi's interests. With regard both to China and to ASEAN, "rather than alienate the Vietnamese by pushing too hard for a solution in Cambodia, Moscow seems ready to accept a slower rate of improvement in relations. . . ."[41]

More recently, the Kremlin played host to Malaysian Prime Minister Mahathir in early August. Although there were continuing differences and no progress on Kampuchea (and Afghanistan), the exchange was a cordial one, and areas of common perceptions were emphasized. Mahathir voiced particular appreciation of Gorbachev's desire "to preserve and strengthen peace in the Asia and Pacific region" as put forward at Vladivostok and the newly pronounced Soviet willingness to remove its medium-range missiles from Asia.[42] This latter move, Gorbachev's acceptance of a "global double zero" in arms negotiations with the United States, was announced only one week prior to Mahathir's arrival and had been advocated by ASEAN states. Significantly, Gorbachev chose to proclaim this concession in an interview with B. M. Diah, editor of the Indonesian newspaper *Merdeka*, contending that it was "an effort to accommodate the Asian countries and take into account their concerns."[43]

Future Soviet policy in Southeast Asia depends on Soviet perceptions. Will the gains from a settlement in Kampuchea be worth the risk of pressuring the Vietnamese? So far, Moscow does not believe so. Only if the Soviets could be assured of holding on to their gains—particularly Cam Ranh Bay in Vietnam—are they likely to push very hard for a settlement. For the ASEAN states, a key factor is the evolving shape of the Soviet-Vietnamese-Chinese triangle. How serious is Moscow about Sino-Soviet normalization? How adamant will Beijing continue to be in demanding an end to Soviet support for Vietnam's occupation in Kampuchea? How much change there and in Chinese policy would it take for Vietnam's sense of siege to dissipate? Finally, for Moscow, how important is it and how likely are the prospects for a significant presence in the ASEAN states? In January the Kremlin reiterated, this time through its ambassador in Kuala Lumpur, that it wants formal talks and desires to be "a regular dialogue partner" with ASEAN.[44] All Indonesian Foreign Minister Mochtar could say later that month about Gorbachev's new Asian offensive, however, was that the Soviet leader "geographically . . . certainly may be right" that the USSR is a Pacific country![45] Thirty years of Soviet efforts have produced only this grudging concession. Mahathir's Soviet visit may mark the beginning of a change in this perception, as he asserted that Malaysia at least "recognizes that the Soviet Union is part and parcel of the Asia-Pacific region."[46] If and when this becomes the prevailing regional perception of the Soviet Union, Gorbachev will indeed have made great strides in his "Vladivostok initiative"; at this point, however, Moscow's diplomacy still has a difficult road ahead to provide for an enhanced Soviet role in Southeast Asia.

NOTES

1. He began his emphasis in this direction during Indian Prime Minister Rajiv Gandhi's visit in May 1985; see *Pravda*, 30 June 1985.
2. *Pravda*, 29 July 1986.
3. See Leif Rosenberger, "The Soviet-Vietnamese Alliance and Kampuchea," *Survey* (Autumn/Winter 1983): 211. *Far Eastern Economic Review* (hereafter

cited as *FEER*), 27 February 1981, 32–34, cites a figure of $3.8 billion. This figure may be based on an extrapolation backwards, as it were, since it appears that the Soviets provided a good deal more economic assistance in 1980, somewhere around $850 million.

4. Foreign Minister Thach cited in Paul Kelemen, "Soviet Strategy in Southeast Asia: The Vietnam Factor," *Asian Survey*, March 1984, 343. For Soviet funding of Hanoi's third plan, see Douglas Pike, "Vietnam in 1981: Biting the Bullet," *Asian Survey*, January 1982, 72; *Christian Science Monitor*, 27 July 1984; *Soviet Analyst*, 29 May 1985.

5. For USSR's assistance to Hanoi's fourth plan, see *Nhan Dan* (the daily of the Communist Party of Vietnam) 18 July 1985 in *Foreign Broadcast Information Service — Asia and the Pacific*, 22 July 1985 (hereafter cited as *FBIS-AP*). For Ligachev's comments, see *Los Angeles Times*, 19 December 1986.

6. *Soviet Analyst*, 29 May 1985.

7. *Pravda*, 1 November 1983. See also *FEER*, 17 November 1983, 46–47.

8. See *Los Angeles Times*, 11 November 1981 and 4 May 1982. For an analysis of the current state of the Vietnamese economy and the issues involved, see K. W. Taylor, "Vietnam in 1984: Confidence Amid Diversity," in Lim Joo-Jock, ed., *Southeast Asian Affairs 1985* (Singapore: Institute of Southeast Asian Studies, 1985), 349–363.

9. *Pravda*, 29 March 1982; *VNA*, 28 March 1982, in *FBIS-AP*, 30 March 1982.

10. *South China Morning Post* (Hong Kong), 1 November 1986.

11. Radio Hanoi, 19 October 1986 in *FBIS-AP*, 22 October 1986. Emphasis added.

12. *New Straits Times* (Kuala Lumpur), 18 and 21 April 1984; *Boston Globe*, 24 April 1984.

13. For statistics on Soviet ships in Cam Ranh Bay, see *International Herald Tribune*, 22 December 1983; *FEER*, 29 December 1983,: 16; *Christian Science Monitor*, 14 May 1985; *FEER*, 30 May 1985,: 45. For deployments of Soviet aircraft to Cam Ranh Bay, see *New York Times*, 2 January 1985. The source was squadron leader Prasong Soonsiri, the head of Thailand's National Security Council.

14. *New York Times*, 25 October 1985.

15. See Sheldon W. Simon, "The Great Powers and Southeast Asia: Cautious Minuet or Dangerous Tango," *Asian Survey* (September 1985), 931–934.

16. *Christian Science Monitor*, 29 September 1982. For Prime Minister Dong's statements, see *Newsweek*, International Edition 14 May 1984.

17. For example, see the report on Brezhnev's meeting with him, Radio Moscow (9 September 1981) in *FBIS-Soviet Union* (hereafter cited as FBIS-SU), 9 September 1981. See also *New York Times*, 22 April 1981; Nayan Chanda, "The Bigger Brother," *FEER*, 5 June 1981, 24–26; Chanda, "Vietnam Back in Front," *FEER*, 8 January 1982, 13–15; "First Round to Hanoi," *FEER*, 11 December 1981, 8–9; "Now a Non-Person," *FEER*, 18 December 1981, 16–17; Rosenberger, 222.

18. From *Xinhua* in *FBIS-SU*, 12 March 1985.

19. *Pravda*, 30 June 1985.

20. Radio Hanoi (16, 17, 19 December 1986) in *FBIS-AP*, 22 December 1986.

21. *Izvestia*, 19 December 1986.

22. *AFP*, 14 October 1986 in *FBIS-PRC*, 15 October 1986; *Kyodo* (Tokyo), 15 October 1986 in *FBIS-PRC*, *15 October 1986*.
23. *Xinhua*, 21 April 1987 in *FBIS-PRC*, 22 April 1987. See also *Pravda*, 21 April 1987.
24. *Xinhua*, 26 April 1987 in *FBIS-PRC*, 27 April 1987.
25. See Nayan Chanda, "Not Soft on Cambodia," *FEER*, 1 January 1987, 13.
26. Nayan Chanda, "Weather Eye on Moscow," *FEER*, 23 October 1986, 24.
27. For a discussion, see Robert C. Horn, "The Soviet Union and Asian Security," in Sudershan Chawla and R. R. Sardesai, eds., *Changing Patterns of Security and Stability in Asia* (New York: Praeger, 1980).
28. *The Nation* (Bangkok), 8 June 1986.
29. For example, see Robert C. Horn, "Anti-Americanism in Southeast Asia: The Malaysian Case," in Alvin Z. Rubinstein and Donald E. Smith eds., *Anti-Americanism in the Third World. Implications for U.S. Foreign Policy* (New York: Praeger, 1985), 151–170; Robert C. Horn, "U.S.-ASEAN Relations in the 1980s," *Contemporary Southeast Asia* (September 1984), 119–134.
30. Radio Moscow, in Indonesian to Indonesia (30 April 1986) in *FBIS-SU*, 6 May 1986.
31. See *FBIS-SU*, 6 May 1986; Radio Moscow (15 October 1986) in *FBIS-SU*, 21 October 1986.
32. For example, see *FBIS-AP* (Thailand), 11 June 1986; *AFP* (Hong Kong) 5 June 1986, in *FBIS-AP*, 6 June 1986.
33. Radio Bangkok, 8 October 1986 in *FBIS-AP*, 10 October 1986.
34. See *FEER*, 20 September 1984, 14–15; Robert C. Horn, "The USSR and the Region," in Lim Joo Jock, ed., *Southeast Asian Affairs 1985* (Singapore: Institute of Southeast Asian Studies, 1985).
35. *Bangkok Post*, 17 March 1986 refers to "the obvious threat to our national security posed by the Soviet military build-up in Cam Ranh Bay."
36. See *AFP*, Hong Kong 28 April 1986 in *FBIS-SU*, 29 April 1986; *AFP*, September 1986 in *FBIS-SU*, 16 September 1986.
37. Perhaps significant, the order in which Gorbachev mentioned them was Indonesia, the Philippines, Thailand, Malaysia, and Singapore. Australia and New Zealand were placed between Indonesia and the Philippines; South Asian nations and Brunei followed Singapore; and Pacific Island states came at the conclusion of the paragraph.
38. Susumu Awanohara, "The Bear at the Door," *FEER*, 26 March 1987, 18.
39. Nayan Chanda, "Soulmates' Dissonance," *FEER*, 11 June 1987, 24.
40. *The Nation* (Bangkok), 13 August 1987.
41. Sophie Quinn-Judge, "Moscow on the Move," *FEER*, 4 June 1987, 10. Another hint of potential progress on Kampuchea surfaced the same day Mahathir arrived in Moscow. Indonesian Foreign Minister Mochtar and his Vietnamese counterpart, Nguyen Co Thach, after two days of talks in Ho Chi Minh City, agreed to a vague "cocktail party" format to begin negotiations on Kampuchea. It remains to be seen whether this was a significant breakthrough or yet another nonstarter. See the Joint Press Release in *FBIS-East Asia and the Pacific*, 29 July 1987.
42. From the Joint Communique in *Izvestia*, 6 August 1987.

43. *New York Times*, 23 July 1987.
44. *Radio Liberty Research*, RL 28/87 (14 January 1987).
45. *Asahi Shimbun* (Tokyo), 1 February 1987.
46. *Pravda*, 31 July 1987.

7

Indonesian-Soviet Relations:
Policy Implications

J. Soedjati Djiwandono

Perceptions of the Soviet Union are likely to vary not only from one Indonesian to another at a given time depending on such factors as the individual's degree of knowledge of the country and sources of information available, but also from one period of time to another. Insofar as perceptions are related to policy, however, it is those of Indonesia's leadership that matter. This leadership's perception has not remained constant. In the short span of Indonesia's recent history, it has been changing; hence Indonesia's changing policy toward the Soviet Union. This chapter attempts to summarize the perceptions of Indonesia's political leadership regarding the Soviet Union that help explain Indonesia's changing policies toward that country.

EARLY INDONESIAN-SOVIET RELATIONS

The Soviet Union formally recognized the newly independent Republic of Indonesia in January 1950.[1] However, there was a delay before actual diplomatic missions were exchanged. For internal reasons it was not until May that the Indonesian government sent a delegation to Moscow to negotiate the exchange of diplomatic representatives.[2]

Indonesia's desire to establish relations with the Soviet Union was motivated by two main considerations. First, Indonesia hoped that friendly relations with the Soviet Union might neutralize domestic communist opposition to the government by the Communist Party of Indonesia (PKI). Second, Indonesia adhered to the nonalignment principle in foreign policy. Furthermore, Indonesia needed both Soviet and U. S. approval for membership into the United Nations. Even though the Soviet Union did not seem to be interested in fostering friendly relations with Indonesia, it voted for Indonesia's admission to the United Nations as its sixtieth member on 28 September 1950.

Developments during the early years of Indonesia's independence were not conducive to closer relations with the Soviet Union. At the time, Indonesian foreign policy was relatively passive, and internal reconstruction took priority. Besides, Indonesia's foreign policy was oriented toward the West. This pro-Western orientation was due partly to the positive role the United States played in the final stages of Indonesia's struggle for independence and the strain between Indonesia and the Soviet Union over the 1948 Communist Madiun revolt, which also contributed to Indonesia's strong anticommunist attitude in its domestic policy.

Diplomatic relations were finally opened between Indonesia and the Soviet Union in September 1954. Following Stalin's death Soviet foreign policy shifted from militancy toward moderation and an accommodation of nonalignment.[3] Meanwhile, in Indonesian domestic politics, a coalition developed between the PKI and the nationalist parties, particularly the Partai Nasional Indonesie (PNI). For the first time since the Madiun revolt, the PKI offered to support the new Wilopo cabinet if it pursued "an independent national policy." The Soviet Union indicated its approval by publishing the PKI's offer in the Soviet press. The implication seemed to be that any Indonesian government that pursued an independent policy would enjoy the support not only of the PKI but also of the Soviet Union. Soviet acceptance of Indonesia's independent policy cleared the way for the future course of Indonesian-Soviet relations. A major factor that contributed to closer relations between the two countries was Indonesia's strained relationship with the West, particularly the United States, under Ali Sastroamidjojo's cabinet. Indonesia, with India, rejected the Manila Pact of September 1954 and denounced military alliances in Southeast Asia.

The 20th Congress of the Communist Party of the Soviet Union (CPSU) in 1956 marked a turning point in Soviet relations with the new, excolonial states of Asia and Africa and ushered in a new era of increasingly cordial Indonesian-Soviet relations. As Indonesia's foreign policy assumed a more anti-Western attitude and relations with the United States deteriorated, the Soviet approach began to appeal to Indonesia. The United States' negative view of nonalignment, intervention in a regional rebellion in 1958, and neutrality on the West Irian issue alienated Indonesia and drove it closer to the Soviet Union.

The West Irian issue represented an apparent convergence of interests that drew the two countries closer together than at any other time in the history of their relations. In a lecture at Pajajaran University in

Bandung in May 1958, President Sukarno stated specifically that Indonesia had turned to the Soviet Union because of the United States' attitude toward the West Irian issue.[4]

Full Soviet support and substantial Soviet arms transfers lent credibility to Sukarno's threats of war against the Netherlands. Concerned over the dangers of an escalation of the dispute, the United States intervened to bring about a negotiated settlement that satisfied Indonesia. Thus Indonesia used the Soviet Union to induce United States diplomatic intervention to achieve a satisfactory settlement to the West Irian dispute.

However, in President Sukarno's subsequent confrontation against Malaysia in 1963–1964, Indonesia failed to induce a corresponding Soviet role as a means of soliciting American mediation in its favor. For a number of reasons, the Soviet Union was reluctant to provide Indonesia with the necessary diplomatic and military support for its confrontation against Malaysia. When Soviet support was finally offered, it was not only too late but also of little value.

Partly in desperate search of a comparable substitute for the Soviet Union and partly out of its international isolation as a result of its militant foreign policy, Indonesia subsequently looked to strengthening relations with the People's Republic of China (PRC). This substantially deteriorated Indonesian-Soviet relations.

By the time the PKI attempted another coup in 1965, Indonesian-Soviet relations were almost at a standstill. The Soviet Union lost little from the virtual destruction of the PKI in the aftermath of the coup attempt since the PKI had sided with Beijing in the Sino-Soviet dispute. Although diplomatic relations between Indonesia and the PRC were suspended in 1967, it did not improve Indonesian-Soviet relations. On the contrary, Indonesian-Soviet relations were subjected to new strains because of the anticommunist orientation of the New Order regime under President Suharto in Indonesia.

Therefore, Indonesian-Soviet relations continued for a time to be almost nonexistent, even though diplomatic relations were never severed.

THE NEW ORDER AND INDONESIAN-SOVIET RELATIONS

Indonesia's bitter experiences with external interference by the major powers explains why the New Order has given top priority to achieving and maintaining internal and regional peace by pursuing national development in its domestic policy and regional cooperation in its foreign policy using the framework of ASEAN.

It is on the basis of Indonesia's independent and active foreign policy that the New Order has maintained its relations with the Soviet Union. However, Indonesia's attitude toward the great powers remains ambivalent. This includes its relations with the Soviet Union because the Soviet Union in the past has interfered in Indonesia's domestic affairs and is a communist state. Although Indonesia rejected communism and banned the PKI, this anticommunist sentiment was not to affect Indonesia's foreign policy. In principle, Indonesia was to continue seeking friendly, mutually benefiting relations with all countries regardless of differences in social, political, and economic systems. Nonetheless, Indonesia's active and independent foreign policy has become more centrist and pro-Western than before. Consequently, apart from occasional strains, Indonesian-Soviet relations under the New Order may be described as correct but cool.

Indonesia's new leaders were concerned with the country's immense economic problems inherited from the Old Order and were interested in improving Indonesia's multilateral relations with Western Europe, the United States, their Asian allies, and pro-Western nonaligned countries. The Western countries were willing to assist Indonesia in rescheduling its debts and to provide economic and financial aid. Furthermore, the West and Japan began investing heavily in Indonesia, and trade with the West boomed.

The Soviet Union did not prove as willing to aid Indonesia with its economic problems. It had been impatient with Indonesia because it had defaulted on its debt carried over from the pre-coup relationship. The Soviet Union made no public statement on the debt issue because of its friendship with the Sukarno regime. But when Suharto became president, the Soviet Union severely rebuked Indonesia for default on its debt repayment and refused to attend the meetings of a consortium that was reviewing foreign aid to Indonesia; instead it demanded immediate repayment. Only in 1970 did the Soviet Union finally accept a settlement of the total Indonesian debt at $750 million and agree to a new repayment schedule.[5] It also offered to resume work on some of the unfinished projects begun during Sukarno's regime.

This debt settlement established a new basis for normalizing relations between the two countries. Visits between the two countries resumed. For instance, in the middle of 1973 a delegation of the Indonesian parliament visited the Soviet Union. In the following year, the late Foreign Minister Adam Malik also visited Moscow.

However, relations became strained again when in early 1982 Moscow radio broadcast a greeting on Brezhnev's birthday from the Central Committee of the Communist Party of Indonesia in Moscow. Indonesia protested and in the following month, expelled a number of Soviet diplomats on grounds of espionage and closed the Jakarta office of the Soviet airline, Aeroflot. It also sent a Soviet chess player home before he competed in an international chess tournament in Indonesia.

It was not long before fresh attempts were made to improve Indonesian-Soviet relations. A Soviet parliamentary delegation and trade mission visited Indonesia in the middle of the same year, 1982, and near the end of the following year. In 1984 Indonesian visitors to Moscow included Foreign Minister Mochtar Kusumaatmadja; Co-ordinating Minister for Economic, Financial, and Industrial Affairs Ali Wardhana; and an Indonesian Chamber of Commerce group. Indonesia's economic problems warranted new attempts to improve trade and economic relations with the Soviet Union and other socialist countries. Because of protectionism in the West and lower oil prices, Indonesia needed to diversify its market for nonoil exports. However, to promote improved trade and economic relations with the Soviet Union, Indonesia needs to overcome bureaucratic, administrative, and technical obstacles as well as the long-established prejudices of both countries.

Indonesia's fresh approach to the Soviet Union indicates that it is balancing its foreign policy. Economically and politically Indonesia perceives the Soviet Union as a counterbalance to its close relations with the West. Indonesia's renewed attempts at improving relations with the Soviet Union also are likely to improve its nonaligned image. This in turn may enhance its credibility and increase its capability of playing a more significant role internationally as a middle power.[6]

IMPLICATIONS OF GORBACHEV'S PEACE INITIATIVE

The Indonesian government's tentative reaction to Gorbachev's peace initiative has been favorable. Foreign Minister Mochtar Kusumaatmadja remarked that "it is a good beginning but there is a long way to go. Much will depend on how the Soviet Union tackles those problems; it is still too early to make a detailed assessment." He regarded the 1986 Vladivostok speech as "a very significant statement which requires careful study because, for the first time, there is no mention of an Asian collective security system. On the contrary, his speech seems to be based on the recognition of the existence in the Asia-Pacific region of very important countries, great nations, with strong economies, with strong national identities." However, he added that "we should also consider Gorbachev's speech in the context of global politics. I wish he was more attentive to Southeast Asia. . . . Gorbachev's statement gave the impression [that] there is no separate assessment of Southeast Asia in its own right, that [it] is just an appendix of China. It does not reflect a true appreciation of Southeast Asia's importance."[7]

It would seem too much to expect more from the USSR. Gorbachev's speech reflects his approach to the Asia-Pacific region as a whole. He will certainly attach greater importance to Soviet relations with the United States, and decreasingly with China, Japan, and with other countries, including those in Southeast Asia and the South Pacific.

It seems superfluous for Gorbachev to try to convince the world that the Soviet Union is an Asia-Pacific power. But on closer examination, he seems to have good reasons to do so. That the Soviet Union is a Pacific power is self-evident. The issue is whether it is also an Asian power. The greater part of the Soviet land mass lies in Asia and a substantial part of the Soviet population is Asian. Therefore, geographically and demographically the Soviet Union is both Asian and European, which explains the Soviet ambivalence. In spite of its Asian land mass, the majority of the Soviet population lives in the European part. In 1955 the Soviet Union wanted to have its Asian republics represented at the Bandung Conference, but not the Soviet Union as a whole. Soviet participation was opposed by then prime minister of India, Nehru.[8]

It seems fair that as an Asia-Pacific power the Soviet Union has legitimate interests in the Asia-Pacific region. Yet in discussions on the Asia-Pacific region, particularly on regional cooperation, there is a strong tendency to exclude the Soviet Union and to treat it as an external power. The Soviet military buildup in the region has invoked cries of the "Soviet threat," while increasing relations between the Soviet Union and the countries of the South Pacific have created concern over "Soviet penetration." These are often related to the problems of security of the sea-lines of communication in the Asia-Pacific region. A Soviet scholar has recently complained that the Pacific Ocean is often treated as though it were an "American lake," and the sea-lanes "American highways." Thus Gorbachev's speech indicates the Soviet intention to gain recognition of and respect for its legitimate presence, role, and interests in the region. His peaceful overtures and emphasis on improving bilateral relations in economic, cultural, and technological cooperation with the Asia-Pacific countries may be intended to repair the damage to the Soviet image resulting from the Soviet military presence in the region.

Whether the Soviet Union will succeed in its efforts to balance its presence here will depend not only on its own capabilities but also on the responses of Asia-Pacific countries. The strategic and political environment in the Asia-Pacific region has certainly been unfavorable for the Soviet Union. The majority of security arrangements involving U.S. commitment and U.S. military bases are in this region and directed at the Soviet Union.[9] Except for the communist Indochinese countries, the majority of the nations in the region are either allied with the United States or favorably disposed to it, including China. North Korea has always tried to balance its relations between Moscow and Beijing.

Perhaps the most important aspect of Gorbachev's peace initiative is the idea of a conference for the Asia-Pacific region in the mold of the Helsinki conference to integrate the region into the establishment of "a comprehensive system of international security."[10] This, of course, is not an entirely new idea. It may be just another version of Brezhnev's idea of an Asian Collective Security System or Gorbachev's own previous idea of an All Asia Forum. Unlike Brezhnev's Asian Collective Security System, which in its initial stage was aimed principally against China, Gorbachev's proposal does not appear to be directed against China or the United States.

However, to apply to the Asia-Pacific region a European type of solution such as the Helsinki Agreement, which is based on typically European experience and conditions, contradicts Gorbachev's own realization of the complexity and diversity of the Asia-Pacific region. Unlike Europe, the Asia-Pacific region is not neatly divided by security alliances, ideological orientations, and sociopolitical and economic systems. Gorbachev's sweeping proposals may easily lead one to suspect his real motives and intentions. Apart from the principles in the Helsinki Agreement, applying such a European design to the Asia-Pacific region would imply that the region be divided according to the influence and perhaps domination of the superpowers involved in it. The inevitable function of a Helsinki type of agreement is to affirm and sustain the status quo.

It must be noted that various conflicts in the Asia-Pacific region, including the territorial disputes between the Soviet Union and China and the Soviet Union and Japan, and the Kampuchea and Afghanistan conflicts, are likely to militate against the achievement of a Helsinki type of dialogue and agreement and a "comprehensive system of international security." Is it then possible that Gorbachev suggested such a proposal precisely with the intent to sustain the status quo in the Asia-Pacific region and hence freeze the territorial issues in favor of the Soviet Union?

Indeed, if a Helsinki type of agreement in the Asia-Pacific region could retain the status quo, which would be in the Soviet Union's favor, the Soviet leadership should then be able to pay greater attention to their domestic problems. And as in Europe, the Soviet Union would become at least for the time being, a "status quo" rather than a "revisionist" power in the Asia-Pacific region.

NOTES

1. For a detailed discussion of early Indonesian-Soviet relations see J. Soedjati Djiwandono, "Indonesia's Changing Perception of the Soviet Union," *Indonesian Quarterly* 15, no. 2 (1987): 278–292.
2. Anak Agung Gde Agung, in *Twenty Years of Indonesian Foreign Policy 1945–1965* (The Hague: Mouton & Co., 1973), discusses the delay in Soviet recognition and also Indonesian reluctance to foster relations.
3. See Charles B. McLane, *Soviet Strategies in Southeast Asia: An Exploration of Eastern Policy Under Lenin and Stalin* (Princeton, N.J.: Princeton University Press, 1966), 464–473.
4. Robert C. Bone, Jr., *The Dynamics of the Western New Guinea (Irian) Problem* (Ithaca, N.Y.: Cornell University Press, Modern Indonesia Project, 1958), 118–119.
5. Wynfred Joshua and Stephen Gibert, *Arms for the Third World: Soviet Military Aid Diplomacy* (Baltimore, Md., and London: The Johns Hopkins Press, 1969), 253.
6. See J. Soedjati Djiwandono, "Relations with the Socialist Countries," *Indonesian Quarterly* 13, no. 1 (January 1985): 3–6.
7. *The Jakarta Post*, 2 August 1986.
8. During the preparations for the projected Second Afro-Asian Conference in 1964–1965 the Soviets wanted to send a delegation to represent the entire Soviet Union. By then the debate over Soviet participation got entangled in conflicts between the Soviet Union and China, between China and India, and between Malaysia and Indonesia. This time India supported Soviet participation, while China and Indonesia opposed it. It was never resolved because the Second Bandung Conference was finally aborted.
9. J. Soedjati Djiwandono, "The Soviet Presence in the Asian Pacific Region," *Asian Affairs* ll, no. 4 (Winter 1985): 21–39.
10. J. Soedjati Djiwandono, "Mr. Gorbachev and the Asia Pacific Region," *The Indonesian Quarterly* 14, no. 4 (October 1986): 464–466.

8

Malaysian-Soviet Relations:
Changing Perceptions?

Pushpa Thambipillai

FUNDAMENTALS OF MALAYSIAN-SOVIET RELATIONS

The new thrust in Malaysian-Soviet relations is best reflected in Prime Minister Mahathir Mohamad's speech in Moscow in July 1987:

> My visit to your country coincides with two important jubilees: the 70th anniversary of the Great October Socialist Revolution and the 20th anniversary of the establishment of diplomatic relations between our countries. . . . A great deal has been accomplished over this period. One of the main aims of my visit to your country is to strengthen our ties and discuss future cooperation between us.[1]

This highlights Malaysia's changing emphasis in foreign policy, and Mahathir Mohamad's direct, practical, and challenging style. The prime minister has assumed an active role in Malaysia's foreign affairs by increasing his contacts with countries in the East (through his Look East Policy) and, later, the South (in his search for South-South cooperation). Although Mahathir's visit to the Soviet Union in 1987 was in a sense overdue, it does reflect both Mahathir's and Soviet General Secretary Mikhail Gorbachev's growing interest in strengthening their relationship. Twenty years of continuous diplomatic relations speak well for the two countries, but do not necessarily imply constructive and favorable interactions throughout the entire period.

Until the mid-1970s Malaysia did not consider strengthening its relations with the Soviet Union for a number of reasons. In the early years of Malaysia's statehood, it needed to maintain a high level of association with its traditional friends in the Commonwealth, especially Britain and Australia. Furthermore, with regards to some other countries like China, Malaysia had to keep constantly alert as to their actions in the region. At the time, the Soviet Union was not immediately threatening and so geographically distant that Malaysia did not have much direct interaction with it.

After the mid-1970s Malaysia regarded the Soviet Union more seriously. A number of factors contributed to this change in Malaysia's attitude. In 1975 communist regimes took hold nearer home in Vietnam, Kampuchea, and Laos, and in 1978 the Soviet presence was felt even more with the Vietnamese invasion of Kampuchea and the Soviet Union's closer cooperation with the Indochina states. The following year, Malaysia was further alarmed by the Soviet invasion of Afghanistan. Although Afghanistan was geographically distant, Malaysia felt strongly about the fellow Islamic state.

In 1979 Prime Minister Hussein Onn visited the Soviet Union—a sign of Malaysia's desire for better communication and friendship in an era of political uncertainty. By the time Mahathir Mohamad became prime minister in 1981, Malaysia was rapidly becoming an economically vibrant country and politically assertive in international and regional issues. Through Mahathir, who took a far greater interest in foreign policy than previous prime ministers, Malaysia grew more politically confident and felt it could be more selective in developing relationships with small or large countries.

Although Malaysian government leaders realized the need to develop the Soviet bilateral relationship, they kept a respectable but watchful distance from the Soviet Union. Ties were maintained and regulated within an ideological framework that stressed the differences rather than the similarities, if any, between the two countries. This is also characteristic of the current Malaysian-Soviet relations.

The Malaysian government's staunch anticommunism does not encourage or permit Malaysian-Soviet ties at the mass level. This chapter thus reflects largely the government perceptions as articulated by the leaders' words and actions, since in Malaysia one usually does not risk expressing private perceptions of the Soviet Union in public.

HISTORICAL BACKGROUND

Malaysia's foreign policies were influenced by its close association with Britain, the Commonwealth, and other Western countries for most of the first decade after its independence. Essentially, its allies were the developed countries of the West and its enemies were the communist states.

From the late 1940s to 1960 Malaysia experienced a communist insurgency initiated by the Malayan Communist Party, which was composed mainly of ethnic Chinese and closely linked to China. Therefore, Malaysia did not seek to establish relations with any communist state that was determined to "export revolution." Although the local insurgency was declared officially over in 1960, it was not until after the formation of Malaysia in 1963 that foreign policy took on a more active role.

Although Malaysia's leaders, especially Prime Minister Tunku Abdul Rahman, frequently proclaimed their nonalignment policy, Malaysia was committed to the West. Although Malaysia believed in the containment of communist expansionism, it did not become a member of any anticommunist organization, such as the Southeast Asia Treaty Organization (SEATO), the U. S.–initiated military alliance in the Asia-Pacific region.[2] Since Malaysia was historically linked to the Commonwealth, it continued to be a member of the defense arrangement with Britain, New Zealand, and Australia (and later Singapore).[3]

Contacts with Afro-Asian countries coupled with the desire to join the nonalignment movement and the realization that international politics consisted of more than East-West relations led to some changes in the leadership's perceptions of foreign affairs. Malaysia established formal trade relations with the Soviet Union in April 1967 in pursuit of new markets for Malaysian commodities, especially rubber. This was surprising considering Malaysia's anticommunist stand and Soviet accusations that the creation of Malaysia was an imperialistic initiative of the Western countries. There had also been some allegations of Soviet support in President Sukarno's confrontation campaign against Malaysia. Tunku Abdul Rahman, who previously had adhered to a pro-West policy, obviously had succumbed to influence from within his government and party to relax the country's strong anticommunist foreign policies, especially regarding the Soviet Union and Eastern Europe. (Yugoslavia was the only communist state with which Malaysia had established relations until 1967.)

Under the initial trade agreement, commodity sales were promoted directly through the Malaysian and Soviet trade missions in each other's capitals. In November 1967 full diplomatic relations were established, and the first Soviet trade office was set up in Kuala Lumpur. An Air Services Agreement was signed, and a Malaysian-Soviet Friendship Society was planned for each country. The interactions were not very visible; this was strictly a government-to-government relationship. The first Soviet ambassador to Malaysia was appointed in April 1968, and the Malaysian deputy prime minister, Tun Razak, officially visited Moscow the following month.

The creation of Malaysia, the resulting Indonesian confrontation, and the formation of ASEAN in 1967 contributed to Malaysia's more active outlook on foreign policy. One initiative, which became the cornerstone of Prime Minister Razak's foreign policy after he assumed office in 1971, was the neutralization of Southeast Asia first suggested by Razak's cabinet colleague, Tun Ismail, in 1968. China, the Soviet Union, and the United States were expected to guarantee the neutralization of the region. The Malaysian leaders tried to popularize this concept, and won endorsement from the ASEAN member governments. It was collectively adopted in November 1971 as the Kuala Lumpur Declaration, which advocated a Zone of Peace, Freedom, and Neutrality.

Prime Minister Razak's second visit to the Soviet Union in 1972 (the first visit by a Malaysian prime minister) resulted in two bilateral agreements: one for economic and technical cooperation and another for cultural and scientific cooperation. This visit occurred soon after the adoption of the Kuala Lumpur Declaration, and Razak emphasized that "I have not come here to seek the formal endorsement of the Soviet Union for this proposal because that would be the responsibility of the Southeast Asian countries themselves acting as a group. But it is my hope that as we in Southeast Asia proceed on this path toward our goal, we shall receive the sympathetic understanding of the Soviet Union."[4]

In keeping with the neutralization concept and the furthering of relations with Eastern European countries, Malaysia also approached China. In accordance with global diplomacy, Malaysia established diplomatic relations with the People's Republic of China in May 1974. Since 1975 was a crucial year in the international politics of Southeast Asia, Malaysia was initially apprehensive about the communist victory in Indochina. Generally, the Malaysians did not subscribe to the theory that predicted the rest of Southeast Asia would also fall to the communists. By 1976 Malaysia had established diplomatic relations with the unified Vietnam.[5]

The new direction adopted by Razak and his team established friendly relations with the communist states. He strengthened relations with the Soviet Union and Eastern Europe for economic reasons and pursued diplomatic relations with China and Vietnam for regional stability.

The Soviet Connection

In mid-1976 the arrests of accused communist sympathizers set off a "witch hunt" for communists in the government and media. A Malay journalist, Abdul Samad Ismail, managing editor of the *New Straits Times*, and an "accomplice" (the government's term) from another daily were arrested and purported to have promoted communism through the media. Two cabinet ministers, who had been Prime Minister Razak's close associates, Deputy Minister of Labor and Manpower Abdullah Majid and Deputy Minister of Science and Technology Abdullah Ahmad, were detained and released several months later after "confessing" to their crimes.

These incidents reconfirmed the suspicion of those in the ruling party, United Malays National Organization (UMNO), that Razak, who died in 1976, had been surrounded by communist sympathizers. Many believed that this communist scare was also a tactic used to identify and purge the inner circle of "Razak boys" who were accused of trying to split party unity. Therefore the entire incident was viewed as an exaggerated vendetta against high-level supporters of the late prime minister. Nevertheless, the communist scare also helped rally public support for the new prime minister, Hussein Onn.

The next administration, led by Prime Minister Mahathir Mohamad, experienced a similar incident. In July 1981, only three days before Mahathir was to be sworn in as prime minister, his political secretary since 1974 Siddiq Mohamad Ghouse was detained by the police for "carrying out activities prejudicial to the security of the country." Siddiq was accused of being a Soviet agent in the employ of the KGB at the Soviet embassy in Kuala Lumpur. This was probably the first time that the Soviet Union was implicated directly in the communist scare. Following the arrest, three Soviet embassy personnel were expelled.

Although the Malaysians were initially shocked with the discovery of a spy so close to the prime minister, neither the Soviet nor the Malaysian government paid much attention to the issue after the initial exposure. There were no public reactions from Moscow on the expulsions, nor was there any immediate retaliation. An editorial reflected the Malaysian attitude, "While Malaysia is prepared to give substance to the professions of improving relationships between both countries, this does not mean that we will be blindly vulnerable to subversion."[6] Similarly, government statements concentrated on how Malaysians ought to guard against communist subversion, be it by the Russians or the Chinese, but claimed diplomatic relations with the USSR were not affected.

A few months later, in October 1981, Abdul Halim Mahmud, a journalist with a Malay weekly, *Watan*, was detained and accused of furthering communist ideas through his writings; the owner of *Watan* was also briefly detained. Halim was later unconditionally released. The government also released Samad Ismail later that year, after he confessed to his "communist activities," and allowed him to rejoin his former daily.

At the diplomatic level, Malaysia clearly demonstrated its friendship toward the Soviet Union and its desire to be nonaligned. Prime Minister Hussein Onn had visited the Soviet Union in 1979 and had noted that "the visit has not only given Malaysia the opportunity to increase trade with the USSR but also in reflecting Malaysia's and ASEAN's concept of being neutral in dealing with major powers."[7] One of the main reasons stated for the visit was to try to persuade the Soviets to urge Vietnam to withdraw from Kampuchea and work toward a peaceful settlement of the conflict.

Malaysia again tried to obtain the Soviet Union's support in an effective political solution to the Kampuchean conflict during Soviet Deputy Foreign Minister Nikolai Firyubin's visit in April 1981. Firyubin laid out the Soviet proposals for international peace made by Soviet President Leonid Brezhnev. Despite these efforts, there was no agreement on an acceptable settlement to the regional problems.[8]

Malaysia tried to expand relations with other Eastern-bloc countries for economic and political reasons. President Nicolae Ceausescu of Romania earned the distinction of being the first communist head of state to visit Malaysia when he arrived in November 1982. Mahathir visited Romania and Yugoslavia in May 1983. He secured an agreement to establish direct barter trade and tried to enlist their support on regional issues, especially Kampuchea.

The Malaysian Citizen and the Soviet

Despite a lack of government encouragement for individual citizens to express their views on sensitive issues, there have been some instances in which Malaysians demonstrated their political feelings toward the Soviets. For example, as early as 1968, about one hundred students sat in front of the newly established Soviet embassy to express opposition to the Soviet invasion of Czechoslovakia. More recently, the Soviet occupation of Afghanistan prompted anti-Soviet anger in Malaysia and most other Islamic countries. A local division of the opposition Muslim political party, Parti Islam Se Malaysia (PAS), called for the severance of diplomatic relations with the Soviet Union in protest against its intervention in Afghanistan.[9] The International Muslim Brotherhood Organization claimed responsibility for gunmen who "took pot shots" at the Soviet embassy one evening, shattering the window panes of the ambassador's reading room.[10] It claimed that "the motive is to warn the Russians to get out of Afghanistan. The next time we strike, we will kill the ambassador or any employees."[11]

Deputy Foreign Minister of Asian Affairs Mikhail Kapitsa became the target of Malaysian anti-Soviet anger when in Singapore in early April 1983 he warned ASEAN nations that the infrastructure of the Southeast Asian countries would erode if ASEAN did not end its confrontation with Vietnam and its allies in Laos and Kampuchea. Furthermore, he stated that Vietnam would have to retaliate and supply arms to insurgents in the ASEAN states if ASEAN continued to support the Khmer Rouge in Kampuchea. About four thousand youth members from the various ruling coalition parties rallied to protest this statement. Deputy Minister Anwar Ibrahim, the UMNO Youth leader, addressed the crowd and stated that the threat issued by the Soviet minister "could not be taken lightly as the Communist Party of Malaya still existed." He found the Soviets' attitude vacillating, "as it had once stated that its foreign policy was not to interfere in the internal affairs of other countries. However . . . the Soviet Union had committed aggression in Afghanistan and supported Vietnam in its aggression in Kampuchea showing that its deeds and words were different. . . . The Soviet Union was not happy with Malaysia's stand and thus threatened it would support the Communist Party of Malaya to erode the infra-structure in the country."[12] The youths at the rally then pledged to defend the country and oppose the threat "to the last." A report even claimed that "never was there a more unpopular name than that of Mikhail Kapitsa. Each time the UMNO Youth leader mentioned the name . . . he had to pause and allow the crowd sufficient time to vent their contempt for that name."[13]

This and several other youth protests were held with indirect government support and actively led by Anwar Ibrahim, an influential cabinet minister. The Soviet ambassador refused to accept a protest note from the Youth leaders when they met him a day after the rally; and another youth delegation had their appointment two days later cancelled. The delegation leader commented that "the embassy's attitude was proof that an iron curtain exists not only in the Soviet Union and East Germany but right here in our own country. . . . I agree totally with Encik Anwar Ibrahim that they [the Soviets] are very arrogant."[14]

For a while, the Soviets were Malaysia's focus of interest. There were calls to reduce the embassy staff of sixteen on diplomatic staff and nineteen on nondiplomatic staff (all of whom were recruited locally). (Ten Malaysians had been assigned to the embassy in Moscow, only seven of whom were in residence at that time.) Subsequently, a regional journal identified two of the men at the Soviet embassy as spies, which prompted the UMNO Youth to call for their expulsion if the allegations were true. Evaluating the excitement, the deputy prime minister, Musa Hitam, stated that the government would not conduct "spy catching" in public especially through the mass media.[15]

The entire Kapitsa incident is an example of an issue taken to emotional extremes. At one meeting Kapitsa's effigy and paper models of weapons and the sickle and hammer were burned.[16] Another rally attracted ten thousand people, who shouted "death to Mikhail Kapitsa; death to Russia" and sang "Malaysia Berjaya," a national song, while an effigy of Kapitsa and the Soviet flag burned.[17]

Anti-Soviet sentiment became public again when the Soviets shot down the Korean Airline jet, which carried a Malaysian passenger. The government and various public groups, including opposition parties, made their indignation about this incident known. The Malaysian government canceled the planned visit that week of a Soviet foreign ministry delegation, while the Kiang and Penang port workers initiated a limited boycott of Soviet ships (one hour per shift). There was to be a boycott of servicing Aeroflot at the international airport, but it was later called off by the Malaysian Airline Systems Employees' Union when it was discovered that the action would not be within the stipulated industrial relations regulations governing the union.

In the mid-1980s the atmosphere improved considerably. Deputy Foreign Minister Kadir Sheikh Fadzir met Mikhail Kapista in Moscow while there to attend Soviet Party Chief Konstantin Chernenko's funeral in March 1985. Later that year, one of the Soviet deputy prime ministers, Iakov Ryabov, visited Malaysia with a trade delegation for consultations. It appeared that the Malaysian government would modify some of its unyielding attitudes toward the communist power if the Soviet Union refrained from any controversial actions. The burden was on the Soviet Union to ensure the stability and continuity of the relationship. Afghanistan and Kampuchea remained an irritant, but Malaysia was willing to explore its trade potentials, especially when access to western markets became uncertain and commodity prices fell. Furthermore, Mahathir was pursuing bilateral economic relations with China and felt it important to keep equal relationships with the two communist powers.

STRENGTHENING MALAYSIAN-SOVIET RELATIONS

As a major commodity-producing country heavily dependent on external trade, Malaysia has sought to expand trade with as many partners as possible, regardless of ideologies (excluding Israel and South Africa). It developed direct trade relations with the Soviet Union in the 1960s, and since then bilateral trade has been a small but constant portion of Malaysia's total trade. Exports to the Soviets have been around 2 percent of total exports since 1984, while imports have been generally less than 0.2 percent of total imports. The Soviet Union buys rubber, palm oil, cocoa, minerals, and other raw materials. About 5 to 6 percent of Malaysia's rubber goes to the Soviet Union.[18] Other than some machinery and fertilizers, the Soviet Union does not have many products that Malaysia wants to import. Therefore the trade balance has been in Malaysia's favor by ten to one.

The surprising announcement in 1984 that Malaysia would consider purchasing Soviet helicopters indicated that incompatible ideologies need not hinder commercial undertakings. Only a few years earlier, the purchasing of Soviet helicopters would not have been considered, but Mahathir stated: "We buy arms from everywhere and I don't see why we can't buy from these countries . . . if they fit our specifications and are cheap."[19] Malaysia usually purchased helicopters from the United States and France. Reportedly, "by considering Soviet weaponry, Malaysia will be able to practice its equidistant relationship between superpowers and an open arms policy. This is not the first buy from a communist nation as Malaysia has been buying mortars and anti-personnel mines from Yugoslavia."[20] This would also indicate to the West that if it (especially the United States and West Germany) does not sell Malaysia high-technology weaponry, Malaysia can shop elsewhere. In late November 1984 a team from the Malaysian air force visited Moscow to study the possibilities of purchasing Soviet helicopters. The study team had to consider such issues as price, quality, availability of spare parts, training of pilots in the Soviet Union, presence of Soviet technicians in Malaysia, and the compatibility of local needs and environment. An initial report was submitted to the cabinet in December 1984; however, no public announcement has been made yet on the purchase of Soviet helicopters.

The Soviet Union took advantage of the slump in commodity prices that affected Malaysia's domestic growth and the general global recession and presented itself as a potential trade partner. In June 1986 the vice-chairman of the Soviet Presidium, Akil V. Salimov, and his delegation visited Kuala Lumpur and stated that the Soviet Union wanted to establish more equitable and mutually advantageous socioeconomic, scientific, and cultural cooperation.[21] This was only one of several delegations that visited the ASEAN capitals as part of the diplomatic initiatives toward Asia associated with Mikhail Gorbachev.

Although regional media and analysts displayed warnings such as "Soviet Union woos ASEAN with trade markets," or "Moscow seeks to bait ASEAN with trade offer," or "the Soviets come-a-calling on ASEAN," the government pursued a practical policy and sought more trade with the Soviet Union.[22] It negotiated bilateral shipping agreements with the Soviet Union and other Eastern-bloc countries, similar to the pacts it had with several trading partners. The proposed agreements were deemed necessary because of the size and growing importance of Malaysia's bilateral trade. When queried about bilateral Malaysian-Soviet relations, Malaysian foreign ministry officials claimed that the main emphasis was on trade relations and that they wanted a strictly economic relationship.

Unofficially, the Malaysian government discourages travel to the Soviet Union. When in late 1985 the government stopped requiring Malaysians to obtain permission before visiting that country, it made it clear that it did not wish to encourage Malaysians to rush to the Soviet Union. Aeroflot, the Soviet airliner, had always provided one of the cheapest links between Kuala Lumpur and London with stopovers at Moscow. It is difficult to assess whether the number of Malaysians visiting the Soviet Union has substantially increased.

Gorbachev's Asian Initiatives and Malaysian Interests

The quiet diplomacy of 1984 and 1985 was jolted suddenly in July 1986 when Soviet Party Secretary Gorbachev stated his plans for new diplomatic initiatives toward Asia and the Pacific in his unprecedented speech at Vladivostok. Only time will tell whether these new directions will actually be executed. Those who recalled similar initiatives articulated during the 1960s were not impressed with Gorbachev's new plans. Leonid Brezhnev, in 1969, proposed a collective security plan for Asia that was not supported by the Asian states.[23] However, international and national issues were different two decades ago, and the new Soviet intentions were appealing.

The Asia-Pacific countries were interested, but cautious. Each country's reaction depended upon its relationship with the Soviet Union; for instance, Japan and China seemed more interested than Singapore or Malaysia. After the initial curiosity most of the Asia-Pacific countries wondered if there was actually anything new about the proposed policies. Malaysia, especially, seemed indifferent. In his Vladivostok speech, Gorbachev referred to three areas of special interest to Malaysia.

1. The Soviet Union is prepared to expand ties with Malaysia and the other Southeast Asian states. "In keeping with its principled policy, the Soviet Union will seek to lend dynamism to its bilateral relations with all countries situated here without exception."

2. In reference to the resolution of the Kampuchean issue he indi-

cated that "here, like in other problems of Southeast Asia, much depends on the normalization of Sino-Vietnamese relations."

3. On relations between ASEAN and Indochina, the Soviet leader commented that "in our opinion, there are no insurmountable obstacles in the way of establishing mutually acceptable relations between the countries of Indochina and ASEAN. Given goodwill and on the condition of nonintervention from the outside, they could solve their problems which would benefit simultaneously the cause of security in Asia."[24]

Clearly, Malaysia's bilateral relationship with the Soviet Union is a function of much larger geopolitical considerations. Malaysia and the rest of ASEAN have been preoccupied with the Soviet role in the Kampuchean issue. Thus Malaysia realized that if the Soviets were willing to facilitate a settlement of the Kampuchean issue, relations could improve between the Soviet Union and ASEAN. Also, no Malaysian leader would disagree with Gorbachev's statement that much of the geopolitical relations in the region depended on the normalization of Sino-Vietnamese relations.

Despite Gorbachev's speech, Malaysian perceptions and foreign policies have not changed significantly since 1986. There is somewhat more economic emphasis in its bilateral relations, but two political issues, Kampuchea and Afghanistan, remain important foci of Malaysian foreign policies and constraints to the further development of its relations with the USSR.

Direct outcomes of Prime Minister Mahathir's official visit to the Soviet Union in July 1987 were an agreement on avoiding double taxation and an agreement on shipping. These would undoubtedly lead to increased economic cooperation, especially in trade. There was a consensus that the trade imbalance should be reduced by increasing imports from the Soviet Union rather than reducing exports from Malaysia; several products were tentatively identified for import by Malaysia. Mahathir assured Gorbachev that "we have a market economy in our country, and your organizations must establish effective business ties with our private sector. You can be sure that my government will support this process."[25] Subsequently, a cooperative agreement was signed by the Soviet Union's Chamber of Commerce and Industry and Malaysia's Chamber of Commerce and Industry. The countries' foreign ministers, Eduard Shevardnadze and Abu Hassan Omar, also signed a Soviet-Malaysian protocol for consultations.

THE FUTURE OF MALAYSIAN-SOVIET RELATIONS

Mahathir's 1987 visit seems to have strengthened bilateral relations. *Pravda* reported:

Mahathir said that the propositions set forth in the Vladivostok speech, as well as in the interview given to the Indonesian newspaper *Merdeka*, were received with interest in Malaysia. Malaysia proceeds from the assumption that the USSR, an Asia-Pacific power, has interests in that region and in the world as a whole. The Malaysian government believes that in showing attention to the Asia-Pacific region, the Soviet Union is guided not by a desire for rivalry, but by the interests of enhancing stability in the region, which is in need of it. The Soviet initiatives do not cause concern in Malaysia. As an independent country, Malaysia has its own point of view and intends to defend it firmly.[26]

According to the Malaysian foreign minister, the visit was "highly successful."[27] Too much emphasis should not be placed on the apparently good relationship between the two countries; it could be contrived by both countries to skillfully accomplish their international and regional strategies.

Malaysia still regards communism as an evil ideology. It has been clearly established that the authorities would not tolerate the slightest indication of subversion either by sympathetic Malaysian or Soviet nationals, nor would they allow publications that favorably portray the Soviet political and economic system. At a time when more and more educated youths are questioning the traditional social systems and values, the government is apprehensive of foreign-inspired alternatives, especially Soviet alternatives.

In summary, Malaysian attitudes and actions toward the Soviet Union are strongly guided by the noninterference of the Soviet Union in its domestic affairs, Soviet actions related to Afghanistan and Kampuchea, and economic interests.

NOTES

1. The prime minister in Moscow, 30 July 1987. *FBIS*, 15 November 1987, 5–8 (quoting *Pravda*, 31 July 1987).
2. For an analysis on the Southeast Asia Treaty Organization see Lezek Buszynski, *SEATO, The Failure of an Alliance* (Singapore: Singapore University Press, 1983).
3. See Chin Kin Wah, *The Defense of Malaysia and Singapore: The Transformation of a Security System, 1957–1971* (Cambridge: Cambridge University Press, 1983).
4. *Foreign Affairs Malaysia* 5, no. 3 (September 1972): 30.
5. It had earlier established relations with North and South Vietnam, Laos, and Cambodia.
6. *New Straits Times*, 15 July 1981.
7. *Foreign Affairs Malaysia* 12, no. 4 (December 1979), 457.

8. *New Straits Times*, 16 April 1981.

9. Ibid., 6 April 1981.

10. Ibid., 14 January 1983.

11. *The Star*, 16 January 1983.

12. Ibid., 18 April 1983.

13. Ibid.

14. Ibid.

15. Ibid., 24 April 1983.

16. Ibid., 29 April 1983.

17. Ibid., 13 May 1983.

18. Malaysia, Ministry of Finance, *Economic Report, 1987/1988*.

19. *New Straits Times*, 9 September 1984.

20. Ibid., 13 May 1984.

21. Ibid., 6 June 1986.

22. Keith Stafford, *New Straits Times*, 22 May 1986; Derek Martin da Cunha, *New Straits Times*, 4 December 1985; Mathews George, *Sunday Star*, 15 June 1986.

23. For a detailed study of Soviet interests in the region and especially on the Soviet collective security proposal see Leszek Buszynski, *Soviet Foreign Policy and Southeast Asia* (London & Sydney: Croom Helm, 1986), 40–96.

24. Translation taken from *News and Views from the USSR*, "Mikhail Gorbachev Talks About International Affairs in Vladivostok," Consulate General, Union of Soviet Socialist Republics (San Francisco, 29 July 1986).

    The July speech did not come entirely unexpected to those in Malaysia or in ASEAN. Earlier in 1986, the Soviet embassy in Singapore had invited newsmen based in the ASEAN countries to a briefing on the latest efforts by the Soviet Union to improve relations with ASEAN.

25. *FBIS*, 5 August 1987, p. D8 (quoting *Pravda*, 31 July 1987).

26. Comments delivered by Mahathir Mohamad at the Kremlin 31 July 1987. *Pravda*, 1 August 1987 (*Pravda* is translated and published in English by Associated Publishers, Inc., St. Paul, Minnesota).

27. *New Straits Times*, 8 August 1987.

9

Philippine-Soviet Relations:
Two Decades of Diplomatic Coquetry

Wilfrido V. Villacorta

Since 1967 when the Philippine Congress called for a softening of relations with the socialist bloc, the Philippines has employed a backward-forward style of diplomacy with the Soviet Union. Such a tentative and cautious approach is rooted in mutual fear. The Philippines feels insecure about a superpower with a different social system and with past links to the underground movement. As a result of Cold War propaganda, the Soviet expansionist image still looms in the Filipino mind. The Soviet Union continues to mistrust the Philippine governments because of their close relationship with the United States. Although the Soviets welcome any development that erodes Philippine-U.S. ties and uses it as an entry point for overtures, they are aware that results will almost always be limited. The relations of the Philippines with the Soviet Union have been a function of Filipino perceptions of the Soviet role in domestic and regional developments. Such perceptions have, in turn, been shaped by the status of the Philippines' relations with the United States.

HISTORICAL BACKGROUND

Since the late 1940s when the country regained its independence, Philippine governments have regarded the United States as their closest and most reliable ally. Faced with a serious insurgency problem, the Philippines looked to the United States for advice and material assistance. The United States readily provided assistance because it considered the pacification campaign essential to the protection of its interests in the country.

The insurgency had its origins in agrarian unrest, although it was by Crisanto Evangelista and Jacinto Manahan, both leaders of the labor movement, that the Partido Comunista was founded in 1930. Its program of action was patterned after that of the Communist Party of the Soviet Union (CPSU). In 1932 the Supreme Court outlawed the party, forcing its members to work in the underground.

The Japanese occupation stimulated the organization of the military arm of the Communist party in 1942. Peasant leaders from Central Luzon formed the Hukbo ng Bayan Laban sa Hapon (People's Army Against the Japanese), which became known as the "Huk."[1] At the end of the war, the United States forcibly disarmed the Huk units and launched mass arrests of its leaders and members. Despite the subsequent release of some leaders and the proclamation of amnesty, government dialogues with the insurgents broke down. It took the charismatic figure of Ramon Magsaysay, who became defense secretary and, later in 1953, president, to neutralize the popular appeal of the Huks. The surrender of Luis Taruc and the capture of other Huk officials deeply damaged the morale of the movement.[2]

Against this backdrop, it can be understood why it took almost twenty years before relations with socialist countries were considered by the national leadership. The first official to urge the review of government policy toward the Soviet Union and other socialist states was Salvador Lopez, the secretary of foreign affairs during the administration of President Diosdado Macapagal. In 1964 he advanced "the need for an Asian policy that would take due account of the emergence of China as a power in Asia" and "the need to reduce our excessive dependence upon the United States by developing a new foreign policy leverage and broadening our options in international affairs."[3] However, the strong anticommunist character of the Macapagal administration militated against expanding the horizons of Philippine foreign policy.

Ferdinand Marcos was elected to the presidency in 1965. He ran on an ostensibly nationalist platform, espousing a more independent foreign policy. In January 1967 Foreign Affairs Secretary Narciso Ramos spoke of the "possible relaxation" of the ban against trading with socialist countries.[4] The following month the Philippine and Soviet delegates held talks at the Economic Commission for Asia and the Far East (ECAFE) meeting in Bangkok. In that same year the Philippine Congress sent a mission to the Soviet Union, Poland, Czechoslovakia, Romania, East Germany, and Bulgaria.[5]

The exploratory mission headed by Congressman Manuel Enverga reported that "socialist Europe is a vast export area for Philippine products of all sorts, and trading patterns and habits do not offer serious obstacles to the Philippines seeking to develop for her products so huge and varied a market."[6] Another mission organized by the Philippine Chamber of Industries recommended lifting the travel ban on Filipinos bound for the socialist countries of Europe and allowing trade with these countries through trade organizations or an interchamber board.[7] In 1968 President Marcos announced his government's readiness to open trade relations with Eastern Europe. The Philippine Congress subsequently affirmed the policy "to engage in trade with countries with which the Philippines has no existing consular or diplomatic relations."[8] According to Alejandro Fernandez, the relaxation of travel and trade restrictions was motivated by both economic and political considerations. The drive to diversify the country's international market was in preparation for the expiration of the Laurel-Langley Agreement, which had provided preferential access to the U.S. market. Socialist countries also offered higher prices for sugar, copra, and coconut oil, the Philippines' major export products. The transformation in the power relationships in Asia was another important consideration, namely, the projected U.S. disengagement from Asia, the detente between the United States and the Soviet Union, the Sino-Soviet schism, and the rise of Japan as an economic power. In his State of the Nation address on 27 January 1964, Marcos prematurely alluded to "an impending American withdrawal in the military sphere, an event of great importance to countries which have hitherto depended upon an American military guarantee."

With Marcos' reelection in November 1969, the president's eyes were set not only on his second term but more importantly on how he could stay in power beyond 1973. The then prevailing constitution did not allow more than two presidential terms. Hence he and his advisers began preparing for the eventual declaration of martial law which would be preceded by a constitutional convention that would usher in provisions for an indefinite tenure for the incumbent president.

In the context of this game plan, we can better appreciate the moves of Marcos to improve relations with the socialist bloc. Obviously, he wanted to utilize these diplomatic overtures as leverage vis-à-vis the United States. Knowing that its Philippine bases were the main concern of the United States in dealing with his government, he found these bases very useful hostages through which he could extract U.S. tolerance for his premeditated authoritarian rule. Marcos also knew about the Soviet Union's keen interest in preventing closer relations between China and the United States and in reducing special U.S.-Philippine relations. Hence he thought it wise to alternately flirt with both China and the Soviet Union.

In 1972 diplomatic relations with Romania and Yugoslavia were established. In a foreign policy statement made in 1975, President Marcos referred to the need "to pursue more vigorously the establishment of diplomatic relations with Socialist states, in particular with the People's Republic of China and the Soviet Union." The following year, he stated that "we seek to pursue more vigorously economic and trade relations with the Socialist states."[9]

Alejandro Fernandez described the move in the 1970s to establish diplomatic relations with socialist countries as "unquestionably the most radical and most significant new direction in the foreign policy of the Philippines."[10] On the other hand, Salvador Lopez thought that it was long overdue: "It has taken President Marcos ten years since the beginning of his first term to pry open long-barred windows that open on the socialist states of the world."[11] Alex Brillantes observed that these overtures were mainly reactive and that "the move towards the establishment of diplomatic ties with the socialist countries was made primarily because the bigger capitalist powers with which the Philippines was aligned and closely identified with had already established relations with them."[12]

This reactive policy toward the socialist states was apparent in the establishment of diplomatic relations with China in June 1975. This step was considered "safe" after President Richard Nixon visited China in 1972. It was hoped that Philippine recognition of the People's Republic of China, ushering in government-to-government relations, would significantly reduce whatever support China was giving to the local communist movement. On the other hand, there was no urgency in establishing diplomatic relations with the Soviets.

Establishment of Philippine-Soviet Relations

In March 1972 First Lady Imelda Marcos visited Moscow to explore the establishment of diplomatic relations. Her visit was followed by the establishment of the Philippine-USSR Friendship Society that same year. In 1974 the counterpart USSR-Philippine Society was founded in Moscow.

From 30 May to 6 June, 1976 President and Mrs. Marcos made a state visit to the Soviet Union. A joint communiqué establishing diplomatic relations between the two countries and a trade agreement were signed on 2 June 1976. Two years later, Mrs. Marcos returned to Moscow to sign a cultural agreement with the Soviet Union.

Cultural relations with the Soviets. Interaction with the Soviets has been most active in the cultural area. Since 1976 three executive agreements on cultural exchanges have been completed. There had been a sustained exchange of artists between the two countries, until the economic crisis brought financial constraints to the Philippine government. The Philippine National Olympic Committee has been receiving assistance from Soviet coaches training Filipino athletes. Moreover, the National Historical Institute of the Philippines signed an agreement with the Institute of Oriental Studies of the USSR Academy of Sciences to promote scholarly works and contacts between historians of both countries.

Economic relations with the Soviets. Although trade began earlier, a formal trade agreement was signed after the 1976 opening of diplomatic relations. The two countries granted each other most favored nation treatment regarding customs duties, internal taxes, and the issuance of import and export licenses.[13]

Philippine exports to the Soviet Union include raw materials; food products; manufactured products; and alcohol products such as beer, rum, and gin. Philippine imports from the Soviet Union include industrial equipment, minerals, tools, machinery, coal, and oil. From 1972 to 1984 the Philippines enjoyed a favorable balance of trade. Since 1985, however, the country has not been able to export a sufficient amount of traditional products to the Soviet Union.

The Soviet Union only accounts for 1 to 2 percent of the Philippines' total trade. Steps were taken to promote economic cooperation in two areas: the shipping and cement industries. A joint venture, the Philippine–Soviet Shipping Company (FILSOV), was formed in 1974 to provide more shipping facilities for the Philippines than those provided by the United States. Many Filipino exporters reportedly preferred to use Soviet ships because of their stable freight charges and reliable schedules. These ships also went to the remote islands.

A feasibility study was launched in 1982 for a joint venture between the Philippines and the Soviet Union in constructing a one-million-ton-per-year cement plant. It would have been the first Soviet industrial project in the country and would have produced a significant increment over the current annual output levels of 4 to 4.5 million tons, enabling the Philippines to export cement. This project did not materialize due to financial handicaps.

Scientific cooperation. An agreement to promote cooperation in science and technology was signed on 8 July 1982. Exchanges of scientists and postgraduate students and contacts among research institutions were envisioned in the agreement; however, to date its programs have not been implemented.

RECENT DEVELOPMENTS

Relations with the Soviet Union are becoming increasingly complex because of the intensified insurgency and the "Red scare" that some groups have promoted. Although the Huks gradually lost their influence after Ramon Magsaysay came to power, the Communist Party of the Philippines (CPP) was founded in 1968 by a new group of younger ideologues. In that year, its armed wing, the New People's Army (NPA), started with some 200 regulars. During the next decade the strength of the NPA increased by tenfold. Before Senator Aquino's assassination in 1983, there were 5,000 to 7,000 estimated guerrillas.[14] In 1985 the strength was reported at 20,000 soldiers.

When Corazon Aquino assumed the presidency, cease-fire talks were given priority during the first year of her administration. Allegations of cease-fire violations by both sides hindered negotiations. Counterinsurgency operations have intensified alongside a general amnesty program. Despite these actions, the number of ambushes and rural guerrillas increased.

There have been reports of Soviet assistance to radical labor groups and the New People's Army.[15] Also denounced were the Soviet embassy's alleged attempts to increase the size of its staff and expand its facilities. These accusations were promptly denied by the Soviets as well as by the radical groups concerned. In the meantime, President Aquino vowed to end "all threats to peace and freedom" and reiterated her call for a "people's war against the communist insurgency and the fascist attempts to destabilize the government."[16]

The most serious attempted coup, on 28 August 1987, exacerbated the crisis. The mutiny so jolted the government that it triggered a revamping of the cabinet. The president accepted Vice-President Salvador Laurel's resignation as secretary of foreign affairs. In turn, Mr. Laurel submitted to the congress on September 30 a list of supposed leftists and communists in the government. An alarming wave of McCarthyism swept the officialdom.

CHANGING PERCEPTIONS

Factors Influencing Philippine Perceptions of the Soviets

A number of Philippine domestic issues influence the nature of Philippine-Soviet relations. First, the Philippines has been plagued with massive poverty and agrarian problems that have resulted in the rise of the communist insurgency and secessionist movements. Second, the majority of the population is Catholic, and Catholicism is against communism and all that it allegedly stands for—atheism, violence, and dictatorship. It must be mentioned, however, that there are elements in the Catholic church that have taken up the cudgels for the rural and urban poor, even if this commitment required the use of Marxist analytical and tactical tools.

The Philippines regional involvement has influenced its Soviet perception. The Philippines' membership first in the Southeast Asia Treaty Organization (SEATO) and, later, in the Association of Southeast Asian Nations (ASEAN) has carried with it deep imprints of Cold War perspectives. Having been allied with the United States in the Korean and Vietnam wars, Philippine governments have always been wary of the Soviet presence in Northeast and Southeast Asia.

U.S. and Japanese economic assistance to ASEAN countries is another factor that shapes Philippine perceptions of the Soviets' role in Southeast Asia. There is expectedly an inverse relationship between anticipated trade with and economic assistance from the United States and Japan and cooperative initiatives with the Soviet Union.

Political Relations

The early days of the Aquino government were not accompanied by pleasant memories of Soviet actions. On the eve of Mr. Marcos' overthrow, he summoned the new Soviet ambassador to Manila to present his credentials. As *Asiaweek* described it:

Faced with a diplomatic boycott, Marcos called in new Soviet Ambassador Vadim I. Shabalin to present his long-postponed credentials. Protocol required congratulations—and a sucker was born. "The Soviet ambassador was the victim of unfortunate circumstances," says a leading European envoy in Manila. It took the Soviets 51 days from Aquino's swearing in to get another chance to congratulate a Philippine president.[17]

In explaining the faux pas, the Soviet embassy in Manila insisted that the ambassador's felicitations were more personal than official. In any case, the government-controlled press greatly publicized the event and proclaimed that the Soviet superpower recognized the legitimacy of the Marcos government.

But ambassadorial follies are conveniently forgotten in favor of international amity. The current official policy of the Philippine government toward the Soviet Union is reflected in the various foreign policy statements made by Vice-President Salvador Laurel, when he was secretary of foreign affairs. He spoke of the need to pursue friendly relations, and to expand ties with the Soviets. "As Asia-Pacific states, [the Philippines and the Soviet Union have national interests that] coincide in many ways. We share the common obligation to contribute in every way we can to the peace, harmony, and prosperity of our region."

Mr. Laurel said that the Vladivostok statement of Soviet leader Mikhail Gorbachev deserved serious consideration.

> We especially welcome his reference to the Philippines as one of the countries with which the USSR is prepared to expand ties. For our part, we are all prepared to explore all avenues to bring about such expansion of ties, and to reiterate our long-standing position that we are a medium size developing country seeking only to safeguard our national interest, and as such we must make no enemy if we can make friends.[18]

In another speech, Vice-President Laurel welcomed Mr. Gorbachev's "expressions of Soviet intent with respect to the reduction of Soviet forces in various places in Asia" and said that the government "eagerly awaits these intentions to be translated into action—moves that we are confident will meet positive response not only from the Philippines but from other countries within our interests in Asia as well."[19] These statements were made in reference to Gorbachev's Vladivostok speech of July 1986 in which he referred to the Philippines four times. This included the following references to the Philippines:

> We are prepared to expand ties with Indonesia, Australia, New Zealand, the Philippines, Thailand, Malaysia, Singapore, Burma, Sri Lanka, Nepal, Brunei, the Republic of Maldives, and the youngest independent participants in the region's political life.
>
> The Soviet Union is a convinced advocate of disbanding the military groupings, renouncing the possession of military bases in Asia and the Pacific ocean, and withdrawing troops from the territories of other countries.
>
> We propose to start talks on the reduction of activity of fleets in the Pacific, above all nuclear armed ships. Restriction of the rivalry in the sphere of antisubmarine activity in certain zones of the Pacific would help strengthen stability. This could become a substantial confidence-building measure. In general, I would like to say that if the United States gave up military presence, say, in the Philippines, we would not leave this step unanswered.

The political relations between the two countries have improved. The Presidium of the Supreme Soviet of the USSR congratulated the president on the ratification of the new constitution, which is attributed to her popularity. President Aquino promptly acknowledged the felicitations. The Philippines and the Soviet Union have also agreed during United Nations deliberations on such issues as opposition to racial discrimination, self-determination of peoples, and assistance to developing countries. They have also supported each other's candidates to important United Nations posts.

Senator Leticia Ramos-Shahani, chairperson of the Philippine Senate Committee on Foreign Relations, spoke of the need "to evolve on our terms a foreign policy with the other superpower, the USSR" and to train "a corps of diplomats expert in dealing with Eastern Europe, a most sensitive area."[20] She further stated that the development of an independent foreign policy requires the capability "to interpret the intentions of the Soviet Union in all its complexity and not just continue indefinitely depending on our allies for information."

This call for more information about Soviet intentions is timely because those who defend the retention of U.S. bases argue that U.S. withdrawal of these bases would invite an invasion of the Philippines by Soviet forces. This view, although simplistic, is nonetheless popular. A deeper and wider understanding of the global and regional strategies of the superpowers is needed to clarify this issue.

Economic Relations

The present government recognizes that Philippine-Soviet trade is minimal. Trade Secretary Jose Concepcion noted that "two-way trade between the two countries has been on a downward slide since 1981, totalling a mere US$44 million in 1985." But he stressed that "the potential is there."[21]

Philippine ambassador to Moscow Alejandro Melchor maintains that the primary reasons for increasing Soviet presence in Asia are to secure technology and capital and to increase trade.[22] He identified certain areas in which the Philippines could pursue expanded relationships with the USSR: power generation, construction of naval facilities, and the labor market. Among the brightest prospects for an expanded Philippine-Soviet economic relationship is the use of Soviet technology to increase the Philippines' power-generating capacity. After the Aquino government decided to stop the operation of the Bataan nuclear plant, it now recognizes the need to build 300-megawatt coal-fired plants in the provinces of Isabela and Batangas. This project would benefit from Soviet technology, since it will use lignite coal, which is abundant and used extensively in the USSR. Since the USSR has a large naval presence in the Southeast Asian region, the Philippines could offer facilities for ship repair and drydocking. The Philippines is exploring the possibility of opening the USSR labor market to Filipino overseas workers because of decreased employment opportunities in the Middle East.

The Soviets have followed up their offers of assistance to the Philippine government. Returning the visit to Moscow of then Deputy Minister of Foreign Affairs Leticia Shahani, Mr. Boris Nikolaevich Koltsov, a ranking official of the USSR State Committee for Foreign Economic Relations, conducted high-level talks with Philippine officials. He headed a team that conducted a survey of the coal-fired power plant in Isabela. Mr. Koltsov reiterated to several officials his government's proposals for assisting in the economic recovery of the Philippines. The Soviets offered to supply the 300-megawatt Isabela Coal-Fired Power Plant and the associated transmission lines and upgrade the Nonoc Nickel Refinery with the introduction of the acid leach technology process. These proposals, he stressed, would not add to the country's external debt burden. As compensation for these two projects, the Soviets expressed their willingness to be paid in kind with Philippine traditional products and services for the repair of Soviet vessels at Philippine shipyards.

Party Relations

The communist movement in the Philippines is split into two major factions: the Moscow-oriented Partido Komunista ng Pilipinas (PKP) and the originally Beijing-oriented Communist Party of the Philippines (CPP). These local communist parties have different orientations toward the Soviet Union.

On the 68th anniversary of the October Revolution, the PKP sent a message to the CPSU extolling the "leading role played by your party, owing to the fact that it is guided by Marxism-Leninism, which has equipped you with the mastery of the laws of social development as interpreted by the genius of Lenin."[23] PKP Secretary General Felicisimo Macapagal warmly congratulated the CPSU during the 27th Congress.[24] The PKP continues to consider the Soviet Union, through the CPSU, the international leader of socialism and the ideal model of a socialist society.

In 1968 younger members of the PKP, who were disenchanted with the party's leadership and policies, established the CPP. The CPP's perception of the Soviet Union is reflected in the *Liberation*, published by the National Democratic Front (NDF), which is related to the CPP. It published an interview with NDF international representative Luis Jalandoni, who was asked about the status of the NDF relations with socialist countries like China, the Soviet Union, and Vietnam. His reply was as follows:

The NDF has at present no formal relations with these countries. But in various international conferences or gatherings, the NDF meets the representative of these countries and there is friendly interaction. In the long-term, the NDF program calls for developing warm and close relations with Third World and socialist countries.

Some socialist countries, such as Vietnam and Cuba, have also shown support and interest by sending representatives to attend the burial of labor leader Olalia, for instance, and some gatherings of patriotic multisectoral alliances in the country. Vietnam, in particular, helps the Filipino people's struggle indirectly by its militant opposition to U.S. imperialist policies worldwide.[25]

The rightist opposition in the Philippines alleged that the Soviet Union has provided more than moral support to the CPP. Right-wing politician Rene Espina charged that Soviet arms were landed in January 1987 for a communist New People's Army camp in the Philippine province of Samar.[26] Former speaker of the Marcos parliament Querube Makalintal echoed these allegations and claimed that Soviet-made Kalashnikov assault rifles were delivered to the NPA rebels in Samar.[27] Another report claimed that the Soviet Union and Vietnam "offered weapons, finance, and training" to the CPP.[28]

Defense Secretary Rafael Ileto stated that this report is not supported by facts.[29] However, the Philippine Senate urged an investigation of alleged Soviet assistance to labor groups and the rebels and of sightings of submarines suspected to belong to the USSR.[30] Such allegations of interference in the internal affairs of the Philippines were vehemently denied by the Soviet ambassador in Manila, Vadim Shabalin, as "flagrantly distorting" the Soviet Union's foreign policy toward the Philippines.

CONCLUSIONS

There has been little progress in Philippine-Soviet relations. What is discernible is a regression in the substance of the relations due to the current political instability. The "Red scare" that is being spread by Philippine right-wing groups further exacerbates the situation. Newspaper reports about alleged agreements between Eastern European parties and the CPP further reinforce policymakers' apprehensions about the Soviet Union.[31]

However, the intelligentsia are becoming increasingly aware of the factors behind the anti-Soviet hysteria. A Philippine diplomat observed that "Filipinos have succumbed to American-inspired Cold War propaganda. They see Red whenever they see Soviets."[32] An editorial in a leading newspaper deplored the prevailing McCarthyist tendencies, which picture communists as monsters and villians.

> Some of us [have been] conditioned through the years of deliberate miseducation, to react antagonistically at the slightest mention of communists, Red or radical. And for as long as we allow ourselves to remain captives of this mind set, we will never understand what compels some Filipinos to rebel, and we will never learn to deal with the insurgency intelligently.[33]

Economic and other forms of dependency on the United States are viewed as additional explanations for the country's perception of the Soviets. Former Philippine Ambassador Narciso G. Reyes wrote that "in Southeast Asia, the Philippines has always functioned in the giant shadow of America."[34] Brillantes makes a parallel observation:

> As long as the Philippines continues to remain heavily dependent on the United States, it will never be a nation that the Soviet Union will seriously deal with. The Russians perceive the Philippines as a very close ally of the United States, but they see no harm in trying to cultivate good relations with the U.S. ally in the event that a falling out with the United States may develop; the Soviets will be there to fill any vacuum that may open up.[35]

The United States' influence plays a role in shaping Filipino attitudes toward the Soviet Union. It is in the United States' interest to drum up the Soviet threat particularly to safeguard the tenure of her military facilities in the Philippines beyond 1991. The dichotomization of humanity into the "good guys" and the "bad guys" must continually be projected into a Cold War type of division into the "free world" and the communist world, the latter to be perpetually painted as the epitome of all evil.

Placing an ally like the Philippines in an ideological quarantine by "protecting" her against contamination from the socialist bloc would also render her safe from the designs of the local communist movement. All these objectives reflect U.S. strategic interests in the Philippines: the maintenance of her military facilities, the obliteration of the local communist insurgency, and the neutralization of Soviet diplomatic offensives.

When Vice-President Laurel gave his first testimony at the hearing of the newly convened Senate, he shared the following insights:

There remains in the Philippines an attitude of suspicion toward any venture that would entail the presence of Soviet personnel in the country. Perhaps, the time has come to weigh seriously the possible political and economic benefits from increased trade with and financing and technology from the USSR against the perceived national security implications of such exchanges.[36]

This statement was reminiscent of the exhortations twenty years ago of President Marcos, Foreign Secretary Narciso Ramos, Congressman Manuel Enverga, and the head of the trade mission to socialist countries, Augusto Caesar Espiritu. The call for a reexamination of foreign policy premises and for a consideration of the benefits of better relations with the Soviet Union is similar, although recent official pronouncements are, in fact, more cautious. Vice-President Laurel spoke of weighing the benefits "against perceived national security implications of such exchanges," while Senator Shahani referred to the need "to interpret the intentions of the Soviet Union in all its complexity." If these diplomatic code words are translated, they relate to the lingering fear among Filipinos of Soviet aggression and interference in domestic affairs. Although the Huk threat disappeared more than thirty years ago, it is still deeply embedded in the memories of the present generation of national leaders. The fear is compounded by bombardments from the Western media about the strategic significance of the Soviets' bases in Cam Ranh Bay and their occupation of Afghanistan. This perception is justified by the Philippine government's support for the United Nations resolution calling for the withdrawal of Soviet troops from Afghanistan and the ASEAN resolutions denouncing Vietnam's invasion of Kampuchea and Soviet warships' maneuvering in Thai territorial waters. These international positions constitute the irritants in Philippine-Soviet relations.[37]

It is therefore not surprising that Philippine-Soviet relations have not gone far. They continue to be characterized by the diplomacy of coquetry, what is referred to in Filipino colloquialism as *jele-jele* (playing coy). Philippine comedies commonly portray traditional courtship situations in which Maria Clara, the demure maiden, shyly hides her face behind her fan and plays *jele-jele*, while the frustrated suitor has to maintain a safe distance, occasionally moving *atras-avante* on the divan. The reason for their mutual fidgeting is because Big Mama beside them is watching.

Is it wise to continue this *comedia* at the official level? If intelligence reports are to be believed, the Soviets are getting impatient and beginning to enter through the back door. And underground movements supported by the Soviets in many other countries have become more formidable and often invulnerable.

NOTES

1. Alfredo Saulo, *Communism in the Philippines* (Manila: Ateneo de Manila University, 1969), 1–28; 36–43.
2. Ibid., 55–61; Alvin Scaff, *The Philippine Answer to Communism* (Stanford, Calif.: Stanford University Press, 1955), 116–140.
3. Salvador Lopez, *New Directions in Philippine Foreign Policy* (Quezon City: U. P. Law Center, 1975), 18.
4. *Manila Times*, 25 January 1967, 22A.
5. For further information on Philippine contacts with the Soviet Union and Eastern Europe, see Alejandro Fernandez, *The Philippines and the United States: The Forging of New Relations* (Quezon City: NSDB-UP Integrated Research Program, 1977), 279; Alex Brillantes, "Perceptions of Philippine-Soviet Relations," Foreign Relations Journal 1, no. 4 (December 1986): 131.
6. Manuel Enverga, *The Enverga Report of the Exploratory Mission to the Socialist Countries in 1967* (Manila: House of Representatives, 1967), 71.
7. Jose Ingles, *Philippine Foreign Policy* (Manila: Lyceum of the Philippines, 1982), 65.
8. Fernandez, 279.
9. Benjamin Domingo, *The Making of Filipino Foreign Policy* (Manila: Foreign Service Institute, 1983), 224.
10. Fernandez, 278.
11. Lopez, 16.
12. Brillantes, 131.
13. Brillantes, 135–140.
14. Carolina Hernandez, "Security Issues and Policies: The Philippines in the Mid 1980s," *Foreign Relations Journal* 1, no. 1 (January 1986), 65.
15. *Manila Bulletin*, 11, 15–16 July 1987.
16. *Manila Times*, 17 July 1987.
17. *Asiaweek*, 10 August 1986, 14.
18. Salvador Laurel, Speech at the Pacific Futures Development Center, 26 August 1986.
19. Salvador Laurel, Speech on "New Directions of Philippine Foreign Policy," 2 September 1986.
20. Leticia Shahani, "An Independent Foreign Policy—Its Implications for the Filipino People." Statement read before the Senate of the Philippines, 24 August 1987.
21. Concepcion is quoted in *Asiaweek*, 10 August 1986.
22. *Business Day*, 23 October 1986.
23. *PKP Courier*, no. 4 (1985), 37.
24. *PKP Courier*, no. 1 (1986), 40.
25. *Liberation*, 15, no. 1 (1 January 1987): 7.

26. *Malaya*, 21 January 1987.
27. *Malaya*, 22 January 1987.
28. *Manila Bulletin*, 14 March 1987.
29. *Manila Bulletin*, 26 August 1987.
30. *Philippine Star*, 25 August 1987.
31. For example, *Financial Post*, 13 October 1987; *Manila Bulletin*, 15, 22 July 1987.
32. *Asiaweek*, 10 August 1986.
33. *Philippine Daily Inquirer*, 6 March 1987.
34. Narciso Reyes, "Dealing with Friends and Allies on an Equal Footing," *Foreign Relations Journal* 1, no. 4 (December 1986) 200.
35. Brillantes, 145.
36. Salvador Laurel, Testimony before the Senate hearing, 8 September 1987.
37. Brillantes, 143.

10

Singapore-Soviet Relations:
Perceptions and Policies

Bilveer Singh

Since its independence the Republic of Singapore has been expressly noted for adopting a pragmatic foreign policy and being friendly to all countries, irrespective of ideology and system of government. Toward the Soviet Union Singapore has generally maintained an equidistant posture. In its early years of statehood, Singapore had a relatively positive evaluation of the Soviet Union. However, as it matured, its perception slowly and steadily shifted and fundamentally changed following the dramatic events in Indochina, especially the evolution of the Soviet-Vietnamese alliance. Today Singapore is one of the most vocal anti-Soviet states in the Asia-Pacific region. Its hardline position toward Moscow developed in late 1978 along with its activist and high-profile foreign policy.[1] Since then Singapore's leaders have viewed Soviet and Vietnamese policies as being in collusion to create a communist world order presided over by the Soviet Union.[2]

SOVIET-SINGAPORE RELATIONS BEFORE GORBACHEV

Soviet-Singapore relations can be described as good, correct, and satisfactory until late 1978. Upon Singapore's independence, its relations with the Soviet Union began well because of Singapore's initial anti-Americanism, its declarations of ardent nonalignment, and its espousal of Democratic Socialism. In fact, in September 1965, Prime Minister Lee Kuan Yew threatened to offer the Soviets a base if Malaysia hosted U.S. troops.[3] Furthermore, the deceleration and the end of *konfrontasi*, and the fall of Sukarno after the attempted coup, provided the Soviet Union with the necessary impetus to develop its relations not only with newly independent Singapore but also with Malaysia.

Singapore was willing to develop its relations with the Soviet Union partly to make its nonalignment more credible, but more importantly to entice the superpower's economic and political interest in Singapore. Three months after Singapore's independence, on 4 November 1965, Deputy Prime Minister Toh Chin Chye led a delegation to Moscow that made agreements to set up a trade mission and a TASS office in Singapore. On 4 April 1966 a trade agreement was concluded, and two years later a protocol was added. In late 1967 agreement was reached on the setting up of a Singapore–Soviet Shipping Agency (SINSOV), which was the first Soviet joint venture in the region,[4] and thereafter the number of Soviet ships entering Singapore tremendously increased, totaling some 2,000 per year. Singapore has become the regional repair center for Soviet ships, especially the Keppel and Sembawang shipyards.

In 1967 Singapore began supporting the U.S. involvement in the Vietnam War, but the Soviets did not criticize Singapore's change in policy because of the insignificance of Singapore's voice in international politics, and they did not want to disrupt the mutually beneficial relationship. In fact, since the fall of Sukarno, Singapore had been the most pro-Soviet state in insular Southeast Asia. However, Prime Minister Lee Kuan Yew was not unaware of Soviet mischief in the region. In November 1967 he pointed out that the "Russians supplied some MIG 19s and 21s to Sukarno. And [if] you start supplying spares [spare parts] again, it will be a very troubled part of the world. How can I be sure? How can the Americans be sure that the PKI (Partai Kommunist Indonesia) cannot make a comeback, and Mr. Brezhnev and Mr. Kosygin, . . .will not supply or resupply all the spares to make the MIG's and the cruisers and the submarines effective again? Nobody knows."[5]

In 1968 the British decision to withdraw from the "East of Suez" and U.S. bombing of North Vietnam signaled a major change in regional power alignments. Partly in response to these developments, Singapore established diplomatic relations with the Soviets in June 1968 at the ambassadorial level. In the same year, the Soviets began their first major naval expansion in the region. The Singapore leaders perceived this as a "natural phenomenon" that was economically important because the British were quickly vacating Singapore's first-class naval bases. The political significance of the Soviet presence was more important. It would fulfill Lee Kuan Yew's call for a multipower presence in the region and could persuade the United States to remain. Despite Singapore's keen interest in the Soviet naval expansion, it did not offer any of its bases to the Soviets. However, Soviet shipping fleets were encouraged to use Singapore's ports. David Wise has indicated that the "Russians do not have Singapore as a naval base, but the next best thing; what is described by Western defence and shipping experts as huge Russian fishing fleets; at large in both waters (surface and underwater), their duties [are] not only to fish but also to act as a vast floating naval base and infrastructure to mother surface and underwater 'teeth' units of the Russian navy out of sight, beyond and beneath the horizon."[6]

In February 1969 Singapore and the Soviet Union signed an air agreement, and in May Aeroflot, the Soviet national airline, opened a branch in Singapore. When, in June, Brezhnev issued a proposal for an Asian collective security system, Singapore responded more favorably than others in the Asian-Pacific region. Prime Minister Lee said that "Singapore had always expressed a positive interest in the proposal and would welcome further elaboration of the way in which peace and security could be consolidated for the countries of Southeast Asia."[7]

The Singapore leadership perceived the emerging Soviet presence in the Asia-Pacific region as a positive development because among other things it served Singapore's interest in keeping the Asia-Pacific waterways, on which it depended heavily for its prosperity, free of any single-power domination. By late 1969 Singapore was becoming wary of Kuala Lumpur and Jakarta's moves to "nationalize" the Straits of Malacca. The Soviet Union, which was also interested in unimpeded navigation, would help keep the Straits of Malacca open for navigation. Prime Minister Lee stated, "I think they [the Soviets] are a force to the good because they want to keep the Straits of Malacca open for navigation."[8] Foreign Minister Rajaratnam said "Singapore welcomes the growing interest shown by outside powers including the Soviet Union and Japan—in both the island Republic and Southeast Asia."[9]

In 1970 the Singapore leadership gained greater insight into the Soviet Union's posture in the Asia-Pacific region. This new insight greatly affected later bilateral relations. In September Prime Minister Lee spent eight days in Moscow and praised the Soviet leaders for displaying a profound understanding of the problems that Southeast Asian countries were facing. In addition, he indicated that "economic relations between Singapore and the USSR will develop on a mutually advantageous basis."[10] However, overall trade has remained insignificant.

In June 1970, commenting on the phenomenal growth of Soviet naval presence and strategic interest in the region, Rajaratnam argued that the Soviets were unlikely to retreat from the Pacific. On the contrary, "all signs indicated a sustained and growing interest in the

Pacific. In fact, of all the superpowers, the Russians appear to have not only a sense of what their global interests are, but also a carefully thought-out strategy of protecting and extending them."[11] This assessment was critical because it reflected the Singapore leadership's awareness of growing Soviet penetration into the Asia-Pacific as the United States gradually retreated from the region, and the growing diplomatic offensive of Beijing. In light of these developments, Singapore would continue to work toward maintaining a multipower presence in the Asia-Pacific region.

In April 1971 Britain, Australia, New Zealand, Malaysia, and Singapore established the Five Powers Defence Arrangements. At the same time, the Anglo-Malaysian Defence Arrangements that involved both Malaysia and Singapore were annulled. This was part of Singapore's adjustment to the post-British era in the Asia-Pacific region. The Soviets ridiculed the new bloc as a "blood relative of NATO, SEATO, CENTO, ASEAN, and ASPAC" and indicated "the new 'bloc' conflicts with the interests of the countries of Southeast Asia, particularly Malaysia and Singapore, which have proclaimed a policy of nonalignment as one of the principles of their foreign policy."[12] After April 1971 the Soviets frequently highlighted the so-called contradiction between the five power arrangements and the nonaligned foreign policy of Singapore.

As the tide in Indochina turned against the United States, the Singapore leadership became apprehensive of its future in the turbulent region. Therefore, Singapore supported United States presence in the region. The Paris peace negotiations and the implementation of the Nixon Doctrine in South Vietnam made the Singapore leadership more nervous. In March 1973 Prime Minister Lee for the first time expressed his apprehension of Soviet expansion and growing influence in the Asia-Pacific region, even though he was well aware of this years earlier. In fact, Lee proposed that a joint naval task force, comprised of the United States, Japan, Australia, and Western Europe, be formed to safeguard the freedom of the Indian Ocean, promote peaceful development in Southeast Asia, and offset the threat of the growing Soviet fleet.[13] This was definitely a major change from the prime minister's previous stance of welcoming Soviet interest in the region. A month later while in the United States Lee pointed out that:

If the Yankees went home, somebody would come in. Russia can and will fill such a vacuum rapidly. China with no blue water fleet cannot. But China would not want to see itself outflanked by Russia in such a way. Nor would Japan be happy to see the Soviet navy astride its critical route to the Gulf from where nearly 90 percent of its oil comes. . . . The vacuum would be filled and if filled by a much more clumsy, more heavy-handed power [the Soviet Union], it would become a great deal more uncomfortable for the smaller countries of the region. So they may not be unhappy to see a Russian presence balanced by an American one.[14]

Despite Singapore's growing apprehension of Soviet power in the Asia-Pacific region, bilateral ties remained correct, though somewhat chilled. In November 1974 Singapore and the Soviet Union signed a cultural and scientific cooperation agreement. The following March a second joint venture was set up, the Singapore Soviet Maritime Company (MARISSCO).

However, events in Southeast Asia confirmed Singapore's fears. In April 1975 Indochina turned totally communist, and the Soviet Union became increasingly important in Indochinese politics. By the end of the year, Vietnam had already tilted toward Moscow, and Singapore's leadership feared that the Sino-Soviet conflict would soon engulf the whole region, eliminating the peace that was so vital to Singapore's prosperity.

In July 1976 Rajaratnam pointed out that "so far as the Soviet Union is concerned, there is no doubt about the role she intends to play in the region. Her policy in regard to Southeast Asia is activist, consistent, and credible. As far as Singapore is concerned, we will continue to maintain good relations with the Soviet Union but at the same time resist on our own or through the collective strength that ASEAN provides any Soviet influence or presence, which we believe is detrimental to our noncommunist way of life."[15] In effect, Singapore's Soviet policy since late 1978 has been the implementation of the above doctrine. With the communization of Indochina, two ideologically opposing blocs developed in Southeast Asia. ASEAN and Singapore tried to extend a hand of friendship to the Indochinese, but little progress was made.

Despite disagreements between ASEAN and the newly communist Indochina, Soviet-Singapore relations remained correct. However, developments in Indochina soon changed this. Though Vietnam and Laos established close and cordial relationships, Kampuchean-Vietnamese relations were strained and grew worse. The Soviet support of the Vietnamese and the Chinese support of the Kampucheans tremendously aggravated the conflict.

Although Singapore did in a way welcome the conflict, because it would give ASEAN some breathing room, it was disquieted by the involvement of the major powers. As the conflict in Indochina intensified, the Soviet Union's role became more important, and this heightened Singapore's fears and suspicions of Soviet intentions in the region. In June 1978 Hanoi joined the Council for Mutual Economic

Assistance (COMECON) and five months later signed a Friendship Treaty, which was in effect a military alliance with the Soviet Union. Consequently, Singapore adopted an increasingly anti-Soviet stance, for it saw a big Soviet hand in the Indochinese conflict. This became obvious when the Soviets supported Hanoi's blatant invasion of Kampuchea. The willingness of Vietnam to invade another sovereign country and the Soviet underwriting role in this aggression was intolerable to the Singapore government. The bilateral political atmosphere between Singapore and the Soviet Union has never been the same since late 1978.

Because of the developments in Indochina, Singapore has adopted an increasingly hostile view of the Soviet policies in the region. Singapore has attempted to label the Soviet Union as an overtly expansionist nation and has hoped to mobilize world opinion to check the Soviets' growing influence and power. Singapore also strongly condemned the Soviet invasion of Afghanistan and described the events in Kampuchea and Afghanistan as "parallel events" aimed at creating a "new communist empire."[16]

Singapore's attitude toward the Soviet-Vietnamese alliance reflects its foreign policy precepts, especially its desire for regional peace and the maintenance of a balance of power in Southeast Asia. Because of the perceived Soviet-Vietnamese threat to the entire region, Singapore called on the United States to restore the military balance of power in Southeast Asia. At the same time, China's experience was evaluated favorably, at least in the short run. In the prime minister's view, "for twenty years and probably more, China will not have the industrial muscle to be a threat to the region."[17] In contrast, "the Soviet Union and Vietnam have got enormously more military muscles than China to bring to bear on Southeast Asia."[18] Therefore Singapore welcomed, at least temporarily, China's crucial role in deterring Vietnamese expansionism.

SINGAPORE-SOVIET RELATIONS UNDER GORBACHEV

Since coming to power in March 1985, Mikhail Gorbachev has instituted reforms both in domestic and foreign policy. His *glasnost* policies at home as well as the adoption of a more personal diplomacy worldwide reflect the new leader's imprint on the country's policies. However, as far as Singapore was concerned, these changes were viewed as nothing more than tactical. They represented changes in form but not in substance.

Since late 1984 Singapore has adopted a more sober and balanced foreign policy posture because of its domestic economic and political problems, the general protectionist environment worldwide, and the stalemate in Kampuchea. Its activist, high-profile foreign policy gave way to one more concerned with creating political and economic stability. Furthermore, there were indications of Singapore's interest in fostering better ties with the new leadership in Moscow, such as the increasing trade relations and the growing number of diplomatic and cultural exchanges. In March 1986 the Soviet Union awarded two contracts worth S$6.3 million to two Singapore shipyards, which partly ameliorated the depressed shipping industry. In September 1986 a senior Soviet foreign ministry official, Rudolf Alexeev, visited Singapore; a month later, Singapore sent a high-level foreign ministry delegation to the Soviet Union. In January 1987 the Riga ballet performed in Singapore. These developments certainly represented a change from the period 1978–1984 in which such exchanges were almost unthinkable. However, it cannot be concluded that Singapore totally turned around and favorably viewed the new Soviet leadership.

In response to the various Soviet attempts to present itself as a more sensitive and respectable superpower, the campaign in Singapore against the Soviet Union and its policies in the region appeared to have died down. Yet Singapore's leadership was not convinced that Gorbachev's Soviet Union was necessarily a positive force in the region. Suspicions, even cynicism, continued in Singapore's Soviet policy, as evidenced in the manner that Singapore's leadership described the Soviet Union and its policies since March 1985. As did most countries in the region, Singapore's leadership admitted that Gorbachev represented a new force in the Soviet Union. For instance, the *Straits Times* editorialized on 4 March 1987 that "Mr. Gorbachev's latest move [a proposal to reduce intermediate missiles from Europe] shows that he is one of the sharpest and ablest statesmen around at the moment. That he is able to conceive of his foreign policy in global terms is shown in the recent wave of Soviet diplomatic moves, which clearly bears his imprimatur. Who else could have pushed for new Soviet positions on such long-standing problem areas as Afghanistan and Cambodia? Or even concessions on the Cambodia 'obstacle' that would give a boost to Moscow's slow-moving normalisation talks with the Chinese?" However, the editorial cautioned the world that it should "read much more into the Gorbachev proposal and not bargain away the security of U.S. allies around the globe."[19] Singapore encouraged apprehension of Soviet action.

Similarly, when Gorbachev announced his Vladivostok initiative on 28 July 1986, Singapore was not too enthusiastic, unlike many regional states. The *Straits Times* editorial stated that "Gorbachev should not be surprised that most states in the region are more than a little suspicious of his offer to build a new era of peace with them" because of the massive Soviet military buildup in the last twenty years. The editorial went on to point out that "it is discomfiting that Moscow has been pounding the Asia-Pacific beat with a big stick; it is disturbing that the Soviet Union is now talking 'law and order' while trying to keep the big stick out of sight. Mr. Gorbachev's new-look foreign policy is sophisticated, it is shrewd, and it is sly; and small states would have to step nimbly through the thicket of initiatives he has so skillfully laid in Vladivostok. For a start, they should be sceptical and suspicious and circumspect."[20] Singapore viewed the Vladivostok initiative as a new Soviet maneuver to win influence in the region, especially because of the negative reactions to Brezhnev's military approach toward foreign policy in the region. First Deputy Prime Minister Goh Chok Tong warned that the Soviet Union has become more "sophisticated" and rather "seductive" in its policy presentation; and while the Vladivostok speech might be "very superficially attractive to Asia," the democratic and market-oriented countries in Asia should unify and counter Soviet policy with their own established policy.[21]

Singapore's Prime Minister Lee Kuan Yew stated that he was "not impressed" by Gorbachev's various moves. Referring to Singapore-Soviet relations, the prime minister stated that "Singapore has extended a welcome mat to the Soviet Union since 1965." The prime minister visited the Soviet Union in 1962 and 1970, and "yet trade with the Soviet Union amounted to only one percent of Singapore's world trade." He argued: "So it is not for want of a welcome mat"; rather, "it is that their society is differently geared. They do not sell us products, which we want to buy at prices cheaper than other peoples." Poor trading relations can be explained by the fact that "either they are not interested in what we sell because their buying agencies have instructions not to use up foreign exchange, or what they want to sell, our people are not interested in buying."[22]

Singapore's broadly cynical and suspicious posture toward Gorbachev's Soviet Union can be explained by a number of factors. First, Singapore believes that the Soviet Union is a major source of mischief in the region. Its support for Vietnam's Indochina policies, its military presence in the region, and its support for Marcos and recognition of the fraudulent elections confirmed the perception that the Soviet Union will always fish in troubled waters. Second, that the Soviet Union has little to offer by way of trade has always ensured Singapore's distance from it. Third, while Gorbachev has said much about changes in Soviet foreign policy, little has been carried out. Until the Soviet Union implements the changes it espouses, there will be little credibility in Gorbachev and his policies. Singapore fears that the Soviet Union may assume dominance in the region through design or default. Already, it has a massive military presence in the region. Since Singapore subscribes to the balance of power approach to international-al politics, its foreign policy entails that any distention of power by any one great power must be contained, especially a communist power. This accounts for the generally cold reception of Gorbachev in Singapore. Finally, the antipathy toward Gorbachev's Soviet Union is also partly a reaction to the policies of Singapore's neighbors. In-donesia and Malaysia generally have been impressed by Gorbachev and his initiatives. For example, Mochtar Kusumaatmadja, the In-donesian foreign minister, described Gorbachev's Vladivostok speech as a "positive development [that] showed [Soviet] readiness to have peaceful coexistence in the real sense [and] a change in direction in its Asia-Pacific policy." Singapore is generally apprehensive of its bigger Malay neighbors both of whom have openly pursued anti-Chinese policies at home and abroad as well as encouraged the Soviet Union. In an effort to counter the Malay policies, Singapore gives as little leeway to the Soviet Union in the region as possible and encourages the other great powers.

SINGAPORE-SOVIET RELATIONS: FUTURE PROSPECTS

One could conclude that the Kampuchean invasion marked the beginning of Singapore's adoption of a strong stance toward the Soviet Union. However, it would be a mistake to infer that Singapore's view of Moscow changed overnight. Singapore's apprehension of Moscow has evolved as the Kremlin's interest, presence, and influence in the region grew. The decreasing U.S. involvement and commitment be-tween 1973 and 1980 and the increasing Sino-Soviet rivalry in the region also contributed to Singapore's apprehension.

Three future scenarios of Singapore-Soviet relations can be postu-lated. First, Singapore could adopt an even stronger stance toward Moscow by suspending diplomatic ties and downgrading all political, economic, and cultural links. This is highly unlikely for it would not benefit Singapore in any way nor serve Singapore's economic and political interests. Futhermore, there is no cause presently to warrant the adoption of such a drastic course. Second, Singapore could adopt a "back to normal" posture by softening its strong stance and verbal attacks on Moscow and taking an equidistant posture. This scenario would entail an increase in political and economic relations with Moscow and indirectly imply that Singapore's hard-line policy had failed. Third, Singapore could maintain its current Soviet policy, bar-ring any change in the Kampuchean situation. While Singapore has toned down some of its past criticisms of Moscow, its basic posture remains unchanged. Until the Soviet Union breaks the Kampuchean deadlock, its role and credibility in the region will continue to be questioned. To do otherwise is to accept the *fait accompli*, and this is something all the ASEAN governments, especially Singapore's, have agreed to oppose.

NOTES

1. For a discussion of Singapore's "activist foreign policy," see S. Dhanabalan's speech given at the National University of Singapore (NUS) on 27 November 1981 in *Singapore Government Press Release*, Release No. 09–1/81/11/27 (Singapore: Ministry of Culture, Information Division). For a discussion of Singapore's "high profile policy," see S. Rajaratnam's speech at the NUS on 21 December 1981 in ibid., Release No. 09–2/81/12/21.
2. See *From Phnom Penh To Kabul* (Singapore: Ministry of Foreign Affairs, September 1980).
3. *New York Times*, 17 September 1965.
4. *Izvestia*, 13 March 1971.
5. *Mirror* (Singapore), 20 April 1976, p. 1.
6. *Far Eastern Economic Review* (Hong Kong), 6 August 1976, 32.
7. Cited in Alex Josey, *Lee Kuan Yew* (London: Angus and Roberton, 1976), 293.
8. *Mirror* (Singapore), 30 June 1969, p. 8.
9. Ibid., 20 October 1969, p. 1.
10. *Soviet News* (Singapore), 14 August 1975, p. 4.
11. *Mirror* (Singapore), 1 June 1970, p. 4.
12. *Current Digest of Soviet Press* 23, no. 16 (18 May 1971),: 178.
13. *Straits Times*, 12 May 1973.
14. *Far Eastern Economic Review*, 23 April 1973, p. 12.
15. *Mirror* (Singapore), 12 July 1976, p. 2.
16. See *From Phnom Penh to Kabul*, 1–22.
17. See Lee Kuan Yew's interview with Kazuo Nishi, managing editor of *Mainichi Shimbun*, at the Istana Annex, Singapore, on 12 September 1980, printed in *Speeches*, 4, no. 4 (October 1980): 5.
18. See Lee Kuan Yew's interview with Derek Davies, editor of *Far Eastern Economic Review*, at the Istana Annex, Singapore, on 12 September 1980 printed in ibid., 15.
19. *Straits Times*, 4 March 1987.
20. Ibid., 15 August 1986.
21. Ibid., 3 September 1986.
22. Ibid., 17 October 1986.

11

Thai Perceptions of the Soviet Union and Its Implications for Thai-Soviet Relations

Chantima Ongsuragz

Thailand currently perceives the Soviet Union as an indirect, yet real, threat to her national security. A number of factors have contributed to this perception: (1) the fundamental values and institutions of the Thai society, (2) the Thai policymakers' attitude toward communism and the Soviet Union, (3) Thailand's policies, (4) Soviet diplomatic style, (5) Soviet activities in Thailand and Indochina, and (6) Soviet involvement in the Kampuchean issue.

THAI PERCEPTIONS OF THE SOVIET UNION

Thai Society and Worldview

Thai beliefs in the monarchy and Buddhism, the state religion, support and unify Thai society. Through various forms of socialization, the authorities try to indoctrinate all Thai to hold these two institutions in the highest regard. For instance, the children in primary and secondary school are required to take civics and morals classes that teach them to accept the monarchy's and Buddhism's special role and status in society. The military, police, and other security-related personnel have been more rigorously inculcated with these social values. They almost instinctively suspect anyone who does not show proper respect for the monarchy and Buddhism as being leftist or communist. Since communism rejects monarchical government and religion and views them as impediments toward a classless society,

Thailand is fundamentally anticommunist. The principal values and institutions of the Thai society make communism appear to be a natural enemy.

Because of its small size and the international situation, Thailand has long accepted the presence of major powers in regional affairs. Before the Second World War, colonialist England and France were the powers that immediately concerned Thailand. Presently the United States, China, and the Soviet Union are all involved in Southeast Asia.

Nevertheless, Thailand regards the demands of the major powers as an opportunity to play one against the other in an effort to preserve her independence. Keeping the balance of power is integral to the policies of the Thai policymakers. Foreign Minister Field Marshal Siddhi Savetsila describes the current situation in Southeast Asia as follows:

> At present, a rough distribution of power prevails in the region. On the one hand there are those who seek to expand their influence or to project their power—Vietnam on land and the Soviet Union by sea. On the other hand, there are ASEAN which aspires to ZOPFAN, the U.S. which seeks to maintain her role in preserving peace and stability in the Asia-Pacific region, and China which is concerned with the protection of her southern flank. Kampuchea happens to be the vortex, in which all sides interface. Kampuchea, therefore, will be the crucible out of which a new configuration of power in the region will emerge. How the Kampuchean question is settled will consequently determine the distribution of power in Southeast Asia for years to come.[1]

Thai Policymakers

The most important policymakers for foreign affairs are the prime minister; minister of foreign affairs; secretary general of the National Security Council (NSC); minister of defense; the commanders of the armed forces, particularly the army and the chiefs of the intelligence services; and the secretary general of the prime minister's office. The military, NSC, and the Ministry of Foreign Affairs have long been in control of the direction of national policies.

Overall, the military's voice appears to carry the greatest weight, since most of Thailand's government leaders have military backgrounds. At the NSC, seven of eight secretary generals held high military rank, and three of them held titles conferred by the king. Only the current secretary general is a civilian.

The NSC plays a central role in policy formation, especially when the policy has strong security implications. The Sino-Thai relations illustrate this. Khien Theeravit, who conducted a survey on the Thai perceptions of the Sino-Thai relationship, found that:

> The Thai government considers that China has an immediate impact on Thai security. For the Thai government holds that communism is currently threatening national security, and that China constitutes a principal agent of the ideology. Accordingly, the most powerful groups in the policy formulation process with regard to China are those which control the national security organs, i.e., the NSC, the Internal Security Operations Command, the Central Intelligence Department, the Special Branch of the Police Department. . . . On important policies the government must have the NSC's consent. . . . The Thai academics, journalists, and the general public do not have any part to play in the formulation of [the country's] Chinese policy. The overall attitude is that the security of the country might be shaken, if these people were allowed to know about or participate in [the process].[2]

This observation remains valid even today and applies equally well to the country's Soviet policy. As suggested earlier, the members of the armed forces have best internalized the basic Thai social values. Consequently, many of Thailand's policymakers are fundamentally anticommunist.

Thai Policies

Thailand's internal and external policies have been directed largely toward countering the influence of communism, especially before the Second World War. In the 1930s a prominent 1932–coup leader, Pridi Phanomyong, introduced an economic program that encountered very strong resistance from the military. Even King Rama VII criticized it and indicated that Pridi's program was "definitely the very same one currently in use in [Stalinist] Russia."[3] The king felt that it would be harmful to the people and the nation as a whole because it "would turn Thailand into a genuine communist country along the line of Russia." Furthermore, implementing the program would have international consequences: "As the program is identical to the one being used in Russia . . . , if our government adopted and implemented it in every detail, it would be just like our government is helping Third International to achieve its goal—which is to communize the world—more easily. . . . We would definitely become communist, if the program were implemented, . . . the second country after Russia."[4] Essentially King Rama VII's policy was to counter communist influence, and the Thai government has adopted it ever since. After Mao Zedong and his communist colleagues ascended to power in Beijing, Thailand considered them the chief enemy—not so much because they are communist or because China is a very large country, but because they supported the Communist Party of Thailand (CPT) that had been trying to take power. When the war in Vietnam expanded, Thailand helped the United States by sending troops to fight against the communist side.

Vietnam replaced China as Thailand's chief adversary after Vietnam invaded Kampuchea in 1978 and toppled the Khmer Rouge regime. Former Ministry of Foreign Affairs (MFA) Permanent Secretary Asa Sarasin told Soviet Ambassador Valentin Kasatkin that Hanoi had designs on Thailand and intended to incorporate a part of her territory in the enlarged federation of Indochinese states.[5] The invasion of Kampuchea made the security-conscious Thai policymakers feel even more suspicious toward the actions of Vietnam and the Soviet Union.

China, meanwhile, has become a strategic friend to Thailand. The two governments now share an interest in countering the expansion of Vietnamese and Soviet influence in the region. According to Foreign Minister Siddhi, "China is now a stabilizing force in Southeast Asia." Sino-Thai relations are "close and cordial" and are based on "sincerity and goodwill towards one another. It makes things easy for both of us . . . , [and] when we are in need of anything, China [has] never failed us."[6]

China, though ideologically communist, has become an ardent opponent of the Soviet Union and Vietnam. Therefore, the Thai leaders tolerate China's ideology because they consider its stance regarding Moscow and Hanoi as being much more vital.

Soviet Diplomatic Style

The Soviet style of diplomacy has also contributed in some measure to the threatening image perceived by certain influential Thai policymakers. For instance, Andrei Gromyko once greeted a visiting Thai diplomat with the following remark: "I hear you have problems in your part of the world. . . . Now, tell me, do you want war or peace?"[7] In 1985 Mikhail Kapitsa, then deputy foreign minister, warned a Thai military delegation that if Thailand, like Indonesia, did not recognize the reality of the Vietnamese occupation of Kampuchea, it would be subjected to Vietnam's "terms of the victor" within three years.[8] A member of this delegation later commented that Kapitsa's words could be construed as a "friendly warning, or perhaps a wedge to divide members of the ASEAN, or an implicit threat."[9] The Soviets' overbearing approach to bargaining also contributed to their threatening image. In October 1985 the Soviet Union offered to buy Thai products and demanded that Thailand invite a Soviet deputy prime minister to Bangkok to sign, presumably in his presence, a trade pact or an agreement to establish a Thai-Soviet chamber of commerce. Then NSC Secretary General Prasong Soonsiri, for one, expressed his dislike for such an attitude.[10]

Soviet Activities in Thailand and Indochina

The Soviet Union's behavior has not inspired trust among the Thai policymakers. On the contrary, the Thai are suspicious of Soviet ulterior motives in its bilateral relationship with Thailand. In their trade relations, the Soviet Union was inclined to make direct contacts with local merchants and tried to lobby against establishing a Thai state trading organization.[11] The Thai government has always been unwilling to allow direct trading contacts and therefore questioned why the Soviet Union, which itself trades with foreign countries through governmental organizations, would want to contact the local traders directly. The Thai authorities also thought it significant that the Soviet Union has concentrated on trading with major companies in a variety of businesses rather than with small firms. A former NSC chief has offered the following explanation:

> Of course, there are reasons behind that. Firstly, executives of such groups of companies can provide access to politicians and even some high-ranking military officers. In certain cases, the businessmen are concurrently politicians themselves. My point is that the Russians are eyeing for political gains apart from trade benefits. Through business ties, they have a good opportunity to recruit agents of influence and by giving legal benefits to the business enterprises, the Russians hope that these companies would apply pressure on the [Thai] government in the interest of the Soviet Union.[12]

The Soviet Union has been pursuing an agreement on cultural cooperation and exchanges but would not consent to the security clause in the Thai draft.[13] Meanwhile, it has been offering Thai students scholarships to study in the Soviet Union.[14] Bangkok later demanded that these scholarships be processed through the MFA. Yet the Soviet Union still bypassed the MFA and directly contacted the applicants. A large number of the applicants were high school graduates who could not pass state university entrance exams, could not afford the private universities, and did not want to enroll in either of the two open state universities perhaps for prestige reasons. Thailand also became suspicious of the Soviet interviewing methods. "As we have learned from the recipient of Soviet scholarships . . . the Russians spent only five minutes in screening and interviewing some applicants. The practice has given rise to our strong doubts about their motives."[15] Thailand fears that the Soviets might recruit Thai students to become their espionage agents. "We have to admit the reality that some young students may not be mature enough to have good judgment, and that is something that can be exploited," remarked a security official.[16] The Soviet Union did later demonstrate its willingness to comply with Thailand's scholarship regulations. This concession coincided approximately with Shevardnadze's stopover in Bangkok for talks with Siddhi in early 1987.[17]

The Soviet Union has also attempted to increase its personnel in Thailand by lobbying to establish a Thai-Soviet friendship society and a Thai-Soviet chamber of commerce.[18] The Thai suspected that these personnel would spend most, if not all, of their time on espionage. According to the NSC, fifty of the eighty-six Soviet diplomats in Thailand in late 1985 were suspected of working for the KGB and the GRU (the KGB's military equivalent).[19] A few days later it added that "up to 90 percent of the Soviet officials here do not have clear missions. . . . Several Soviet representatives to ESCAP [have been] doing nothing but photocopying all the ESCAP documents."[20]

Lately the traditionally hawkish NSC has been less outspoken and blunt in its criticisms of the Soviet Union. This may be attributed to (1) differences in style between Suvit Suthanukul, appointed secretary general in 1987, and his predecessor, Prasong Soonsiri; (2) the Soviet Union's friendly gestures overall since Gorbachev's Vladivostok speech in July 1986; and (3) Thailand's effort to respond positively to those gestures. According to Suvit, Thailand now does not fear socialist countries and their professed ideology as much as before. "In the past, we did not understand them very well and [thus] were very apprehensive. Thailand was not well established then. We fear that we could not control the flow of socialism into Thai society. Now we believe we are stronger. We have a better understanding of the socialists and at the same time they have changed. So our fears have been lessened." However, it would be a mistake to presume that Thailand has modified her basic perception of communist countries. Suvit warned, "We still have to be careful, since we have an ideology different from theirs. We can't afford to be too liberal in our ties with them."[21]

Thailand is also very concerned about the Soviet Union's activities in the region, particularly in Indochina. According to Prasong Soonsiri, the Soviets have deployed more than 100 SS-20s in the Asian region of the Soviet Union. They are also expanding the naval and air bases at Cam Ranh Bay and Da Nang, which they constantly use. Furthermore, "all security guards in the compound of the Cam Ranh Bay base are Russians," and the Soviets do not have to inform the Vietnamese authorities of their MIG 23s' flight schedules for prior approval. "Is this Soviet or Vietnamese territory?" he quipped.[22] Prasong also pointed out that Soviet land mines, artillery, and ammunition used by Vietnamese forces in Kampuchea have killed and injured Thai soldiers and civilians. As a result, Thailand regards the Soviet Union as a military threat to her security. Foreign Minister Siddhi commented that apart from the deployment of nuclear missiles to the Asian continent,

> Vietnam's acquiescence to the utilization of its strategic bases as important outposts of the Soviet Pacific Forces has significantly increased the Soviet military capabilities in the region for intelligence monitoring and projecting naval power with potentially grave consequences to the security of all Asian countries. . . . Never has the Soviet threat been as *veritable* as it is today.[23]

Soviet Involvement in the Kampuchean Issue

The Soviet stance on the Kampuchean issue has helped mold the Thai perception of the Soviet Union. However, since Thai authorities consider Vietnam's occupation of Kampuchea to be an immediate threat to Thai security, they want Vietnamese troops withdrawn and believe that the Soviet Union holds an important key to the settlement. A Foreign Ministry spokesman declared that without Soviet assistance the Kampuchean problem could be solved much more easily.[24] Consequently, Thailand has repeatedly requested that the Soviet Union terminate its aid to Vietnam. The Soviet Union, however, firmly supports Vietnam's position and contributes both economic and military aid. It justifies this support to Vietnam by claiming that Vietnam needs help to recover from inherited difficulties and that it wants to help Vietnam ward off "the northern threat," China.[25] It would not stop military aid to Vietnam, for such a move would be "complete nonsense," according to Kapitsa. The Soviet Union further contends that Thailand's (and ASEAN's) proposal to settle the conflict through the

United Nations–sponsored International Committee on Kampuchea is an "unrealistic" approach.[26]

Kapitsa once summarized the Soviet position as follows: "We are not for confrontation. We are for negotiation. . . . We are not for appeasement. We are for détente. And as far as that is concerned, we shall always be your [Thailand's] friend and Vietnam's friend. They [the Vietnamese] help us, therefore we would like to help our friends. . . . You [Thailand] help your friends, too."[27] Thailand considers such a stand unacceptable for its security. Then MFA Permanent Secretary Arsa Sarasin stated, "I told him [the Soviet ambassador to Thailand] that the Soviet double-standard policy towards Thailand in particular and towards ASEAN in general is unacceptable to the Thai people. On the one hand, the Soviet Union wants to foster political, economic, and social ties with ASEAN. On the other hand, it still lets Vietnam use the huge war machine, equipped by Moscow, to make incursions into Thailand."[28]

IMPLICATIONS FOR THAI-SOVIET RELATIONS

Diplomatic Relations

As a result of Thailand's perception of the Soviets and its suspicion of their ulterior motives, Thailand's strategic foreign policy leans toward the "free world," namely, the United States. The United States has always been Thailand's principal ally in international politics. Depending upon the balance of power at the time, Thailand's secondary allies are the countries that the United States regards as strategic friends. The Soviet Union, however, has consistently remained one of Thailand's major adversaries. Realizing that it could not possibly resist the Soviet demand for involvement in Thailand and in the region, Thailand reluctantly agreed to establish diplomatic ties with the Soviet Union in 1946.[29] Before Gorbachev's Vladivostok speech and the Shevardnadze-Siddhi dialogues in early 1987, their diplomatic relations were minimal and businesslike, but stagnant.

When Thailand applied for membership to the UN in 1946, the Soviet Union at first objected because there were still no diplomatic ties between the two countries.[30] The Soviets demanded that the Thai government establish formal diplomatic ties with them, repeal its anticommunist statutes, and apologize for having been anti-Soviet. Thailand conceded to the first two conditions but refused to yield to the third. The Soviet Union finally approved Thailand's membership in December 1946.[31] Meanwhile, Thailand tried to regain its anticommunist posture regarding the Soviet Union as quickly as possible.

The Soviet Union began working toward expanding its bilateral ties with Thailand by beginning with cultural exchanges. In March 1974 the Soviet Union proposed a Thai-Soviet cultural pact. Thailand responded favorably because rejecting the proposal would have been diplomatically inappropriate, but with two important conditions.[32] First, the Soviet Union had to accept a security clause that allowed Thai authorities to search members of the Soviet cultural teams visiting Thailand. Second, Foreign Minister Gromyko had to come to Bangkok to sign the pact. Thailand, of course, realized that the Soviet Union probably could not comply with these conditions, particularly the second one. Would Thailand take such a position, if she genuinely wanted the pact and, therefore, more intimate ties with the Soviet Union? Even when the Thai-Soviet ties were at their best, during General Kriangsak Chomanan's tenure in the late 1970s, Thailand refused to sign the cultural pact, arguing that it was unnecessary.[33] Thailand preferred to consider Soviet cultural proposals on a case-by-case basis.

The Soviet Union continues to organize cultural and artistic exhibitions in Thailand, but Thailand has allowed very few events, such as ballet performances, films, trade and industrial exhibitions, and exchanges of parliamentary delegations. Thailand has opposed the establishment of a Thai-Soviet friendship society.[34]

Economic Relations

Thailand has not been very enthusiastic about pursuing expanded trade agreements either, even though trade constitutes the only area in which Thailand concretely gains from Soviet ties. From 1975 to 1984 bilateral trade increased 44.3 percent per year, more than fivefold. Thai exports to the Soviet Union increased tremendously, by 93.4 percent per year, and imports from the Soviet Union increased 13.8 percent per year. Trade balance, already in Thailand's favor, rose 20.8 percent per year. However, during this period, Thai-Soviet trade constituted only 0.7 percent of Thailand's total world trade, and the Soviet Union absorbed only 1.0 percent of Thailand's total export.[35]

In recent years Thailand has sought to boost trade with the Soviets largely because of increased international protectionism and the Soviets' apparent willingness toward resolving the Kampuchean issue. During Siddhi's official visit to Moscow in May 1987, Thailand agreed to establish joint trade commissions.

The Soviet Union has also proposed to help Thailand in technical areas. As noted earlier, it offered a large number of scholarships to Thai students for study in the Soviet Union. In 1975 it offered to send a team of experts to advise the Thai government on shale oil exploration and to train Thai personnel either in Thailand or in the Soviet Union.[36] When General Kriangsak visited Moscow in 1979, a preliminary understanding was reached on a Thai-Soviet scientific agreement; however, the agreement has never been signed. Thailand has not been very enthusiastic toward the Soviet offers mainly because Thailand values more highly the technical achievements of the major noncommunist industrial countries.

The Future of Thai-Soviet Relations

The Kampuchean issue is the major chasm between Thailand and the Soviet Union. The two countries have not been able to reach an understanding on this issue. For instance, in 1981 Deputy Foreign Minister Arun described his meeting with his Soviet counterpart Firiubin as follows: "We could go together well on general topics, but when it comes to the Kampuchean problem we seemed to go different ways."[37]

Although the Soviet Union showed a keener interest in the problem, it insists that it is not a party to the conflict and that China and Vietnam need to settle the issue through dialogues with ASEAN.[38] However, the Soviets did state during Foreign Minister Siddhi's Moscow visit in May 1987 that they were willing to promote such dialogues and act as guarantor to a "mutually acceptable solution."[39] Thailand regards the Soviet willingness to help end the Kampuchean conflict as a "test" of Soviet sincerity.

The fact that the Soviets have softened their position on Kampuchea since the Vladivostok speech and expressed more willingness to help resolve the conflict in a manner acceptable to all concerned certainly helps improve the Thai-Soviet ties. Two top Thai officials, Prime Minister Prem Tinsulanonda and Army Commander General Chaovalit Yongchaiyut, are scheduled to visit the Soviet Union. General Chaovalit was reportedly eager to make the visit: "After all the Soviet Union is a super power. We want to show our friendship." Significantly, Thailand has minimized the 1987 arrest and deportation of two alleged spies on the Soviet payroll. Prime Minister Prem merely commented that there is nothing extraordinary about spying; every country practices it. The NSC and the MFA refrained from publically commenting on the incident. Also contributing to the warming up of the bilateral ties is that both Prasong and Kapitsa are no longer directly involved in their country's foreign policy-making process.

Presently, Thailand wishes to foster good relations with the Soviet Union, hoping that it will help resolve the Kampuchean issue. As long as the Soviets continue working in that direction, Thai-Soviet ties will progress. Thailand's strategic policy, however, remains unchanged: the Soviet Union is still regarded as a major adversary, along with Hanoi, and a real, though indirect, threat to Thailand's national security. Consequently, it seems certain that should Thailand become convinced of the Soviet Union's unwillingness or inability to help solve the Kampuchean conflict, Soviet-Thai ties will return to their level before the Vladivostok speech—minimal, businesslike, but stagnant.

NOTES

1. Siddhi's speech to the Foreign Correspondents Club of Thailand, 11 December 1986.
2. Khien Theeravit, *Sino-Thai Relations: The Thai Perceptions* (Bangkok: Institute of Social Research, 1978), 67–68.
3. Chai-anant Samutvanich and Kattiya Kannasutr, eds., *Documents of Thai Politics and Government* (Bangkok: Thai Wattanapanich, 1975), 354.
4. Ibid., 354–355.
5. *Bangkok Post*, 18 January 1985.
6. See ibid., 1 January 1987; MFA, Department of Information, *Press Release*, No. M37 2528, p. 5.
7. *Bangkok Post*, 10 September 1986.
8. *Nation*, 5 November 1985.
9. Ibid.
10. *Far Eastern Economic Review*, 21 November 1985.
11. See Khien Theeravit, *Sino-Thai Relations: The Thai Perceptions* 18.
12. *Nation*, 24 October 1985.
13. See ibid., 6 September 1975, 1 October 1975, 23 February 1976, 6 July 1978, 7 July 1978, 31 July 1978.
14. *Bangkok Post*, 31 January 1974; *Nation*, 18 April 1974.
15. *Nation*, 1 December 1985, 24 October 1985.
16. Ibid.
17. Ibid., 9 March 1987.
18. See Prasong's interview in ibid., 24 October 1985.
19. See Prasong's interview in *Far Eastern Economic Review* (21 November 1985): 36ff.
20. *Nation*, 27 October 1985.
21. Ibid., 13 July 1987.
22. Ibid., 24 October 1985. For Thai perspective of Soviet military activities in Laos and Kampuchea, see *Bangkok Post*, 19 September 1982.
23. *Bangkok Post*, 22 July 1983; *Nation*, 23 July 1983. Emphasis added.
24. *Nation*, 28 July 1985.
25. Ibid.
26. Ibid.
27. *Post*, 17 March 1985.

28. MFA Permanent Secretary Asa Sarasin's statement in *Nation*, 6 April 1983. See also Siddhi's similar remark in *Bangkok Post*, 20 December 1986.
29. Although diplomatic ties had been agreed upon in 1946, Thailand delayed the dispatch of an envoy to Moscow until two years later, and then closed the three-man legation within just over a year. The legation reopened in 1953.
30. Direk Jayanam, *Thailand and World War II* (Bangkok: 1967), 668, 674 (in Thai).
31. *Soviet News*, 7 January 1947.
32. Nation, 19 August 1975, 9 September 1976, 7 July 1978; *Bangkok Post*, 4 September 1975.
33. *Nation*, 31 August 1978.
34. For Prasong's reason see *Bangkok Post*, 21 October 1985.
35. Department of Business Economics, Ministry of Commerce, *State and Problems of Trade Between Thailand and the Soviet Union* (Bangkok, 1985, 1987), 17–18.
36. *Japan Times*, 23 September 1975; *New York Times*, 28 September 1975.
37. *Nation*, 18 April 1981.
38. Ibid., 23 June 1987.
39. Ibid., 19 May 1987.

12

Vietnam and the Soviet Union:
Perceptions and Policies

Carlyle A. Thayer

HISTORICAL BACKGROUND TO PRESENT RELATIONS

Vietnam's relations with the Soviet Union may be traced to the early years of the Bolshevik Revolution and the founding of the Communist International. These two events led to the introduction of Marxist-Leninist ideology and party organization into French Indochina. It was in 1919, for example, that Ho Chi Minh began to read Marx and Lenin in a systematic way.

Vietnam's first contacts with the Comintern date back to mid-1923 when Ho journeyed to Moscow to study Marxism-Leninism. After his arrival, Ho was appointed a member of the presidium of the Krestintern (Peasant International) and a delegate to the 5th Congress of the Comintern (held in July 1924). In 1925 Ho was assigned to the Comintern's Far East Department in Canton, China. There he successfully established contacts inside French Indochina and recruited cadres for the anticolonial cause. That same year, as a result of his organizational efforts, the Revolutionary Youth League (RYL) was founded. In February 1930, acting in the name of the Comintern, Ho presided over a conference in Hong Kong that formally established the Vietnam Communist Party (VCP).[1]

While Ho's role was pivotal, the role of other Vietnamese revolutionaries during this early period should not be underestimated. Between 1932 and 1935 some forty Vietnamese cadres, who had been trained in the USSR, were sent back to Vietnam to undertake clandestine duties. In the decade preceding 1941, these Moscow returnees played a dominant role in party affairs. However, the record of the 1930s suggests that the VCP's relationship with the French Communist party was more substantial and important than with the Comintern or Communist Party of the Soviet Union (CPSU).

During the Second World War contact with Moscow was broken, and the influence of the Chinese Communist Party (CCP) rose accordingly. Several key Vietnamese leaders quartered in Yunnan. The CCP, and later the People's Republic of China (PRC), became the main backers of the VCP's armed struggle. Chinese military support was decisive in the post-1949 period and directly contributed to the Vietnamese victory at Dien Bien Phu in 1954. There is little evidence that the CPSU or the Soviet Union took a major interest in the VCP's armed struggle against the French during the First Indochina War (1945–1954).

Formal state-to-state relations between the Soviet Union and the Democratic Republic of Vietnam (DRV), then an insurgent movement fighting to gain power, were established on 31 January 1950. After the battle of Dien Bien Phu and the 1954 Geneva Conference, a communist regime was established in North Vietnam, and a Soviet embassy opened in Hanoi. Nevertheless, Vietnam did not rank high on Moscow's list of diplomatic priorities.[2] In 1955, for example, when Nikita Khrushchev and N. A. Bulganin made a much publicized trip to Asia, visiting Afghanistan, Burma, and India, Vietnam was omitted from the itinerary. In 1956 the USSR, as one of the cochairmen of the Geneva Conference, offered only *pro forma* protests at the failure to hold reunification elections. The following year, Moscow even proposed admitting both parts of divided Vietnam into the United Nations.

Economic relations between Hanoi and Moscow date back to July 1955, when President Ho Chi Minh first visited the Soviet Union as head of state. At that time, he obtained the DRV's first grant of Soviet economic assistance. In 1958, when Vietnam launched its First Three-Year Plan, the Soviet Union increased its level of support, overtaking China for the first time as Vietnam's largest donor of economic aid. The Soviet Union also contributed the lion's share of finance for the DRV's First Five-Year Plan (1961–1965).

Before 1965, Soviet-Vietnamese political relations do not appear particularly close. Any momentary upturn in Soviet interest was related more to Nikita Khrushchev's new activist policy toward the Third World and to Sino-Soviet rivalry than to any warming in bilateral relations with Hanoi. In April 1956 Deputy Premier A. I. Mikoyan became the highest-level Soviet official to visit Vietnam. In 1957 Ho visited the USSR twice, while President K. Y. Voroshilov journeyed to Vietnam (the last visit by a Soviet official with Politburo rank until February 1965). However, as Khrushchev's flirtation with the Third World quickly waned, so did Soviet-Vietnamese relations.

Because of differences over support for just wars and wars of national liberation, and Vietnam's refusal to sign the Non-Proliferation Treaty at this time, Soviet-Vietnamese relations began to decline in 1963 and reached an all-time low in the summer of 1964.

Two events precipitated a reappraisal of Soviet policy, the August 1964 Gulf of Tonkin incident and Khrushchev's ouster in October. In early 1965 Premier Kosygin was dispatched to Hanoi to convey Soviet policy changes. His visit coincided with the onset of the U.S. air war against North Vietnam. Moscow took this opportunity to come to Vietnam's assistance, providing expensive antiaircraft equipment such as radar-controlled guns and surface-to-air missiles (SAM). In April VCP First Secretary Le Duan traveled to Moscow and signed a joint communique agreeing to an expansion in Soviet aid. By the end of the year, Soviet military assistance was estimated to have reached US$550 million, and Soviet personnel were manning SAM sites.

During the subsequent years of the Vietnam War, the USSR surpassed China as Vietnam's main source of military aid. Soviet assistance did not necessarily translate into increased political influence, as Vietnam doggedly stuck to its "straight zig-zag" path between its two major allies. For example, in 1971, after China and the United States signaled their mutual desire to improve relations, the Soviet Union offered to sign a Treaty of Friendship and Cooperation with Vietnam. Hanoi declined. Also, according to Daniel Papp, Hanoi was able to launch the 1972 Spring Offensive despite Soviet concerns that this would disrupt the scheduled summit between Richard Nixon and Leonid Brezhnev.[3] After the summit, the USSR continued to provide military assistance to Vietnam. Hanoi nevertheless continued to demonstrate its independence by turning down a Soviet offer to provide the latest SAMs with Soviet operators. In June 1972 Nikolai Podgorny[4] was sent to Hanoi to brief leaders there on the outcome of the summit, but the restrained language of the joint communiqué clearly indicated differences over Moscow's policy of détente.

As the war neared its end, the Soviet Union was provided an opportunity to consolidate its political position in Hanoi as a result of increasing Sino-Vietnamese differences over strategy. Following the signing of the 1973 Peace Agreements, when Beijing urged Hanoi to pursue unification as a long-term goal, Moscow provided the military assistance that enabled the Vietnam People's Army to launch the victorious Ho Chi Minh campaign.

In August 1975 VCP Secretary General Le Duan went to Beijing and Moscow to thank Vietnam's wartime allies for their assistance and to ask for continued aid. Despite this, Sino-Vietnamese relations continued to experience strains, as China halted all military assistance and cut back on long-term economic aid. The following year, when

China attempted to enlist Vietnam in a campaign vilifying "great power hegemonism," Vietnam declined. By contrast the Soviet-Vietnamese relationship firmed up. Immediately after the end of the war, the Soviet Union cancelled all of Vietnam's outstanding debts. In April 1976, when Soviet Deputy Premier I. Arkhipov visited Hanoi, it was announced that Soviet economic assistance would be increased. Later that year, Mikhail Suslov led a CPSU delegation to attend the VCP's 4th Congress. Le Duan visited Moscow two more times during this period, in February 1976 to attend the 25th Congress of the CPSU, and again in October 1977. Le Duan also stopped in Beijing on each of these occasions.

Vietnam's attempts to maintain cordial relations with Beijing foundered in the face of China's continued support for Pol Pot's Democratic Kampuchea. This then set the stage for armed confrontation between Beijing and Hanoi. In late 1977, when Democratic Kampuchea suspended its diplomatic relations with Vietnam, China supported the Phnom Penh regime. The following year, citing Hanoi's mistreatment of its Chinese minorities, the PRC suspended most of its aid programs and recalled its advisers from Vietnam. Beginning in August, China increased its shipments of military supplies to Democratic Kampuchea and, at the end of the year, cut the flow of petroleum to Vietnam by closing its pipelines.

Vietnam, left with no other options, responded by firming up its relationship with Moscow. In June Vietnam became a full member of the Council for Mutual Economic Assistance (CMEA). In November Soviet-Vietnamese relations were transformed by the signing of a twenty-five year Treaty of Friendship and Cooperation that laid the foundation for all subsequent forms of cooperation between the two states. An unpublished protocol to the treaty reportedly granted the Soviet Union military access to Vietnam's air fields and ports.[5]

With the protection afforded by this document, Vietnam invaded and occupied Kampuchea. China responded by launching a limited two-month assault on Vietnam's northern provinces (February–March 1979). The Soviet Union support for Vietnam included the prompt sending of Tu-95 reconnaissance aircraft. These were followed by a naval flotilla that was stationed in the Gulf of Tonkin. Further, the Soviet Union embarked on a massive sea and air lift of emergency shipments of military supplies and equipment. Soviet dock workers were also posted to Vietnam to expedite the unloading of these supplies. The events of late 1978–early 1979, dubbed the Third Indochina War by analysts, ushered in a new phase of Soviet-Vietnamese relations, that of alliance partners.

Since 1980 the nature of the Soviet-Vietnamese relationship has changed qualitatively and quantitatively. The top leaders of both countries are in frequent contact; VCP Secretary General Le Duan made at least eight Moscow trips in the period from July 1980 until his death in 1986, and Foreign Minister Nguyen Co Thach logged up twelve visits to Moscow in the same period. Economic cooperation and Vietnamese dependency on the USSR have grown concurrently. By 1985 the Socialist Republic of Vietnam (SRV) imported all of its POL (petroleum oil lubricants) requirements and between 80 to 100 percent of its cotton, fertilizer, iron, cast iron, steel, and nonferrous metals from the Soviet Union. At least 60 percent of Vietnam's trade was with the USSR, and three-quarters of Vietnam's outstanding debt of US$6 billion was owed to CMEA members. In the military sphere, Vietnamese reluctance to grant the Soviet Union military access to its ports and airfields gave way to regular deployments of Soviet ships and aircraft to Cam Ranh Bay. In April 1984 both countries conducted their first joint amphibious operations near Hai Phong. In all other fields, such as the hosting of guest workers and the training of Vietnam's scientific and technical elite, Soviet-Vietnamese collaboration grew closer.

Within this alliance relationship, certain strains have become evident. At least three major issues stand out: Sino-Soviet normalization; Vietnamese accountability in using Soviet aid; and a peaceful settlement of the conflict in Kampuchea. According to a detailed study undertaken by Robert Horn, it took the Soviet Union two years, from September 1981 to October 1983, to obtain Hanoi's public endorsement of Moscow's efforts to normalize relations with Beijing.[6] As early as Vietnam's 5th Party Congress in March 1982, the Soviet Union began voicing its dissatisfaction over Vietnamese misuse of Soviet aid and demanded stricter control and supervision. Only in 1986, before the VCP's 6th Party Congress, did Vietnam's leaders publicly admit that corruption and inefficiency were major problems. Finally, regarding Kampuchea, Gorbachev's 1986 Vladivostok initiative caused anxiety and possibly misgivings among some of Vietnam's leaders.

Since 1980 both Vietnam and the Soviet Union have experienced changes in the ruling party leadership. Brezhnev, who died in November 1982, was succeeded briefly by Andropov (November 1982–February 1984) and Chernenko (February 1984–March 1985) before Mikhail Gorbachev assumed power in March 1985. Vietnam experienced a major leadership transition in 1986 when long-serving Secretary General Le Duan passed away, and three of the old guard, Pham Van Dong, Truong Chinh and Le Duc Tho, stepped aside. The interregnum between Brezhnev and Gorbachev produced some turbulence in Soviet-Vietnamese relations, especially Andropov's openings to China. However, Le Duan's successor, Nguyen Van Linh, was a reforming leader comparable in many ways to Gorbachev himself.

As a result of several Moscow summits, the two leaders now appear in agreement on the three major issues: normalization of relations with China, the efficient use of Soviet aid, and a peaceful settlement of the conflict in Kampuchea.

Soviet-Vietnamese relations currently are more businesslike than previously and are dominated more by economic than political or military issues. For example, at the 6th Congress of the Vietnam Communist Party in December 1986, the USSR announced it would double its aid to Vietnam to an estimated 8–9 billion rubles over the next five years. The following year, the Soviet economic aid package to Vietnam was estimated at US$1.5 billion per year.[7] Vietnam hosts approximately 2,500–8,000 Soviet advisers and officials.[8]

VIETNAMESE PERCEPTIONS

Any discussion of Soviet-Vietnamese relations, including Vietnamese perceptions of those relations, with Vietnamese in Vietnam is an extremely sensitive matter. Ordinary people are enjoined from discussing such subjects with visiting foreigners. Vietnamese officials usually confine themselves to approved rhetoric.

In 1981 the author raised the question of Soviet-Vietnamese relations with Vietnamese Foreign Minister Nguyen Co Thach. He commented as follows:

> There are many big powers now. If there were no Soviet Union, there would be only China, and we would have to pay tribute. Without Soviet aid there would be no independence. We are second to none in defending our independence. In the past, it was not our intention to rely solely on the Soviet Union. . . . We are not in a military alliance with the Soviet Union. We are a member of COMECON and the World Bank. The Soviet Union is not a member of the latter. Neither the Soviet Union nor other socialist countries criticized us for joining the World Bank. The Soviet Union never threatened to cut aid unless we quit the World Bank. The West wants a monopoly in Vietnam. We are a most diversified country. . . . We have no foreign bases. We give facilities to the Soviet Union similar to those provided by Singapore [to the USSR] before 1979.

Vietnam's present ruling elite are first-generation revolutionaries, who adopted Marxist-Leninist ideology in their struggle to expel the French and were greatly influenced by Ho Chi Minh, a man who had extensive experience in the USSR. From the very beginning, Vietnam's communist leaders saw themselves as part of a worldwide revolutionary movement. They are firm believers in the concept of proletarian internationalism. They unabashedly adhere to the notion that Vietnam is a member of the socialist commonwealth headed by the Soviet Union. In their view, the USSR, as the first communist state, deserves to be studied and emulated for the experiences and lessons it can offer.

The USSR has not been, of course, Vietnam's only source of aid and inspiration. During much of Vietnam's struggle against the French, Japan, and the United States, China played a vital role.[9] Many members of the Vietnam Communist Party and the Vietnam People's Army were trained in China. Vietnam also values and studies the experiences of other socialist states, including its neighbor to the north.

Notwithstanding these external influences, Vietnam's leaders are also ardent nationalists. They have spent their entire lives fighting for their vision of an independent and modern Vietnam. During the Sino-Soviet dispute they attempted to follow an independent path between Moscow and Beijing, always weighing Vietnamese national interests with the other issues at stake.[10] The breakdown of Vietnam's relations with China after 1975 and Vietnam's current pro-Soviet alignment may be traced to Vietnamese resistance to Chinese pressures to take sides.[11]

The Soviet-Vietnamese relationship is not without its problems. First, Vietnam is overwhelmingly dependent on the Soviet Union for its military and economic aid. The Vietnamese sense of pride and independence rankles at this relationship. Also, the Vietnamese are aware that the Soviets lag far behind the West in certain areas of technology. The present state of dependency is, in some cases, seen as an impediment to the modernization of Vietnam. Second, the Vietnamese system has shown itself prone to inefficiency, mismanagement, and corruption in the manner in which Soviet aid is handled. Repeated Soviet attempts to inspect and control the disbursement of aid, from central down to project level, often meet Vietnamese resentment. Third, the Soviet military presence at Cam Ranh Bay is a source of embarrassment.[12] Vietnam would prefer a less tight and dependent relationship.

As indicated by the Vietnamese foreign minister and reiterated recently at the 6th VCP Congress,[13] Vietnam would prefer a greater diversity in its foreign relations and counterbalancing inputs of foreign assistance. However, the ongoing conflict with China, a continuing U.S. trade and aid embargo, and world condemnation of Vietnam's occupation of Kampuchea preclude a lessening of Vietnam's dependency on the Soviet Union in the short run.

There is a view held outside Vietnam that the Soviet-Vietnamese relationship is not robust and will not endure over time.[14] According to proponents of this view, there is little substance in the relationship other than a momentary congruence of national interests. Soviet culture is considered to be alien and unattractive to the Vietnamese. The Soviets are allegedly perceived by the Vietnamese as racist and overbearing. In time, it is argued, these differences will surface, and the relationship will break up in much the same fashion as Soviet-Egyptian or Soviet-Indonesian ties were broken. The development most likely to cause this rupture will be the normalization of Sino-Soviet relations at the expense of Vietnam.

None of the historical cases cited involves two countries with such a history of intimate party-to-party ties. The Soviet-Vietnamese relationship is fundamentally different from these other examples because Vietnam is a socialist country and is a full-fledged member of the socialist commonwealth and the Council for Mutual Economic Assistance. The weight of bureaucratic linkages and interests spread across all areas of Vietnamese life is too great to permit the relationship to deteriorate to the point of being broken off completely.

The only survey of Vietnamese perceptions of the Soviet presence in Vietnam was conducted in refugee camps outside the country and concerned both North and South Vietnamese, as well as several Soviet-educated intellectuals.[15] That survey portrayed an image of despair and disenchantment with communism and an attitude of hostility and almost racist rancor toward the ill-bred Soviet advisers.

But a different picture can be presented, one that modifies some of the sweeping generalities of that survey. If one moves from the realm of officialdom downward and outward into Vietnamese society, one encounters a different set of perceptions. Attitudes toward the Soviet Union vary between town and country, between north and south, and between individuals. In the north, the following observations can be made on the basis of three field trips there.[16]

The Soviets were the first foreigners in any number (excluding the Chinese) to come to northern Vietnam after partitioning in 1954. They came as friends, technical experts, and as aid donors. By those Vietnamese who interacted with them, the Soviets were perceived as basically competent and hard-working persons. Middle-level Vietnamese cadres express gratitude for Soviet assistance and for the opportunity to go to the USSR for work, training, or education. Visiting Soviet academicians and technical experts are respected, and their views are given close attention. Soviet culture is seen as adding diversity to an otherwise drab life. Soviet literature is sought out avidly, and Soviet technical books are valued highly. Visiting Soviet troupes are popular.

Close personal relations between the Soviets and Vietnamese after work hours are discouraged, if not forbidden. Both parties keep much to themselves and interact only at officially sanctioned gatherings.

When differences and awkward moments arise, these are politely tolerated and attributed to the fact that the Soviet is a foreigner who does not speak Vietnamese and understand local custom.

To the northern peasant, the Soviet is a foreigner, a person encountered only rarely. He is an object of curiosity because of his physical size, clothing, and appearance. He is called *lien-xo* (Soviet), but not in a derogatory sense.[17] The northern peasant has been told to accept the visiting Soviet as a friend. Some peasants are flattered by this interest.

Vietnamese attitudes toward the Soviets differ in the south and are the legacy of the Vietnam War and anti-Communist propaganda. These attitudes have been intensified also by declining socioeconomic conditions, the perceived costs of Vietnam's occupation of Kampuchea, and dependency on the Soviet Union. The following examples are illustrative[18]: In Dalat, northeast of Ho Chi Minh City, a crowd of hostile Vietnamese shouting "lien-xo" fell in behind a pair of white foreigners and began pelting them with stones. In Da Nang, a group of European students got off a train and found themselves surrounded by a crowd of threatening Vietnamese. Fortunately, some of the students spoke enough Vietnamese to convince the crowd that they were Swedes, not Russians. In Ho Chi Minh City, another European walking along the sidewalk narrowly escaped being run down by two young Vietnamese on motorbikes, shouting "lien-xo".

SOVIET POLICY UNDER GORBACHEV

It can be argued that the significance of Gorbachev's 1986 Vladivostok speech for Vietnam and a possible settlement of the conflict in Kampuchea lies in what was not said rather than what was. While Gorbachev's speech contained no basic change in the USSR's previously announced public position that Kampuchea was an issue best left to China and Vietnam,[19] it did signal a Soviet willingness to play a role, however indirect and ambiguous, in achieving a settlement. Left unstated was how Moscow intended to encourage Sino-Vietnamese reconciliation. This led to a period of Vietnamese anxiety that was only assuaged later in the year.[20] Vietnamese anxiety was aroused when Gorbachev and his then deputy foreign minister, Mikhail Kapitsa, omitted in public remarks the usual caveat that Sino-Soviet normalization would not be at the expense of a third country, meaning Vietnam.

Significantly, Gorbachev listed Kampuchea first among the five conflict areas that he singled out for possible resolution as part of a general conference on Asia-Pacific issues.[21] His comments on the Kampuchean conflict were brief.[22] Kampuchea, he said,

Through its suffering . . . won its right to choose its friends and allies, and it is unacceptable to try to draw it back into the tragic past and decide the future of this state in distant capitals, or even in the UN. Much here, as in other problems of Southeast Asia, depends on the normalization of Sino-Vietnamese relations. This is the sovereign affair of the governments and leaderships of the two countries. We can only express our interest in seeing the border between these socialist states becoming again a border of peace and good neighborliness, and a comradely dialogue renewed, with unnecessary suspicions and distrust being removed.

Gorbachev's Vladivostok speech commenced a new phase of heightened Soviet diplomatic activity in Asia, which has been described elsewhere in the volume.[23] Quite clearly, in the year after Gorbachev's Vladivostok speech, Southeast Asia entered a period of cautious optimism with respect to the prospects for a negotiated settlement of the Kampuchean conflict. Laos undertook initiatives designed to improve relations with Thailand and China.[24] Some observers saw these moves as harbingers of a possible improvement in Sino-Vietnamese relations. Vietnam, for its part, sent out secret peace feelers to Norodom Sihanouk to entice him into "national reconciliation" talks with the regime in Phnom Penh. India undertook quiet diplomatic soundings, while Indonesia renewed its efforts to find a framework for discussions suitable to all parties.

Vietnamese Reactions

At the very moment Gorbachev was delivering his speech, Truong Chinh, then secretary general of the VCP, was in Moscow on "vacation" at the invitation of the Central Committee of the CPSU.[25] They later met on 12 August in an atmosphere of "complete mutual understanding, fraternity and cordiality," according to official accounts.[26] Soviet and Vietnamese reports of this meeting suggest that a wide range of issues were discussed, such as trade, economic, scientific, and technical matters, in addition to Gorbachev's Vladivostok address. After Truong Chinh expressed Vietnam's determination to overcome "certain [domestic] difficulties," Gorbachev reaffirmed the USSR's continued support and assistance to Vietnam.

The two party leaders also reached an "identity" of views on all international matters discussed, including relations with China. According to TASS, "[t]he Soviet Union and Vietnam reiterate their readiness for the normalization of relations with the PRC, which would be of much importance for the improvement of the situation in the Asia-Pacific region."[27]

Truong Chinh also took the opportunity to issue a *pro forma* endorsement of Gorbachev's Vladivostok speech. The party's newspaper reported: "Comrade Truong Chinh expressed the stand of our party, government and people to support whole heartedly the latest initiatives put forward in the very important statement by Comrade Gorbachev in Vladivostok to normalize the situation in the Asia-Pacific region, lead this region's development in the general direction of establishing a global security system, and favor the convening of an Asia-Pacific conference with the participation of all countries in the region to achieve the above goal."[28] On his return to Vietnam, Truong Chinh's support of the Soviet position not unexpectedly received the endorsement of the VCP politburo.[29]

However, close observers reading between the lines noted that Truong Chinh had received a "cool reception" while in Moscow. Publicly the relationship appeared normal, while in private the Vietnamese had misgivings. According to veteran Indochina watcher Nayan Chanda, "[t]he communique issued at the end of his talk avoided the standard phrase about both sides achieving 'complete identity of views." Also conspicuous by its absence in the communique was the standard assurance that Sino-Soviet normalization would not be at the expense of "third countries."[30]

Vietnam and the Soviet Union share a particularly close relationship that involves the coordination of their foreign policies. Therefore, it should not be a surprise that the official Vietnamese media chose to report and endorse the broad outlines of Gorbachev's Vladivostok speech uncritically. Vietnam's domestic radio broadcast extensive extracts from the speech, both party and army newspapers carried supportive editorials, and the Vietnam Peace Committee issued a general statement of approval, while no less a figure than Pham Van Dong, then a member of the VCP politburo, granted an interview to TASS to offer his endorsement.[31]

On 14 August a symposium was held in Hanoi "in support of the new peace initiatives" set out by Gorbachev in his Vladivostok speech. According to the Vietnam News Agency, "the participants warmly welcomed the Soviet leader's peace initiatives and expressed their determination to do their best to contribute to the cause of peace, security, and equitable cooperation in the region."[32]

The initial reportage of Gorbachev's speech was mainly factual; both radio and press carried the key paragraphs on Kampuchea when reporting to their domestic audience. The Vietnamese media also highlighted a specific reference made to Vietnam, namely, that Vietnam was a major country in Asia and the Pacific alongside the USSR, United States, and other countries of the region.

Vietnamese media endorsement was also couched in general terms. For example, on 30 July an editorial in *Nhan Dan* declared: "[o]ur people warmly welcome and fully support Comrade Gorbachev's July 28 statement and the Soviet Union's correct position and series of important new proposals for establishing new fair relations and creating an atmosphere of peace and stability in the Asia-Pacific region, in response to the aspirations and interests of various nations in the region."

It was left to Pham Van Dong, acting in his capacity as chairman of the Council of Ministers, to give the official Vietnamese government view: "[t]he Socialist Republic of Vietnam fully supports the Soviet Union's initiatives and will coordinate its actions with the Soviet Union to implement those noble objectives." When asked specifically for his views on Gorbachev's "concrete initiatives and proposals aimed at solving regional issues [i.e. Kampuchea]," Dong replied:

The essential things of these proposals are peace, security and cooperation that have become a historical trend in Asia and the Pacific, and the world as a whole, and Comrade Mikhail Gorbachev has worked out concrete measures to turn this trend into reality. . . . It is [the] right time for all nations in Asia and the Pacific to embark on constructive dialogue aimed at settling all regional issues on the basis of honoring each other's independence and sovereignty, shirking confrontation, limiting and reducing weapons and military activities.

The Vietnamese media, in contrast to the Soviet press, left no doubt as to who was to blame for continuing tensions. *Nhan Dan* observed, "[t]o realize its neo-globalism, U.S. imperialism has put forward its extremely reactionary doctrine for Asia and the Pacific with the aim of maintaining its imperialist position, developing hegemonism, and impeding and opposing revolutionary movements and the ongoing new changes in this important, increasingly important, region." Turning to China, the same newspaper declared that "the responsibility for the worsening relations between the two countries and the continuing tension along the Vietnamese-Chinese border rests completely with China."

Vietnam's 6th Party Congress

In December 1986, prior to the VCP's 6th Party Congress, Truong Chinh journeyed to Moscow on his second trip in three months to seek reassurances of continued Soviet economic assistance. Once again he held wide-ranging discussions with Gorbachev. According to an official account, both leaders reached "total unanimity" of views on domestic and foreign issues. Nayan Chanda quoted analysts as concluding that Chinh and Gorbachev "reached a compromise by which Gorbachev gave his blessings to the party congress plans, in return for Hanoi's backing for his Asian initiative."[33]

None of the reports or speakers at Vietnam's 6th Party Congress indicated that any radical shifts would occur in Vietnam's foreign policy, especially on the Kampuchean question. Rather, the Central Committee's political report reiterated long-standing views: Vietnam would maintain its close ties with the Soviet Union and develop its "special relationships" with Laos and Kampuchea as the cornerstone of its foreign policy.

Nayan Chanda also assessed the implications of the 6th Party Congress for a settlement of the Kampuchea issue in negative terms.[34] He noted that the 1990 date set by Vietnam for the withdrawal of its troops from Kampuchea was omitted from the political report, although it was mentioned by Vice Minister Vo Dong Giang outside the congress hall at a press conference. Chanda interpreted the political report's references to Indochinese solidarity as implying "that Hanoi would not accept any settlement that weakens Vietnam's security cooperation with Cambodia (or Laos) and allows hostile countries a foothold there." Further, in Chanda's view, the CPSU delegate "seemed to offer his blessing to the solidarity of Vietnam, Cambodia and Laos." While in Hanoi, CPSU delegate Yegor Ligachev twice mentioned that the Soviet Union's desire to seek a normalization of relations between China and Vietnam would not be at the expense of Vietnam's interests, and neither would the Soviet Union mediate.[35] The matter was, in his view, best solved by dialogue between Beijing and Hanoi.

Unexpectedly, both Soviet and Vietnamese speakers alluded to the need for Vietnam to improve the efficiency of its handling of Soviet aid. Quite clearly, the Soviet Union's generous offer to double assistance over the next five years was tied to Vietnamese willingness to reform conditions at home.

Did the 6th Party Congress signal a hardening of the Vietnamese position? In Chanda's view, the congress "set back a timid improvement of atmosphere in recent months. But a closer look suggests that an apparent hardening of positions is tactical and not a prelude to escalation."[36] Chanda also argued that the elevation to the politburo of two officials with direct experience in Kampuchea "could instill greater realism in Hanoi's approach" and that "[d]omestic political considerations may dictate a hard-line position on Cambodia at this stage." Subsequently, as leadership changes unfolded in Hanoi, and as Vietnamese officials began to focus almost exclusively on the parlous state of the domestic economy, some leading ASEAN officials began to adopt a more upbeat attitude about the possibilities of a negotiated settlement.

Shevardnadze's Regional Visit (March 1987)

Expectations about a new Soviet role in settling the Kampuchean issue were raised in early 1987 when it was announced that Foreign Minister Eduard Schevardnadze would make his first visit to Southeast Asia and Australia. After stopping in Thailand and visiting Australia and Indonesia, Shevardnadze also paid his first visit to Indochina, briefly touching down in Laos and Kampuchea before traveling to Vietnam.

Press and radio reports later indicated that the foreign minister was mainly interested in listening to regional views and had not presented any new Soviet initiatives on ending the war in Kampuchea.[37] In Hanoi the main topic of discussion was "renovation" in the relationship between the Soviet Union and Vietnam, meaning that Vietnam would push ahead with its plans for economic liberalization and would improve its handling of Soviet economic aid. For his part, Shevardnadze supported the strengthening of the alliance of the three countries of Indochina, as well as their efforts to normalize relations with China.[38]

Since Gorbachev's Vladivostok speech, the Soviet Union has intensified its efforts to normalize relations with China and ASEAN. As both have set the resolution of the Kampuchea problem as a precondition, Shevardnadze's visit to Thailand, Australia, Indonesia, and Indochina may indicate that Moscow is trying to play a role in resolving that conflict. Certainly Mochtar's assessment of Shevardnadze's regional visit bears this out. The Indonesian foreign minister was quoted as stating that Shevardnadze's visit marked the "first concrete steps" toward the implementation of Gorbachev's Vladivostok initiative. According to Mochtar, it was too much to expect that Shevardnadze could achieve some "drastic or concrete" result just yet. His purpose was first to ascertain how firm the regional countries were that the settlement of Kampuchea was a prerequisite for improved Soviet relations with the region. His visit was only "the first act"[39] in the "Vladivostok process."

Nguyen Van Linh's Moscow Visit (May 1987)

Significantly, Nguyen Van Linh, the newly elected VCP secretary general, paid his first visit to the Soviet Union at the same time that

Thai Foreign Minister Siddhi was in Moscow (7–22 May 1987). Linh was accompanied by Foreign Minister Nguyen Co Thach. The VCP secretary general was received by Gorbachev on 18 and 19 May. To all outward appearances, the visit appeared "routine," with Soviet aid the main topic.[40] A closer examination suggests the Soviets continued to try and persuade the Vietnamese to seek an early resolution of the Kampuchean conflict by opening a dialogue with China and by adopting a more flexible policy on what would constitute an acceptable government of "national reconciliation" in Phnom Penh.[41]

At a dinner speech welcoming Linh, Gorbachev called for a political solution based on "the unification of all their national patriotic forces" in Kampuchea.[42] Later, both Gorbachev and Linh called for an improvement in relations with China, stating that "[t]hey would also greet China's active involvement in the search for ways of solving the complex problems of the Asian continent." Linh later told Gorbachev that Vietnamese military withdrawal from Kampuchea was as important as the elimination of the Khmer Rouge leader, Pol Pot, and foreign interference in that country.[43]

The Soviet-Vietnam joint statement left no doubt that Hanoi, whatever its earlier misgivings and anxieties, had been persuaded to support Moscow's efforts to woo China. The communique stated that "[t]he participants in the talks pointed to a desire by their countries to normalize and improve relations with the PRC, which would be a major positive factor for stronger stability in Asia and in international life in general. They would also greet China's active involvement in the search for ways of solving the complex problems of the Asian continent. The Soviet side supported Vietnam's initiative for holding Vietnamese-Chinese talks with a view to settling contentious issues as soon as possible."[44]

Vietnam has long been concerned about the pace of Sino-Soviet normalization and the implications for itself. Hanoi has reacted, in part, by initiating as many as six confidential diplomatic approaches to Beijing since Gorbachev came to power.[45] China has reportedly rejected each one, citing the occupation of Kampuchea as the main stumbling block. Reports in early 1988 that Vietnam and China reached a five-point agreement to improve relations and to institute a cease-fire along the border remain unconfirmed.[46]

Since his Vladivostok address, Gorbachev has shifted ground and agreed to discuss this "third country matter" with China. Soviet officials have encouraged the national reconciliation talks between Sihanouk and Hun Sen, of the People's Republic of Kampuchea (PRK). On the eve of the second round, Gorbachev, in remarks to a Chinese-language publication, stated that sufficient progress had been made toward a settlement in Kampuchea, and the time was now ripe for a Sino-Soviet summit.[47]

In Soviet eyes, the Kampuchean conflict need not remain a zero-sum game between Vietnam and its opponents. Rather, a key feature of Soviet diplomacy has been to use the prospect of a peaceful settlement as a means of enticing China into participating in a new Asian socialist community.[48] In such an arrangement, Kampuchea could remain both "independent" and socialist, and neither Vietnam nor China would lose prestige over such an outcome.

FUTURE PROSPECTS

The Soviet-Vietnamese relationship has expanded considerably since Ho Chi Minh first made contact in the 1920s. The nature of the Soviet-Vietnamese relationship can be characterized as both extensive (it covers a wide variety of fields) and intensive (it has considerable depth). There are three main pillars that support this relationship: shared history, geopolitical reality, and ideological affinity.

The intensification of Soviet-Vietnamese relations is a reflection not only of Chinese hostility toward Vietnam but also the growing momentum of genuine bilateral Soviet-Vietnamese relations. For example, the political and scientific elites of both countries have developed patterns of cooperation for nearly four decades. This process has naturally intensified with the signing of the 1978 Treaty of Friendship and Cooperation.

Vietnam cannot escape from the tyranny of its geographical position. It is a fact of life that Vietnam shares a common border with China and that China is presently hostile toward Hanoi. This geopolitical situation intensifies Soviet-Vietnamese military and security cooperation as well as cooperation in other fields. The relationship is not all one-sided, as the Soviet Union gains considerably from its strategic position in Cam Ranh Bay astride the lines of communication between the Indian and Pacific oceans.

Vietnamese and Soviet leaders share the same ideology. This reinforces the relationship, as they both confront roughly similar domestic and international problems.[49] The leaders of both countries consult regularly on ways to coordinate their responses. At lower levels, the relationship has developed into an extensive network of crosscutting ties developed by party and state bureaucratic organs. The sheer weight of these connections serves to be self-perpetuating.

The nature of the Soviet-Vietnamese relationship is not an exclusive one. Both states are currently engaged in efforts to expand their relations with other countries outside the socialist commonwealth.

Since 1981, for example, the Soviet Union has been normalizing relations with China. Vietnam has been hampered by world reaction to its invasion and occupation of Kampuchea. Nevertheless, at Vietnam's 6th Party Congress, there were signs that Hanoi's leaders had given priority to opening ties with the West, if not with China.

Vietnam hopes to eliminate the Kampuchean problem as the key issue blocking improved relations with Western capitalist states in the near future, citing 1990 as the target date. Within this time frame, Vietnam hopes to secure either a negotiated settlement favorable to its interests or to have created a Kampuchean regime sufficiently viable to stand on its own with minimal Vietnamese assistance.

Vietnam's leaders also remain hopeful that Soviet diplomatic support and economic assistance will continue to be forthcoming. At the end of the current five-year plan period, around 1990, a series of Soviet-funded power projects will come on stream ushering in a new period of industrial production. While the Soviet Union is expected to continue funding such projects, Vietnam is presently advertising its new foreign investment code to entice Western capital back into the country.[50] None of these developments will alter significantly the state of Soviet-Vietnamese relations that can be expected to remain on course at much the same speed and direction in the near future.

NOTES

1. The Vietnam Communist Party was renamed the Indochinese Communist Party (ICP) in October 1930 and has since undergone several name changes. The ICP was ostensibly dissolved in November 1945; it reemerged in March 1951 as the Vietnam Workers' Party (VWP; Dang Lao Dong Viet Nam). The VWP was renamed the Vietnam Communist Party in December 1976; this designation will be used throughout this chapter.
2. A review of Soviet-DRV relations in the 1954–1960 period may be found in Carlyle A. Thayer, *The Origins of the National Front for the Liberation of Viet Nam* (Ph.D. thesis, The Australian National University, 1977).
3. Daniel S. Papp, "Power or Pawn? The Soviet Role in Vietnam." Manuscript located in the SRV, Foreign Relations, USSR (General) File (University of California at Berkeley, Indochina Archive, September 1986).
4. Podgorny previously visited Vietnam in October 1971, making him the highest ranking visitor from Moscow since Kosygin in February 1965.
5. See remarks attributed to Soviet Deputy Foreign Minister Nikolai Firyubin at the opening session of Soviet-Japanese talks. UPI dispatch from Tokyo, *International Herald Tribune*, 15 May 1979; "Firyubin Defends Soviet Bases, Pact Obligation,'" *Japan Times*, 15 May 1979.
6. Robert C. Horn, "Vietnam and Sino-Soviet Relations: What Price Rapprochement?" *Asian Survey*, 27, no. 7 (July 1987): 729–47.

7. Suwit Suthanakun, secretary general of the Thai National Security Council, remarks to Jiji Press quoted by *The Nation* (Bangkok), 15 May 1987.
8. See Brendan M. Greeley, Jr., "Soviets Extend Air, Sea Power With Buildup at Cam Ranh Bay," *Aviation Week and Space Technology* 126, no. 9 (2 March 1987): 76; S. Bilveer, "Soviet Military Presence in Indochina," *Asian Defence Journal*, August 1985, p. 29.
9. Cf. Carlyle A. Thayer, "Vietnam: Ideology and the Lessons from Experience," in William S. Turley, ed., *Confrontation or Coexistence: The Future of ASEAN-Vietnam Relations* (Bangkok: The Institute of Security and International Studies, Chulalongkorn University, 1985), 49–74.
10. Gareth Porter, "Vietnam and the Socialist Camp: Center or Periphery?" in William S. Turley, ed., *Vietnamese Communism in Comparative Perspective* (Boulder, Colo.: Westview Press, 1980), 225–64.
11. In 1976 Vietnam experienced great pressures from the Maoists in China to subscribe to "Chairman Mao's Theory of the Three Worlds," an ideological formulation that ranked the United States and the Soviet Union together as the chief enemies of the world's people. When Vietnam refused to take sides, China unilaterally severed its aid program.
12. Vietnamese spokesmen are unconvincing in their denials about the Soviet military presence in their country at Cam Ranh Bay and elsewhere. One senior official, attending a conference in Italy, reacted to an extremely well-documented paper on the Soviet presence in Vietnam by denying it completely, much to the embarrassment of other conferees. The paper in question was Sheldon W. Simon, "Soviet Policy Toward Southeast Asia: Emphasizing the Military." Conference on Southeast Asia—Moving from the 1980s to the 1990s, sponsored by the Center for International Policy and the Institute of International Studies, The University of South Carolina, Rockefeller Foundation, Bellagio, Italy, 2–6 December 1985.
13. Carlyle A. Thayer, "Vietnam's Sixth Party Congress: An Overview," *Contemporary Southeast Asia*, 9, no. 1 (Singapore, June 1987): 12–22.
14. Pike, 162–78, 224–47.
15. Harry H. Kendall, "Vietnamese Perceptions of the Soviet Presence," *Asian Survey* 23, no. 9 (September 1983): 1052–61.
16. This includes field trips made in August–September 1981 (Hanoi, Yen So, Hai Phong, Ha Long, Hon Gay, Lang Son, and Ho Chi Minh City), November 1985 (Hanoi, Hoa Binh, Ho Chi Minh City, Vung Tau, and Cu Chi), and October–November 1987 (Hanoi, Phuoc Tho and Hai Phong), as well as interviews with Vietnamese who have left Vietnam and do not intend to return.
17. *Lien-xo* is short for *Lien Bang Cong Hoa Xa Hoi Chu Nghia Xo Viet* (Union of Soviet Socialist Republics). As most Westerners in post-1954 Vietnam were Soviets, the term was used similarly. *Lien-xo* is a Vietnamese word with Chinese roots; it is not a foreign-sounding word to the Vietnamese ear, unlike the terms used for other Western nationalities. As used in the north, the expression *lien-xo* is not considered derogatory. Kendall, p. 1054, argues the opposite.

18. Keyes Beech, "Hostility to Russians Runs Deep Among Xenophobic Vietnamese," *International Herald Tribune*, 4 January 1982.
19. This conclusion is reinforced by press conference remarks made later by Mikhail Kapitsa, USSR deputy foreign minister. According to TASS, on 6 August, Kapitsa drew the journalists' attention to the section of Mikhail Gorbachev's speech in Vladivostok expressing the interest in the restoration of the Kampuchean conflict. Neither Gorbachev nor Kapitsa, however, restated the caveat that Sino-Soviet normalization would not be at the expense of Vietnam. Richard Nations, "Moscow's New Tack," *Far Eastern Economic Review*, 14 August 1986, pp. 30–40, concluded that "Moscow apparently sees no need for Hanoi to make concessions to the tripartite anti-Vietnamese Cambodian resistance coalition."
20. Nayan Chanda, "Not So Soft on Cambodia," *Far Eastern Economic Review*, 1 January 1987, p. 12.
21. After Kampuchea, Gorbachev nominated the following areas in his priorities: halting nuclear proliferation; reducing nuclear armed naval fleets in the Indian Ocean; radically reducing armed forces and conventional weapons; and discussing confidence-building measures.
22. The text of Gorbachev's speech in Vladivostok is taken from Soviet Television and Moscow Home Service, 28 July 1986. For an excellent, concise analysis, consult Richard Nations, pp. 30–40.
23. See for instance, Chapter 6., this volume.
24. Late in 1987 Laos and China formally agreed to upgrade diplomatic relations by exchanging ambassadors, see Robert Grieves' dispatch from Beijing, *The Australian*, 2 December 1987.
25. Vietnam News Agency dispatch from Hanoi, 26 July 1986
26. Moscow Home Service and TASS, 12 August 1986.
27. TASS and Hanoi Home Service, 12 August 1986.
28. Editorial, "New Brilliant Manifestation of the S.R.V.-USSR Militant Solidarity and Comprehensive Co-operation," *Nhan Dan*, 13 August 1986.
29. Vietnam News Agency dispatch from Hanoi, 19 August 1986.
30. Nayan Chanda, "Weather Eye on Moscow," *Far Eastern Economic Review*, 23 October 1986, p. 24.
31. Respectively, excerpts were broadcast by Hanoi Domestic Sevice, 30 July 1986; "Tam Cuong Cao Ca Dau Tranh Cho Hoa Binh, An Ninh Va Hoc Tac Quoc Te" (A Noble Example of Striving for the Cause of International Peace, Security and Cooperation), and "Phat Bieu cua Dong Chi M.X. Gooc-Ba-Chop tai Vla-De-Vo-Xtoc ve Nhieu Van De Quan Trong trong Nuoc va The Gioi" (Speech by Comrade M. S. Gorbachev in Vladivostok about Many Important Problems in the USSR and the World), *Nhan Dan*, 30 July 1986; "Just Stand, Lofty Responsibility," *Quan Doi Nhan Dan* carried by Hanoi Domestic Service, 1 August 1986; Vietnam News Agency, 1 August 1986; and Pham Van Dong interview with TASS carried by Vietnam News Agency dispatch from Hanoi, 4 August 1986. Subsequent references are from these sources unless otherwise indicated.
32. Vietnam News Agency dispatch from Hanoi, 4 August 1986.

33. Nayan Chanda, "Communist Compromise?" *Far Eastern Economic Review*, 25 December 1986, p. 15.
34. Nayan Chanda, "Not So Soft on Cambodia," *Far Eastern Economic Review* 1 January 1987, pp. 11–12.
35. Moscow Home Service, 17 December 1986.
36. Nayan Chanda, "Southeast Asia: More Smoke Than Fire Amid the Maneuvering," *International Herald Tribune*, 22 January 1987.
37. Reuter dispatch from Bangkok, *Sydney Morning Herald*, 12 March 1987.
38. Associated Press dispatch from Bangkok citing Vietnam News Agency, *Sydney Morning Herald*, 13 March 1987.
39. Michael Byrnes citing remarks made by Mochtar on visit to the Philippines, *Australian Financial Review*, 29 April 1987.
40. A series of agreements on cooperation in industry and agriculture were signed. The USSR pledged continued cooperation with the SRV. AP and UPI dispatches from Moscow, *The Nation* (Bangkok) 21 May 1987.
41. Sompong Kittinaradorn in *The Nation* (Bangkok), 5 August 1987.
42. TASS, 19 May 1987.
43. *Bangkok Post*, 22 May 1987.
44. Text of the Soviet-Vietnamese Joint Communique as carried by TASS, 21 May 1987.
45. Sompong Kittinaradorn in *The Nation* (Bangkok,) 28 May 1987.
46. The story was broken on 20 January by *Yomiuri Shimbun*, which cited unnamed Hanoi-based officials. For details consult AP dispatch from Tokyo, *The Nation* (Bangkok), 21 January 1988; and AP dispatch from Beijing, *International Herald Tribune*, 22 January 1988.
47. Radio Moscow, 11 January 1988.
48. For a fuller discussion of this point see Carlyle A. Thayer, "Kampuchea: Soviet Initiatives and Regional Responses," in Ramesh Thakur and Carlyle A. Thayer, eds., *The Soviet Union as an Asian Pacific Power* (Boulder, Colo.: Westview Press, 1987), 171–200.
49. Although Vietnam embarked on domestic economic reforms before Mikhail Gorbachev became the general secretary of the CPSU, it is evident that Nguyen Van Linh and other reformers draw comfort from Gorbachev's attempts to restructure Soviet society.
50. See, for example, the comments by Tony Hill, Radio Australia, 1 January 1988, and Peter Nettleship, Radio Newsreel, BBC, 12 January 1988; AFP, AP, and Reuter dispatches from Bangkok, *Straits Times*, 13 January 1988; Barbara Crosette dispatch from Ho Chi Minh City, *International Herald Tribune*, 23–24 January 1988; "Viet Nam Loosens Up," cover story in *Time*, 1 February 1988, pp. 4–11.

13

Australian Perceptions and Policies Toward the Soviet Union

Graeme Gill

THE HISTORICAL DIMENSION

A visitor to Sydney or Melbourne would find, on wandering around the bays on which both cities are located, the remains of forts or gun emplacements that date back more than 125 years. The presence of such fortifications reflects the sense of isolation and fear of invasion that pervaded the Australian colonies since the beginning of white settlement in 1788. Many of these fortifications were completed in anticipation of a Russian attack during the Crimean War of 1854–1856.

Russia was not the only major source of Australian concern during the colonial period. Apart from the British, other European colonial powers were well established in the region by the 1880s, and the French and German intentions, particularly the French, were a source of continuing concern in colonial capitals. In addition, toward the end of the century, Japan was emerging as a strong regional power. However, a more pervasive concern has continually infected white Australian society, the fear of being overwhelmed by the Asian population of the north. The desire to guard against this has been a continuing theme of Australian policy and one which at times has, paradoxically, influenced attitudes toward the Soviet Union. Because of the threatening Asian environment and the physical proximity of outposts of Britain's European challengers, concern about Russia tended to remain low priority except during times of Russo-British tension, such as 1875–1878 and 1884–1885.[1]

Contacts between Russia and Australia remained insignificant after the federation of the Australian colonies in 1901. The general fear of Bolshevism that swept Europe after the Bolshevik Revolution echoed in Australia. Two direct links did exist with the new Soviet regime for a short time. The prominent but middle-ranking Bolshevik Artem-Sergeev worked in Australia from 1911 to 1917, and the Bolshevik government named a Russian emigré in Australia as consul general for the new government. He was, however, soon expelled.[2]

A more permanent link developed with the establishment of the Communist Party of Australia (CPA) in 1920. This party, like its counterparts elsewhere, was formally affiliated with the Comintern and characteristically followed Moscow's direction.[3] The CPA was prevented from operating openly in the main working-class party, the Australian Labor Party (ALP), so its main area of activity was in the broad industrial movement through the trade unions. Party work in the industrial movement added to industrial disruption caused by strike activity. The conservative governments in the interwar period (the ALP held national office only in the 1929–1931 depression years), used this to belabor their political opponents and to stimulate an unsympathetic attitude toward the Soviet Union. Seeking to link presumed Soviet aspirations to world conquest with the CPA, leading conservative figures presented industrial disruption as fundamentally a function of Moscow's wishes. Although there were some on the left who were not communists but were sympathetic toward the Soviet experiment, the overwhelming popular attitude toward the Soviet Union was almost universally negative, and thereby paralleled the view presented by the conservative politicians.

This evaluation changed with the war. Australian admiration and respect for the Soviet people's war effort was widespread, and the kindly "Uncle Joe" image associated with the Soviet Union overshadowed earlier doubts. It was during this flush of pro-Soviet sentiment and in the context of the wartime alliance that formal diplomatic relations were established with the dispatch of a legation in January 1943. Australian failure to establish formal relations with the USSR earlier did not reflect Canberra's desire not to sup with the devil. Prior to 1940 Australia had no diplomatic missions in foreign states; Australian interests were looked after by the British representatives. The first foreign mission was established in Washington in 1940, but only seven others preceded the one in the Soviet Union. Clearly, once Australia began to look at the world through its own eyes, the Soviet Union was high on the list of those to be observed.

The increased popularity of the USSR induced by the wartime conditions was also reflected in the improved position of the CPA at this time. By the end of the war, party membership had peaked, and it seemed to have gained a new sense of respectability.

Postwar Relations

The wartime enthusiasm for the Soviet Union soon waned in the postwar period. Although the ALP government under Joseph Chifley did not evince an openly anti-Soviet attitude, international and domestic developments caused the public mood to shift as it did elsewhere in the Western world. The establishment of Soviet control in Eastern Europe, particularly in Czechoslovakia in 1948; the communist victory in China; the outbreak of communist insurgencies in Southeast Asia; the onset of the Cold War symbolized most graphically by the Berlin Crisis of 1949; and the outbreak of conflict in Korea, all helped to propel the popular mood in an anti-Soviet direction. Also significant was the domestic disruption caused by industrial unrest in which the CPA had a hand, particularly on the coalfields in 1948. The defeat of the Labor government in 1949 and its replacement by the Menzies-led Liberal Country Party (LCP) coalition government, politically reflected this shift in mood to the right.

The LCP government remained in office until 1972, and throughout most of that period anticommunism remained a principal electoral tactic. The "Reds under the beds" syndrome argued that a vote for the ALP constituted a vote for its left wing, which effectively controlled the party and which was itself either controlled or heavily influenced by Moscow or its local clients. This simplistic argument was inaccurate and distorted, but it seems to have struck a responsive chord among sections of the Australian populace.[4] It would, however, be wrong to assume that the government's attitude toward the USSR remained unchanged throughout this period. Particular events and changing perceptions among government leaders caused shifts in official attitude.

The Menzies government came to power espousing a hard-line attitude toward the Soviet Union. One of the planks of its electoral platform was the banning and dissolution of the CPA, a proposal justified partly in terms of a presumed likelihood of war with the Soviet Union in the future, and the potential for the party to act as a fifth column under such circumstances.[5] Although this proposal ultimately was defeated by popular referendum, due mainly to concerns about civil liberties, the proposal itself reflects the suspicion and hostility that characterized the government's attitude toward the Soviet Union and its intentions. This is reflected in External Affairs Minister Spender's comments in the House of Representatives in March 1950: "Soviet Russia's foreign policy is essentially global in character. . . . Its ultimate objective is world communism, a universal form of communism with Moscow as the controlling center either inspired by a belief that only by the destruction of other forms of government can communism be secured, or inspired by no other motive than aggression. . . . Its immediate purpose is to work toward its ultimate objective by communist infiltration in all democratic countries—organized from the centre, Moscow—so creating unrest, causing economic disruption and discrediting governments."[6] This view, which was common in Western capitals at this time, characterized all LCP governments during this period, although it was not always as forcefully presented as this.

This view of Soviet expansionism lay at the heart of the vision of a dangerous monolithic communism that was staple fare for conservative governments of the period. It lay behind the commitment of Australian troops to Korea and to the construction of the Australia-New Zealand-U.S. Security Alliance (ANZUS) (1951) and SEATO (1954) alliances, both of which were designed to ensure that Australia did not remain isolated in a potentially unstable region and confronted by an expansionist force whose aims conflicted with Australian interests. The generally perceived threat posed by Moscow seemed to be given substance by the Petrov affair of 1954. Third Secretary and Consul Vladimir Petrov of the Soviet embassy defected and testified that the Soviet embassy had been the center of espionage activities in Australia. As a result, diplomatic relations between the two countries were ruptured; both diplomatic missions, which had been upgraded to embassy status in 1948, were withdrawn in April 1954. Formal relations at this level were not renewed until July 1959.

In the years following the Petrov affair, the anti-Soviet strand of public debate was strengthened. In 1955 the ALP split, principally due to the attitude toward communism (especially in the labor movement). Most of the Roman Catholic strong anticommunist elements in the party left to form the Democratic Labor Party (DLP). The new party became a major voice of anti-Soviet sentiment within the political system, and because the electoral system enabled it to obtain a position of power in Parliament and in the political debate generally far in excess of its popular support, it constituted an important barrier to any attempts to improve Soviet relations.[7] Furthermore, Khrushchev's de-Stalinization campaign and the invasion of Hungary ruptured the unity of the extreme left, severely weakening the small but committed pro-Soviet contingent. Many of those who, while not pro-Soviet at least maintained an open mind about the USSR, were also repelled by these developments, while for the population at large the Soviet invasion of Hungary was brought home graphically by the bloody Soviet-Hungarian water polo final at the Melbourne Olympic Games of 1956.

But while the USSR continued to be perceived as the heart of communist expansionism, in a more immediate sense it was China that came to be perceived as the spearhead of this. The perception of Chinese communism as the main enemy was fueled by the deep-seated racial fears of a hostile Asian environment. Consequently, the Soviet Union became less of an immediate public concern, although there appears to have been little slackening of the more generalized suspicion and hostility.

The emergence of the perception of China as the more immediate threat was accompanied by an improvement in relations with the USSR, even while the view of a monolithic communism with Moscow at its center remained unshaken. Formal diplomatic relations were resumed in 1959 and became so firmly based that the expulsion of the Soviet diplomat, Ivan Skripov, for espionage activities merely resulted in the Soviet expulsion of an Australian diplomat of equivalent rank. In 1964 External Affairs Minister Hasluck became the first minister to visit Moscow. He was followed by a trade mission and, in October 1965, by the signing of a most-favored-nation trade treaty. But despite these obvious signs of improvement, relations remained correct rather than cordial.

The limits to which domestic political opinion would allow governments to move in terms of the relationship with the USSR were graphically illustrated in the second half of the 1960s. As in much of the West, Australian official opinion was slow to recognize the existence, dimensions, and implications of the Sino-Soviet split. Australian acknowledgment of its presence coincided with the escalation of the conflict in Vietnam and the commitment, in 1965, of Australian forces to that conflict. The fracturing of the monolith enabled Australian policymakers to ascribe responsibility for the Vietnam conflict to the Chinese, in the process virtually absolving the Soviet Union of any responsibility at all. This thinking reached its paradoxical and bizarre conclusion with the suggestion in 1965–1966 by External Affairs Minister Hasluck that the Soviet Union might counter Chinese expansionism.[8] While this suggestion was never considered seriously in the government's foreign policy outlook, it was indicative of some flexibility in the officially acceptable perception of the Soviet Union. But the limits to this were shown by the Freeth affair of 1969.

In August 1969 External Affairs Minister Freeth delivered a speech dealing with the appearance of Soviet naval vessels in the Indian Ocean. Freeth declared that although Australia needed to be watchful, it "need not panic whenever a Russian appears. . . . The Australian government at all times welcomes the opportunity of practical and constructive dealings with the Soviet Union. . . . In principle it is natural that a world power such as the Soviet Union should seek to promote a presence and national influence in important regions of the world such as the Indian Ocean area."[9] This recognition of the possibility of common interests and of the existence of legitimate Soviet interests in the region caused a furor of protest and criticism. Although the press and the leadership of the ALP received the speech favorably, the cry from other quarters was deafening. The charge that Freeth was being "soft on the Russians" issued from the backbenchers of his own Liberal party, from the Country party, and from the DLP, whose electoral support the government wanted in the forthcoming election. Many on the left who had been swept up in the romantic attachment to Mao's China also criticized him for taking an overtly anti-Chinese stand by supporting the USSR. That these criticisms found a resonance within the general population is suggested by the fact that Freeth lost his seat in the national elections at the end of the year.

The vigorous negative reaction to Freeth's speech tapped into the latent popular suspicion of the Soviet Union. What had brought this to the surface was the higher Soviet profile in the Australian public eye caused by the invasion of Czechoslovakia in August 1968, and a number of other developments closer to home: the July 1968 incidents involving a Soviet vessel and Australian fishing vessels in the Gulf of Carpentaria; and the Soviet diplomatic and trade offensive that was under way in Southeast Asia, highlighted in June 1969 by Brezhnev's call for an Asian collective security system. Concern over this negative reaction apparently increased Soviet interest in the area, which became more urgent with the beginning of the withdrawal of British forces from East of Suez and the appearance in March 1968 of Soviet ships in the Indian Ocean.

The public debate on the Soviet presence in the Indian Ocean was, for a short time, heated but not very enlightening. The government sought to tread a cautious path between what many saw as the sensible Freeth position and the more hard-line anti-Soviet position of some of its supporters on the right. The government was fortified by the finding of the Parliamentary Joint Foreign Affairs Committee in December 1971 that the Soviet naval presence did not pose any immediate threat to Australia but that any naval buildup was not in Australia's general interests.[10] Nevertheless, reflecting its distrust of the USSR and to protect itself against criticism from the right, the government encouraged the United States to match the level of Soviet forces, even to the extent of offering facilities for U.S. vessels at the naval base at Cockburn Sound near Perth. Even when the Whitlam Labor government came to power in 1972 and supported the principle that the Indian Ocean should be a zone of peace, and therefore one in which Soviet vessels should not be permanently located, its support for the continuing joint Australia-U.S. facility at Northwest Cape in western Australia compromised its ability to take a clear stand against superpower involvement in the region.[11]

Under the Whitlam government (1972–1975) the process of normalization of relations with the USSR was continued. Under the previous government, Soviet trade and shipping offices had been established in Australia, an Australian trade office was established in Moscow, and provision was made for the greater exchange of visits by ministers and parliamentary delegations. The Whitlam government upgraded diplomatic and consular staff in Moscow, signed cultural exchange and scientific and technological agreements, and presided over increased trade between the two countries; and Whitlam became the first prime minister to visit the Soviet Union.[12] The government recognized Soviet sovereignty over the Baltic states in August 1974, but Whitlam raised questions about Jewish emigration and the treatment of political prisoners in the USSR and rejected a Soviet proposal for a joint space science facility in Australia in April 1974.[13]

It was the election of the Fraser Liberal-National (formerly Country) Party coalition government at the end of 1975 that ushered in the post-Petrov nadir in bilateral relations. In the initial stages of the new government's life it was characterized by two strands of opinion on relations with the Soviet Union. A moderate position was espoused by Foreign Minister Andrew Peacock and Trade Minister Peter Nixon, but the harder line associated with Prime Minister Fraser and Defence Minister James Killen prevailed in government thinking.[14] Fraser attributed the deteriorating world situation directly to the USSR. In a visit to China later the same month, Fraser suggested that Australia, China, Japan, and the United States had a common interest in containing Soviet military expansion.[15] Within a decade, the view of which communist power was expansionist and which a potential buffer had been reversed.

The hawkish rhetoric emanating from Canberra was reflective not simply of the different perceptions of a new government and the conservative disposition of the new prime minister, although these were clearly important parts, but also of changed international realities. The decline of détente was proceeding apace during the second half of the 1970s, leaving behind a legacy of distrust and suspicion on both sides. Furthermore from the Australian perspective, the Soviet Union seemed to be even more intrusive into the region than it had been in the past. The Soviet navy continued to maintain a presence in the Indian Ocean, and Soviet interest in the South Pacific was also becoming evident both in terms of increased diplomatic efforts to isolate China and attempts to gain greater access for Soviet fishing fleets to the region's resources. Moreover, there was a disturbing permanence about the Soviet presence in Southeast Asia. Soviet vessels gained port facilities (although not permanent rights) at the former United States naval base at Cam Ranh Bay in Vietnam; and when that country invaded Kampuchea, it received substantial assistance from the USSR. A diplomatic offensive was also mounted to woo the ASEAN states.[16] Thus, in the latter half of the 1970s, the view from Canberra was one that encompassed a much higher Soviet regional profile than had been evident in the past.

The rhetoric of the Australian government was not matched by the adoption of significant measures directed against the Soviet Union. Upon coming to power, the Fraser government reversed its predecessor's recognition of Soviet sovereignty over the Baltic states, barred two Soviet diplomats from working in Australia as a result of their KGB activities, and temporarily froze relations following the discovery of bugging devices in the Australian embassy in Moscow in July 1978. For their part, the Soviet government took offense at the convening of hearings by the all-party Joint Parliamentary Committee on Foreign Affairs and Defence focusing on human rights in the Soviet Union.[17] However, the relationship became most strained following the Soviet invasion of Afghanistan in December 1979. The Australian government was in the forefront in condemning that action. Exchange agreements were canceled, attempts were made to persuade athletes not to attend the Moscow Olympic Games, and official visits were suspended or postponed; but there was no withdrawal of diplomatic representatives, and no meaningful embargo on trade was imposed. Indeed, wheat sales to the USSR seem to have peaked during this period, as the government's selective response to the Afghanistan invasion was meant to ensure that no politically powerful or sensitive sector of Australian society had to share the weight of its moral outrage.

THE CONTEMPORARY SCENE

Relations began to return to normal after the election of the Hawke Labor government in March 1983. Trade relations were normalized in May 1983; and at the end of 1984, a new cultural exchange agreement was signed. Despite a major domestic political issue at the beginning of the new government's term when a Soviet embassy official sought to "entrap" former ALP national secretary and would-be lobbyist David Combe,[18] the Hawke government's position has been much more moderate than that of its predecessor, both in language and content. Foreign Minister Hayden visited the Soviet Union in 1984 and has called for a realistic approach based upon analysis of Soviet actions instead of a simple, ideological response. He has declared that the basis upon which relations rest is sound and that those relations should be extended and strengthened. Furthermore, he has argued that although the USSR would seek to take advantage of favorable opportunities in the Third World, it would be wrong to blame all instability on Soviet machinations. Indeed, despite its superpower status, Hayden argued that the USSR had serious weaknesses both domestically and in its alliance relations.[19]

With the election of Mikhail Gorbachev as general secretary in March 1985, the Soviet profile loomed much larger in the Australian consciousness. Particular aspects of Soviet developments have been covered significantly by the Australian media, including the Chernobyl disaster and the changes being implemented in the USSR. Both the print and electronic media have endeavored to improve and expand their coverage of events in the Soviet Union. Much of the reportage has been factual, but it has been underpinned by a skepticism about the meaning of the changes. Some observers have expressed doubts about Gorbachev's ability to carry the reforms through. Others have questioned the reforms themselves, labeling them purely cosmetic and designed for foreign consumption. It has been suggested that no real changes in human rights policy can have taken place until all are allowed freely to emigrate.[20]

The continuing flow of arms control proposals from Moscow also served to keep the Soviet Union at the forefront of public attention. This issue, with the associated question of foreign threat, captured the attention of the Australians in 1986 because of the publication of the Dibb Report, a review of Australia's defense force capabilities.[21] One of the chief assumptions of this report is that Australia's strategic environment is benign and that "there is every prospect that [these] favourable security circumstances will continue." Although the report also declares that Australian policy should seek "to discourage Soviet naval visits or other unwelcome military access in the South Pacific," it does not portray the Soviet Union as a major direct threat in the absence of full-scale East-West conflict. The government has accepted the basic thrust of this assessment. Defence Minister Beazley has publicly downplayed the Soviet presence at Cam Ranh Bay, declaring it to be a political rather than a military threat.[22] The government also welcomed Soviet signature of the Treaty of Rarotonga establishing a nuclear-free zone in the South Pacific.[23]

The Dibb Report and the Treaty of Rarotonga promoted the ongoing discussion in Australia about Soviet involvement in the region, focusing on the Soviet fishing agreements with Kiribati and Vanuatu and their implications for regional stability and Australian interests. The government's position as enunciated by Foreign Minister Hayden accepts that the Soviet Union has legitimate interests in the Pacific region but is wary about the way such interest could develop. He declared that the Australian government "has some concerns" over the implications of the Kiribati fishing agreement, but "it cannot be said, however, that Australia's security is threatened by any such recent developments."[24] The concerns were revealed in comments he made in 1986: "Where we are concerned is, if the Soviets got onto the ground . . . and were out of control, because they will try to intrude and promote their political interests."[25] He feared that once the USSR gained ground rights in the microstates of the region, it would "engage in activity other than commercial activity . . . which could erode the political base of the host state."[26] Prime Minister Hawke was more forthright. He is reported to have said in a radio interview, "I find it difficult on the basis of Soviet activities around the world over the past couple of decades to accept that they would limit their interests to purely fishing. You would have to think on the evidence of the past that that could be a cloak for other activities."[27]

The Opposition has not accepted the legitimacy of Soviet interests or actions in the region and are alarmed by them. Shadow Defence Minister Sinclair criticized virtually all aspects of the Dibb Report, including its failure to recognize what he believed to be the threat constituted by the expanding Soviet role in the Pacific Ocean. Shadow Foreign Minister Peacock condemned the fishing agreement with Vanuatu and declared that the ultimate Soviet goal is to destabilize the peace of the region.[28] Suspicion of Soviet motives and no recognition of legitimate Soviet interests remain significant perspectives in the Opposition's foreign policy line.

The increased Soviet interest in the region was signaled by Gorbachev's Vladivostok speech on 28 July 1986. In itself, this speech was not a major subject of debate in Australia,[29] but all political sides recognized its implications in terms of the heightened Soviet profile in the region. This has also been reflected at the diplomatic level in Australia by the much more public profile adopted by Soviet diplomats and by the visit of Soviet Foreign Minister Shevardnadze on 3–5 March 1987.[30] Although not the first Soviet minister to visit Australia, Shevardnadze is the most senior, and he is the only serving Politburo member to have made such a visit. His visit did not incite a major public debate,[31] although it was attended by a series of demonstrations against Soviet policy on human rights and Afghanistan. It was, however, an opportunity for the differing perspectives of the various political sides to be aired.

Andrew Peacock accused the government of surreptitiously changing Australian policy toward the USSR and of upgrading relations in a way that "can only undermine our commitment to and reliability as a member of the Western alliance."[32] In the light of what he perceived to be "an increasingly pro-Soviet position," Peacock outlined an agenda of questions that the government should raise with its visitor and called upon it to make clear Australian "opposition to recent Soviet attempts at becoming a major Pacific power."[33] While the stridency of Peacock's statements may have owed something to the combative nature of electoral politics, the logic behind them was quite consistent with the established stance of the Opposition on Soviet matters. While not opposing Shevardnadze's visit, the Opposition saw this as an opportunity for Australia to show its basic hostility toward Soviet aims and actions.[34]

The government's approach to the visit was also consistent with its previous attitudes. The talks between a series of ministers, including the prime minister, and Shevardnadze encompassed the whole gamut of issues, including trade, regional affairs, arms control, human rights, Afghanistan, Kampuchea, and even space cooperation. The contrast between the government's public position as espoused by its foreign minister and that of the Opposition is encapsulated in the comments made by Hayden. "The Soviet Union should be encouraged to take a more constructive and productive economic role in the South Pacific."[35] Both the Australian and Soviet governments evaluated the trip in a cautiously positive light.

Both major parties' perspectives on the Soviet Union have therefore remained basically unchanged in the face of the post-Vladivostok, higher Soviet regional profile. Governmental acceptance of a legitimate Soviet role is accompanied by a wariness about the possible implications of such a development.[36] The Opposition is much more inclined to be openly suspicious of Soviet motives and to deny any legitimacy to their involvement in the region. While some of the differences between the government and the Opposition reflect the exigencies of parliamentary and electoral conflict, the effect of established ideological positions and argumentative lines is also evident.

THE BASIS OF ATTITUDES TOWARD THE SOVIET UNION

In seeking to understand the differing party positions on the USSR, it is important to consider basic party orientations in foreign affairs. There is a strong tradition within the ALP supporting an independent stance for Australia in foreign affairs and expressing an element of skepticism about the value of the alliance with the United States. Neutralist and disarmament sentiments have been prominent within the party, while an emphasis upon the dangers associated with the existence of U.S. communications facilities on Australian soil (at Northwest Cape, Pine Gap, and Nurrungur) has been a continuing theme in party debate. As a result of this general orientation, the party and its leaders have usually been at pains to treat the Soviet Union in a way similar to the United States, seeking to apply similar standards of behavior and lines of criticism to both superpowers.[37] In this regard,

Prime Minister Hawke is an exception. His deep personal emotional commitment to Israel and his experience from the mid-1970s when he believed he had negotiated an agreement for the emigration of substantial numbers of Soviet Jews only to be publicly humiliated when this did not occur have left him distrustful. The more even-handed approach has not meant that the party has muted its criticism of Soviet actions with which it has disagreed. Party members participated in the parliamentary investigation into human rights in 1977–1979, they criticized Soviet intervention in Afghanistan, and have raised questions publicly and privately regarding family reunions and the fate of dissidents. But this approach does mean that the party has been less alarmist and less negative in its public attitude toward the USSR.

In contrast, the position of the Liberal party and its coalition ally has consistently been one that has emphasized the importance of the U.S. alliance and of Australian participation in the Western world. The positive value of the alliance and the U.S. facilities has been continually emphasized. But this does not mean that Liberal party leaders have always merely followed the alliance leader in Washington; in some respects, the position of the Australian government at the end of the 1960s and in the second half of the 1970s was even more hard line than that of the United States. Nevertheless, this sort of orientation has encouraged the party to adopt positions that are much more antagonistic toward the Soviet Union than those of its rival, although they have been concerned as far as possible to insulate the commercial aspects of the relationship from the more overtly political. The party has continued to support expanded trade despite its distrust and dislike of the USSR.

The positions characteristic of both parties are also related to the nature of the Australian political scene. The reservoir of natural support for the Soviet Union is very small in Australia. Despite the impact of Soviet cruise ships on the Australian holiday scene, the visits of Soviet performers, and the numbers of Australians who have visited the USSR, that country does not have a warm place in the hearts of much of the Australian populace. Organizations like the Australia-USSR Society and commercial outlets for Soviet publications and goods seek to improve the Australian perception of the Soviet Union, but their success has been limited. The extreme left is fractured with the result that the solid constituency the USSR enjoyed in the CPA prior to 1956 has gone. Disillusionment over the events of 1956 and 1968 and the romantic attachment of many on the left to China have resulted in the disarray of Soviet support.

The opposite pole of the political spectrum has been much more influential in politics. The DLP had suspicion of the USSR as one of its major policy planks and was able to exercise considerable influence on the course of government policy during the period of its parliamentary existence. But at the community level, too, the organization of the right has been much more extensive and effective than that of the left. This organization has, in part, had an ethnic base. Australia has been the destination for large numbers of refugees from the USSR and Eastern Europe following the war, the Hungarian and Czech invasions, and the difficulties in Poland at the beginning of the 1980s. Some Soviet Jews also emigrated to Australia in the 1970s and 1980s.[38] Many of these ethnic groups have organized their own cultural associations, set up their own newspapers and periodicals, and become active in the political arena on those issues directly concerning them. The views they have expressed have tended to be hostile to communism and to the USSR,[39] and they and their communities have constituted a potent source of anti-Soviet sentiment. But it would be wrong to limit the organization of the right to such ethnic groups. Unlike the left, the right has for a long time had a major publication that consistently has taken a conservative, anti-Soviet line. *Quadrant* stems from the Australian section of the Congress for Cultural Freedom and expresses views consistent with the outlook of that organization. Such views are also consonant with those of wide sections of business and the media, although it is true that many rural producers and businessmen temper their lack of sympathy with the USSR with an eye to the profits that can come from trading with that country. Nevertheless, the "establishment" view of the Soviet Union is overwhelmingly negative, and, given the nature of this group, the influence of this view is considerable.

THE FUTURE

It is difficult to foresee any dramatic improvement in Australian-Soviet ties at the political level. While the Shevardnadze visit clearly marked an improvement in bilateral relations, it did not represent a fundamental shift in the attitudes of either side to the other. From the Soviet side, the visit was part of the wider process of the new diplomacy unfolding under Gorbachev, a diplomacy that is more sophisticated in differentiating between the component actors in the Western alliance systems and accepts the need for different styles of approach in relations with these individual actors. Thus, while accepting that Australia's alliance ties place her firmly in the U.S. camp, Soviet foreign policymakers could acknowledge commonalities between the Soviet and Australian positions on a variety of issues. The most important issues are Australian opposition to SDI and its generalized support for nuclear disarmament and Australian support (against U.S. opposition) for Soviet participation in the Pacific

Economic Cooperation Conference in Vancouver in late 1986. But the central factor behind the visit relates to Gorbachev's Vladivostok speech and the new focus upon Asia and the Pacific that that embodied. Increased Soviet interest in the South Pacific must embrace the major regional capitals; and, within this context, Canberra is the major capital. An extension of Soviet interest and an improvement in its position in the region would hardly be credible if there were no improvement in relations with the major regional power. In this context, the visit to Australia was part of the broader Soviet interest in the region as a whole.

On the Australian side, the visit was an opportunity to give substance to the government's oft-expressed view that, as a medium power, Australia could play an active part in world affairs and could have its voice heard and taken into consideration by the superpowers. It also provided an opportunity to obtain a firsthand look at the changes underway in the USSR and to press the Soviet government on a range of bilateral issues including family reunions and trade. The latter was particularly important given the established Soviet market for grain and the difficulties being experienced by Australian cereal producers as a result of the U.S.-EEC trade war.

The results of the visit were modest but positive. An agreement was signed on regular bilateral consultation, and provision was made for Soviet scientific studies of fish stocks to be undertaken in Australian Antarctic waters. Furthermore, Shevardnadze undertook to follow up a list of cases of Soviet citizens seeking family reunions in Australia; and, accordingly, in July 1987 the Soviet authorities announced that eighty-nine people would be permitted to emigrate to join their families.

The modest results of the Shevardnadze visit accord with the relative standing of both parties. With both firmly entrenched in their existing alliance stances, the possibility of significant improvements in the relationship is negligible. Direct conflicts of interest separate from the more general East-West relationship are few. What is likely is that there will continue to be improvements at the margins of the bilateral political relationship, principally in terms of expanded opportunities for political discussion and possibly for family reunions. But for both parties, the relationship with the other will remain only a minor aspect of their foreign policy outlook.

In the economic sphere, there is greater scope for expansion, although this is principally a function of the low level at which the economic relationship currently rests. Although trade turnover has more than doubled in the 1980s, Australia still imports little from the USSR, and in overall terms the USSR is a minor purchaser of Australian goods. Over the last fifteen years, imports from the USSR have never amounted to more than .07 percent of all Australian imports and exports 5.1 percent of all Australian exports.[40] Little vigorous marketing of its products has been done by either side, and clearly more could be done here. The Soviet market for primary produce, although variable, is quite significant, and Australia's share of this is small. Soviet sale of industrial products has also been retarded in the Australian market,[41] partly because of competitiveness problems with other suppliers and difficulties associated with servicing and spare parts availability. Nevertheless, an organizational vehicle now exists for fostering trade between the two countries, the Australia-USSR Business Council;[42] and Australian businesspeople have been showing increased interest in expanding commercial links with the USSR.[43] With the economic changes underway in the USSR, scope exists for an expansion of this type of interest in the future. In other areas of life, for example in academic and cultural exchanges, the relationship is likely to continue at a moderate level.

Ultimately, improved relations depend upon political figures in both states being able to react in a meaningful fashion to the advances of the other. The new flexibility evident in Soviet policy and associated in the West with the term *glasnost* raises new challenges for Australian policymakers. Those who assume that the Soviet Union has not changed may find themselves out of date, responding in ways that are no longer relevant to the conditions. But similarly, policymakers must not assume that everything has changed, that there are no constants and therefore simply take at face value the positions espoused by the Soviet authorities. To chart an acceptable course between these two alternatives constitutes a real challenge for Australian policymakers. Similarly, the Soviet foreign policymakers need to establish their own constants in the shifting foreign policy environment, and they must be able accurately to signal their positions to their counterparts abroad. If they are unable to do this, the USSR will continue to appear as a lumbering colossus whose internal processes are inadequate to meet the changing foreign policy demands of its leaders and the shifting international environment. Thus a major challenge confronts the foreign policymakers of both countries, and their success in surmounting this challenge will do much to structure the future of Australian-Soviet relations.

NOTES

1. The Russo-Turkish War in which the British supported the Turks, and the Russian push into Central Asia that brought it close to the boundaries of British possessions in India.

2. Teddy J. Uldricks, *Diplomacy and Ideology: The Origins of Soviet Foreign Relations 1917–1930* (London: Sage Publications, 1979), 23.

3. For the best history of the party, see Alastair Davidson, *The Communist Party of Australia: A Short History* (Stanford, Calif.: Hoover Institution Press, 1969).

4. This does not mean that anti-Soviet or anticommunist sentiment was the major reason for the ALP's failure to gain national office during this period. A variety of factors in domestic Australian politics and within the ALP itself were instrumental in the party's continuing lack of success.

5. P. G. Tiver, *The Liberal Party: Principles and Performance* (Brisbane: The Jacaranda Press, 1978), 170–71.

6. Cited in T. B. Millar, *Australia in Peace and War: External Relations 1788–1977* (Canberra: ANU Press, 1978), 343–44.

7. The system of proportional representation used for the Senate meant that the DLP was able to gain representation in this house and, through playing a balance of power role, have a major influence on government policy.

8. See the extracts from some of his speeches cited in Hedley Bull, "Australia and the Great Powers in Asia," Gordon Greenwood and Norman Harper, eds., *Australia in World Affairs 1966–1970* (Vancouver: University of British Columbia Press, 1974), 343. In 1969 Prime Minister Gorton seemed to think the same way; see Millar, 425.

9. Cited in Millar, 344.

10. Ian Clark, "Indian Ocean," in W. J. Hudson ed., *Australia in World Affairs* (Sydney: George Allen & Unwin, 1980), 308.

11. Attempts were made to dissuade the superpowers from extending their rivalry into this region, including the U.S. expansion of its facilities at Diego Garcia, but the government's efforts in this regard were fruitless. Neville Meaney, "The United States," in Hudson, ed., 200.

12. Henry S. Albinski, *Australia's External Policy Under Labor* (Brisbane: University of Queensland Press, 1977), 153–54.

13. Ibid., 259.

14. V. Kubalkova and A. A. Cruickshank, "Australia and Eastern Europe," in P. J. Boyce and J. R. Angel, eds., *Independence and Alliance. Australia in World Affairs 1976–80* (Sydney: George Allen & Unwin, 1983), 175–78.

15. Millar, 424.

16. *Pravda*, 14 August 1978 and 4 October 1978.

17. Report of the Joint Committe on Foreign Affairs and Defence, *Human Rights in the Soviet Union* (Canberra: Australian Government Publishing Service, 1979).

18. This is the term used by the Australian Security Intelligence Organization to describe the relationship between Valerii Ivanov and David Combe.

19. Bill Hayden, "The Soviet Union: Image and Reality, " address to the Australian Institute of International Affairs, Sydney, 25 October 1984; and his ministerial statement,"Australia's Foreign Policy," 26 November 1985.

20. For example, the editorial in *The Sydney Morning Herald*, 18 February 1987 (hereafter cited as *SMH*); *The Australian*, 27–28 December 1986.

21. The complete executive summary is published in *Current Affairs Bulletin* 63, no. 2 (July 1986): 4–18.

22. *SMH*, 5 March 1987.
23. Minister for Foreign Affairs news release, 16 December 1986.
24. Questions asked 13 September 1985. House of Representatives Debate, 30 November 1985, pp. 4063, 4081.
25. Press conference, Kiribati, 15 May 1986.
26. Press conference, Auckland Airport, 13 December 1986.
27. *SMH*, 9 March 1987. This more hard-nosed view may be shared by the Defence Department. See the report that talks of differences between the approaches of the Foreign Affairs and Defence Departments on this issue in *SMH*, 27 March 1987.
28. Press release, 12 December 1986.
29. Although there was a major well-reported conference on the speech and its implications at the Australian Defence Force Academy in March 1987 and one leading daily ran a special "one year after Vladivostok" survey on the anniversary of the speech. *SMH*, 28 July 1987.
30. For example, see the interview with Soviet Ambassador Evgeny Samoteikin, *The Age*, 28 January 1987.
31. Although one capital city daily did run three editorials on the visit. *SMH*, 14 January 1987, 4 March 1987, and 10 March 1987.
32. Press release, "Peacock: Australia-Soviet Relations," 14 January 1987.
33. Press release, "Peacock: An Agenda Urgently Needed for Talks with Soviet Foreign Minister Schevernadze [(sic)]," 21 January 1987.
34. See the report of the meeting between Shevardnadze and Opposition leader Howard in *SMH*, 6 March 1987.
35. *SMH*, 5 March 1987.
36. It may be significant in this regard that a Defence White Paper under consideration by the government at the time of the Shevardnadze visit emphasized Australia's role in the Southwest Pacific, including increased military surveillance in the region. See the report in *SMH*, 18 February 1987.
37. A good example can be seen in the discussion between Foreign Minister Hayden and Soviet spokesman Joe Adamov on a leading television current affairs program. Sydney, Channel 9, 19 November 1986.
38. In 1971, 2.4 percent of the Australian population had been born in Eastern Europe. According to one calculation, some 2,500 people from Eastern Europe, including Soviet Jews, entered Australia in the second half of 1980. Millar, 350, and Kubalkova and Cruickshank, 347.
39. For example, see the publications *Baltic News* (Estonian, Latvian, and Lithuanian Peoples [HELLP]) and *Australian-Ukrainian Review* (Ukrainian Research and Information Center). During 1986 and 1987 there was considerable discussion in some of these publications about the danger of using Soviet evidence in war crimes investigations in Australia.
40. See the figures in successive volumes of *Australian Yearbook* and J. L. Holmes, "Trading with Eastern Europe," *Current Affairs Bulletin*, 62, no. 8 (February 1986): 18.
41. For suggestions by Trade Minister Dawkins that Australian farmers should look at purchasing Soviet farm equipment, see *The Australian*, 9–10 August 1986.

42. For a report of a visit to the USSR by Australian businesspeople, see *Pravda*, 15 May 1985.
43. For example, see the report in *The Australian*, 1–2 August 1987.

14

New Zealand–Soviet Relations

Dalton A. West

THE PERCEPTIONS

Traditionally, four enduring parameters conditioned most New Zealanders' attitudes toward the outside world: its location, size, foreign trade, and British heritage (cultural factors). These have produced the distinguishing characteristics of New Zealand's external policies—a sense of isolation, need for collective security, economic dependency, and Russophobia.[1]

New Zealand's vital statistics are almost the definition of a small state. The population of 3.3 million is geographically isolated from the major centers of power and commerce, and the nation is without significant military or industrial strength. Furthermore, New Zealand is surrounded by great stretches of ocean, and its nearest neighbor is a large, underpopulated, oceanic island continent.

New Zealanders' aspirations reflect the instincts of a practical people not given to many frills, apart from a stunning physical environment, or high-flown ideas.[2] Until the 1970s the New Zealand economy produced a relatively high standard of living but was somewhat dependent on selective markets, especially the United Kingdom, until its entry into the Common Market. Although New Zealand's economy has produced a reasonable standard of living for its citizens in the past, it is far from clear whether this will continue. The economy is fragile and narrowly based on the maintenance of an intensive agricultural industry in a world in which most industrial nations sanction the protection of their own agriculture while continuing to press for the dismantling of barriers to industrial trade. Thus, facing protectionist practices, New Zealand has to diversify its trade through new markets and products.[3] Since the mid-1970s there has been great economic uncertainty, and the Soviet Union came to play a significant role as a necessary alternate market.

It was the imperial, later Commonwealth, connection that determined how New Zealand responded generally and officially toward Russia and later the Soviet Union. Britain was, over much of the nineteenth century, locked in an imperial contest with Russia and, by extension, so was New Zealand. Later, when New Zealand began to take control of its own foreign affairs, these attitudes continued.[4] For instance, New Zealand's Security and Intelligence Service established in the postwar years was modeled on Britain's, and some of the first personnel in New Zealand were British while many more were British trained. The early preoccupations of that service reflected the British and Western anti-Soviet attitudes in the Cold War years.[5]

During the post-Vietnam period, New Zealand was forced to undertake a major reevaluation of its foreign and defense policies. Even before the end of that conflict, the United States had helped to initiate this reevaluation with its 1970 declaration of the Guam (Nixon) Doctrine. The result for New Zealand (and Australia) was the twin policy that focused on "greater self reliance" and keeping "close to home." The first focus is essentially a foreign policy idea expressed in geographical terms. The second is a defense policy with foreign policy implications.[6]

The "close to home" focus was a policy clearly enunciated in the formal foreign policy and defense reviews undertaken by the national government in New Zealand in 1978 and 1983. However, the idea had made its appearance in public debate at the beginning of the 1970s.[7] Following its accession to power late in 1984, the new Labour government appeared to accept this focus in its major pronouncements and incorporated the "close to home" policy in its own review of defense policy completed in 1986.[8] In "The Defence Question: A Discussion Paper," the document that laid out the terms of reference for the full review, the government stated that one of four "key elements" is that "New Zealand's security is indissolubly linked to the stability of the South Pacific." Therefore, at least one key element of New Zealand security thinking—the close to home, Pacific island focus—is emerging as a consistent element regardless of changes in government. It appears to have become a new parameter that must be taken into account when assessing New Zealand–Soviet relations.

The Pacific island region for the most part is made up of micro- or ministates greatly in need of technical and economic assistance. Therefore, this regional focus deserves some special consideration because it makes New Zealand's regional strategic circumstances somewhat different from, say, Europe or even other parts of the Asia-Pacific region. Unlike other parts of the Asia-Pacific region, where nation-building was and is affected by a sense of insecurity and instability, New Zealand's "close to home" area has been virtually politically trouble free until the mid-1980s. The vital question today is whether this condition will continue.

New Zealand's general situation is not a source of either comfort or strength as it looks outward to the world. It has always been apparent to New Zealand that it could not stand alone; and while isolated, it has never been isolationist.[9] Formerly, when the West had a preponderance of nuclear weapons, most (though not all) were reassured by the West's nuclear arsenal and therefore accepting of the weapons in it. But with nuclear parity in the 1970s, this situation changed. Today, many people no longer regard "the enemy" as the source of insecurity; now the enemy is the weapons themselves.[10]

Paradoxically, having reached the point where a nuclear war could not be fought and won, many people feared it might happen. In New Zealand, this new uncertainty simply deepened the insecurities already produced by the country's isolation and deteriorating economic performance. The result was widespread support for separating New Zealand from nuclear relationships on the international scene. This inevitably meant a change in New Zealand–U.S. affairs. Unfortunately, this was incorrectly interpreted by many outside of New Zealand as a tilt away from the United States and a tilt toward the Soviet Union or neutrality.

In New Zealand today many tend to perceive West and East in similar terms. This might be described by the expression "a plague on both your houses." Despite the undeniable influence of Moscow-aligned socialist groups in New Zealand,[11] the mood in the country is not pro-Soviet; indeed, it is probably just the opposite. From the antinuclear perspective, the Soviet Union's status as a nuclear superpower simply made an already unattractive country just that much more so.

The 1986 Defence Committee report titled "Defence and Security: What New Zealanders Want," with its accompanying statistical appendix, is the most comprehensive study of New Zealand attitudes ever undertaken on matters of defense, security, threat, and related matters. It is the most important collection of poll results ever assembled in New Zealand. The results relate to three broad areas: New Zealanders' worldview, threats, and the antinuclear feeling. When questioned on how well New Zealanders feel they could get along with people from different countries, 69 percent said they would get along with the Soviets either not very well (10 percent), rather poorly (8 percent), or didn't know (51 percent). This contrasted sharply with New Zealanders' attitudes about whether they would get along either quite well or very well with Australia (90 percent), South Pacific island countries (69 percent), Britain (90 percent), or the United States (77 percent). When asked which country posed a military threat to New

Zealand, 31 percent answered the Soviet Union, followed by the United States (14 percent), and France (13 percent). However, it should be noted that 11 percent didn't know if any of the countries listed posed a threat, and 32 percent felt outright that there was no threat to New Zealand.[12] When questioned on alliances involving Australia, the United States, or some third party, 72 percent considered that New Zealand should remain in alliances, and of these 66 percent wanted alliances with Australia and the United States.

SOVIET POWER IN THE PACIFIC

Against the background of four historically enduring features in New Zealand's worldview (location, size, foreign trade, British heritage) and two more recent ones (close to home regionalism and the nuclear dilemma), a series of recent international developments reveals New Zealand's current attitudes. Four are particularly relevant regarding the current state of New Zealand–Soviet relations: (1) the growth of Soviet power in the Pacific; (2) New Zealand–Soviet trade; (3) Soviet–South Pacific economic and political initiatives; and (4) recent bilateral political "crises" ("*Lermontov*," diplomatic initiatives, spying).

The Soviet leadership in the last two decades has recognized the value of a powerful navy and other elements of maritime strength to the Soviet Union's international policies and position. A force designed for power projection has highly visible and generally capable surface combatants, organic aviation, and an amphibious capability. These characteristics, which generally were not present in the Soviet navy in the early 1960s, began to appear in the Soviet fleet by the 1970s and increased significantly in the 1980s.[13]

Concern for the buildup of Soviet naval forces in the Pacific has been reflected in the past two defense reviews in New Zealand, the briefing papers prepared by defense staff for the Minister of Defence in October 1984 (later made public by the minister) as well as information prepared by the External Intelligence Bureau for the Parliamentary Committee on Defence. Most New Zealand military intelligence analysts would agree that Soviet forces constitute a "threat" to New Zealand's national interests.[14]

It is not clear that this concern is shared by the Labour government. Because the government has completed its own formal review of these questions but declined to release the background analyses of Soviet power, it is possible to state the government's position but not its analysis.

In "The Defence Question: A Discussion Paper," the government stated that the third most likely of the estimated "threats to New

Zealand territory" was "interference with New Zealand's trade routes, including the mining of New Zealand harbors, by a hostile external power seeking to put pressure on New Zealand, or as a result of a wider regional conflict." It is reasonable to infer that the unidentified power is the Soviet Union. As to the immediacy of the threat, the paper states that "no apparent threat currently exists, but it could arise as a result of a major alteration in the political and strategic environment in South East Asia and the wider Pacific Basin."[15] Therefore, New Zealand's current official threat assessment and that of Australia and the United States differ only in tone and degree and not on whether the Soviet Union is a threat.

NEW ZEALAND–SOVIET TRADE

The diplomatic links between the USSR and New Zealand began in 1944. On the Soviet side, these have remained in some form or another unbroken for more than forty years. On the New Zealand side, the Cold War attitudes (and the Korean War) led to the closure of the New Zealand mission to the USSR in 1950. It was reopened in 1972, following the election of the Labour government under Norman Kirk, and trade increased spectacularly in subsequent years, rising from 1.7 percent of New Zealand's total trade to 5.3 percent by 1982.[16]

From New Zealand's point of view, the composition of trade is even more significant than its size. The bulk of New Zealand's exports have been wool, mutton, and butter with smaller and less regular sales of beef, barley, and cheese. With the exception of wool, these are products New Zealand has had great difficulty in marketing in recent years. The most dramatic example is fatty mutton. In some years, the USSR purchased as much as 75 percent of New Zealand's mutton exports—a commodity for which there is almost no other market available.

The trade is consistently in New Zealand's favor by ratios ranging from 30:1 to 40:1. The trade appears to be unaffected by political disputes between the two countries. New Zealand is a marginal supplier of food materials for the Soviet Union , and the Soviets buy according to their domestic considerations, such as harvest failures, trade embargoes, and other factors that produce shortfalls. New Zealand's relatively low prices have also given it a competitive advantage. Occasionally, it ranks ahead of some COMECON suppliers (for example, Mongolia, Romania, and Bulgaria) as a supplier of meat to the Soviet market.

Because the Soviets tend to ship their trade in their own vessels to save hard currency, the great expansion in Soviet–New Zealand trade has increased merchant ship visits. Two Soviet shipping companies (Baltic and Far East) regularly service New Zealand. New Zealand in turn provides repair and maintenance facilities for the Soviet merchant marine and fishing fleets. In 1972, nine Soviet-registered ships departed from New Zealand ports; in 1983, this had increased to 306. In the peak year of 1981, there were 377 Soviet vessels, about 1 in 7 vessels in New Zealand ports.[17]

The Soviet Union and New Zealand have had both gains and losses in their trade relationship. As that relationship has stimulated the growth of more positive attitudes within the public and among New Zealand officials, the Soviets have to some extent reaped significant rewards. For example, although New Zealand condemned the Soviet invasion of Afghanistan, the conservative prime minister, Robert Muldoon, was reluctant to follow the United States' example of trade sanctions. He told the United States that "New Zealand has no intention of committing economic suicide."

The growth of Soviet shipping in the region, however, has generated some anxieties. Apart from the ships' potential military intelligence roles, there is some concern that New Zealand could become too dependent on its overseas trade in Soviet ships. New Zealand authorities are also concerned about what are considered unfair shipping practices of the Soviet and Eastern-bloc countries, notably in competitive pricing, which will undoubtedly continue as an irritant in bilateral trade relations.

However, the New Zealand government's immediate concern is maintaining bilateral trade at a high and even level. To this end, Overseas Trade Minister Mike Moore led a thirty two-member trade mission to the Soviet Union in September 1986. This was the first New Zealand ministerial-led mission (thus underscoring its importance), although this was not the first visit by a trade mission or by a trade minister. New Zealand hoped to upgrade trade relations with its seventh-largest trading partner and dampen the massive fluctuations in trade (as much as $100 million in any given year).

New Zealand's Soviet mission toured the Soviet Far East as the Soviet Union tried to impress upon New Zealand the importance of that region for their future economic relations. The Soviets wanted to tie trade to other arrangements, including dry-docking and repair facilities for their ships in New Zealand and Aeroflot landing rights for crew exchanges. New Zealand refused, saying this would seriously compromise New Zealand's relations with the islands, notably Kiribati and Vanuatu but also Fiji and Papua New Guinea. The Soviet Union had made similar offers to the island countries but was rebuffed partly because of New Zealand pressure.

Soviet economic interest in New Zealand includes fishing. Its fishing in New Zealand waters has been substantial. Between 1971 and 1977 the Soviets harvested an average of over 70,000 tons annually.

Since 1978 with the introduction of the New Zealand 200–mile economic zone and licensing, this level has been reduced. The Soviets have sought joint ventures with New Zealand companies to increase their access to New Zealand fishing.[18]

The overall official New Zealand attitude toward the Soviet Union's trade, fishing, and significant scientific interests in the Antarctic is most clearly reflected in the annual (up to 1984) communiqués of the ANZUS Council, composed of Australia, New Zealand, and the United States. While continuing to deny or limit Soviet military and political participation in the South Pacific, for a decade or more the three powers recognized the economic, scientific, and other rights of the Soviet Union in the area. Without wishing to encourage wider Soviet participation in the region, particularly with the smaller island countries, the three ANZUS powers hoped that the Soviet Union would pursue its rights openly and legitimately. This policy has been confirmed repeatedly since 1984 by the new Labour government.

NEW SOVIET INITIATIVES

Between 1980 and 1984, despite the progress in trade relations, political affairs between New Zealand and the Soviet Union were at a low ebb. Disapproval of Soviet activities in Afghanistan and Poland led New Zealand to cancel planned meetings of the Joint Trade Commission in 1980 and 1982. The Soviet ambassador was expelled for passing money to the pro-Moscow Socialist Unity Party of New Zealand in 1980, and the New Zealand ambassador to Moscow was recalled.

It was not until 1984, on the eve of Labour's electoral victory, that Soviet and New Zealand ambassadors were exchanged once again. Therefore, Soviet initiatives during the current Labour government took place against a background of renewed diplomatic presence, difficulties in the ANZUS relationship that gave the Soviets opportunities they clearly hoped to exploit, and difficulties in relations between some of the island countries and the United States that the Soviet Union also sought to take advantage of.[19]

In addition to a considerable increase in cultural exchanges involving entertainers, academics, politicians, and trade unionists—interest groups the USSR traditionally seeks to influence—there has been a noticeable increase in visits by students, church leaders, and peace groups.[20] Not all of these visits produce the desired results for the Soviet Union. A New Zealand delegation returned from youth and student gatherings in the Soviet Union convinced that the Soviets' relations with the United States, Europe, and Asia took priority over the Pacific. The New Zealanders doubted that the Soviet Union could make any significant diplomatic or strategic headway in the South Pacific until its priorities changed.[21]

Politically, the Soviet Union stated its support for New Zealand's position on ship visits and supported the concept of a South Pacific Nuclear-Free Zone for the Pacific (SPNFZ), although not without serious reservations. The Soviets had been so anxious to take advantage of the ANZUS controversy that they misrepresented New Zealand's position on a number of occasions and forced the New Zealand government to make an official protest. Although the Soviet Union has both supported and been supported by a considerable section of the New Zealand peace movement on the SPNFZ, ship visits, and the legislation related to these issues, it would not be correct to imply that the New Zealand government has been equally supportive.[22]

In 1986 the Soviet Union launched two significant political initiatives that directly involved New Zealand. The first resulted from the new Soviet policy of *glasnost* and concerned the new Soviet attitude toward public relations. It began with the first news conference by the Soviet ambassador to New Zealand in March 1986. The second was the visit to New Zealand by Soviet Deputy Foreign Minister Mikhail Kapitsa in August.

Although the Soviet ambassador was appointed in June 1984, he held his first formal press conference in March 1986 confirming the Soviet policy of *glasnost*. He spoke openly about the new policy of media openness, stating the embassy's willingness to hold regular press conferences twice a week. He also called for greater political cooperation with New Zealand, including regular political consultations and exchanges of "parliamentarians," noting that the USSR's political relations with Australia were ahead of New Zealand.[23]

This 1986 public relations initiative coincided with a greater involvement in the political dialogue in New Zealand. The most obvious involvement was increased Soviet commentary in New Zealand on the views of the National Party Opposition and a campaign of full-page advertisements in local newspapers on key issues.[24]

The visit by Mikhail Kapitsa was significant for two reasons. First, he indicated that the Soviet Union would sign the relevant protocols to the South Pacific Nuclear-Free Zone (SPNFZ). This seemed to compliment New Zealand on the role it played in supporting the Treaty of Rarotonga. However, it was a curiously placed emphasis, since Australia had played the leading role in the effort.[25] He also raised the issue of possible military collaboration with New Zealand. Specifically, in an initiative modeled somewhat on the confidence-building aspects of the Helsinki accords of the mid-1970s, he proposed an agreement between the two countries on early notification of ships' movements into each other's waters.[26]

Kapitsa's trip occurred in the wake of Gorbachev's 28 July 1986 Vladivostok speech and was designed to promote the ideas outlined in that speech. The New Zealand prime minister rejected the idea of military collaboration, saying that New Zealand was still in ANZUS. The prime minister further stated that the best thing the Soviet Union could do was to keep its vessels as far away from New Zealand as the Royal New Zealand Navy was kept from the Soviet Union.[27]

A "nonevent" that was possibly significant was the nonvisit by Foreign Minister Eduard Shevardnadze and some of his entourage, including the propagandist Joe Adamov, who made it to Australia but not across the Tasman to New Zealand late in 1986. It was widely believed that New Zealand did not wish to welcome a Soviet delegation at this level. The only high-level member of that visiting team to visit New Zealand was Vsevolod Ovchinnikov, a deputy editor of *Pravda*, who clearly attempted to appeal to two of New Zealand's prevailing moods, nationalism and neutralism: "New Zealand must be New Zealand . . . to be outside the rivalry of big powers is for the benefit of all the nations in the South Pacific."[28]

THE SOVIET UNION, NEW ZEALAND, AND THE PACIFIC ISLANDS

The role of the islands and their presumed vulnerability significantly affect New Zealand's attitudes toward the Soviet Union. Because New Zealand has a statutory security responsibility for Niue, Tonga, and the Cook Islands, New Zealand's perception of the Soviet threat to these islands is different from and apparently more significant than the threat it perceives to its own national security. The islands are deemed much more vulnerable than New Zealand.

Soviet activities in the smaller island countries began in a concerted way with the Soviet attempt to establish full relations with those nations in the early 1970s. These efforts were blunted by a series of moves by the ANZUS powers.[29] New Soviet initiatives in the 1980s are discussed elsewhere in this volume. Because of New Zealand's concern about the small island states' vulnerability, it opposed the granting of shore rights to the Soviet Union when the USSR negotiated a fishing agreement with Kiribati. In this action, New Zealand enjoyed the full support of the United States and Australia. In taking this position on Soviet activities in the islands, the New Zealand government is following its customary, bipartisan policy that has two dimensions: concern over what a Soviet presence could bring and a desire to avoid superpower competition in the region.

New Zealand's opposition to Soviet initiatives in the islands (and similar objections to Libyan activities) has not had a happy effect on New Zealand's relations with some island countries. To many islanders, New Zealand's attitude seems to be quite hypocritical since New Zealand has a fishing agreement with the Soviet Union and enjoys diplomatic relations with a wide variety of nations. They ask why they should not do the same.

Clearly, two of the effects of Soviet initiatives have been to reveal New Zealanders' deep-seated suspicions about Soviet behavior and to create frictions between New Zealand and its island neighbors. These suspicions were aggravated by the circumstances surrounding the February 1987 sinking of the Soviet cruise liner *Lermontov* just off New Zealand, an affair in which the two sides traded accusations regarding the nature and degree of their culpability. New Zealand's expulsion of the Soviet diplomat Sergei Budnik as a KGB officer in April of that year together with the Soviet retaliatory expulsion of the New Zealander David Nicol from Moscow did not help matters.

CONCLUSION

Despite the Soviet efforts to improve relations with the Asia-Pacific region as a whole, and the specific gestures toward New Zealand, New Zealanders' current attitudes continue to show a mixture of feelings of geographic isolation, vulnerability and dependency, and preference for collective security in association with the Anglo-American part of the Western community. However, a historic Russophobia seems to be giving way to new concerns and attitudes that combine elements of regionalism and parochialism at the official level, though at a much higher level of understanding of the Soviet Union than a decade earlier,[30] with a continuing lack of knowledge and, perhaps, indifference in the general public.

NOTES

1. In a larger study some effort must be made to understand Soviet perceptions of New Zealand and the Southwest Pacific, the context of those perceptions, and the policy objectives that the Soviet leadership sets for itself in the region. Paul Dibb, *Soviet Strategy Towards Australia, New Zealand and Oceania* (Canberra: Strategic and Defence Studies Centre, Australian National University, 1984) is thorough but slightly dated; see Dalton A. West, "Soviet Perceptions of the South Pacific: Context and Policy Objectives," in Owen Harries, ed., *The Red Orchestra*, (Stanford, Calif.: Hoover Institution, 1988).
2. D.B.G. McLean, "New Zealand's Defence and Strategic Interests in Asia," paper presented at United States-Asia Institute, Washington, D.C., 1984. Many caught up in the debate of the moment over nuclear issues might

dispute this last point, but they forget that it is the antinuclear feelings in the world that have projected New Zealand to center stage, momentarily, and not the reverse.

3. Sir Frank Holmes, *New Zealand at the Turning Point*, report of the Task Force on Economic and Social Planning (Wellington, 1976), 166–89; David Lange, "The Fourth Labour Government: New Directions in New Zealand Foreign Policy," in Hyam Gold ed., *New Directions in New Zealand Foreign Policy* (Dunedin: Otago University, 1985), 27–35.

4. Richard Kennaway, *New Zealand Foreign Policy, 1951–1971* (Wellington: Hicks Smith & Sons, 1972), 13–31; Michael Stenson, "The Origins and Significance of Forward Defence in Asia," *New Zealand in World Affairs* 1 (Wellington: Price Milburn, 1977): 177–86.

5. Although flawed in some respects, the most comprehensive treatment of this subject is Michael Parker, *The SIS: The New Zealand Security Intelligence Service* (Palmerston North: The Dunmore Press, 1979), 44–46.

6. Sir Alan Watt, "The Interests of the Great Powers," in Mary Boyd, ed., *Pacific Horizons: A Regional Role For New Zealand* (Wellington: Price Milburn, 1972), 56–60; Dalton A. West, "The 1983 Defence Review: Prospects and Implications," *New Zealand International Review* 9, no. 3 (May/June 1984): 2–6.

7. Norman Kirk, "New Zealand and its Neighbours," (Wellington: New Zealand Institute of International Affairs, 1971) (Kirk was Labour prime minister from 1972 until his death in 1974); F.L.W. Wood, "Political and Strategic Background," *Defence Perspectives* (Wellington: Price Milburn, 1972), 21–35.

8. See New Zealand government, *The Defence Question: A Discussion Paper* (Wellington, 1985) (hereafter cited as *Defence Question*); New Zealand, Defence Committee of Enquiry, *Defence and Security: What New Zealanders Want: Report of the Defence Committee of Enquiry* (Wellington, 1986) (hereafter cited as *Defence and Security*); New Zealand government, *Defence of New Zealand: Review of Defence Policy, 1987* (Wellington, 1987) (hereafter cited as *Defence Policy*).

9. D.B.G. McLean, "New Zealand's Strategic Position and Defence Policies," in Desmond Ball, ed., *The ANZAC Connection* (Sydney: Allen & Unwin, 1985), 1–14 and D.B.G. McLean, "New Zealand: Isolated But Not Isolationist," paper presented at the International Studies Association Conference on Small Countries in Large Alliances, Philadelphia, 1981.

10. Michael Howard, "Reassurance and Deterrence: Western Defense in the 1980s," *Foreign Affairs* 61, no. 2 (Winter 1982/1983): 309–324; Helen Clark, "Establishing a Nuclear-Free Zone in the South Pacific," in Hyam Gold, ed., *New Directions in New Zealand Foreign Policy* (Auckland: Benton Ross, 1985), 121–26.

11. On activities of the Socialist Unity party see Barry Gustafson, "New Zealand and the Soviet Union," in H. Albinski and L. Vasey, eds., *Strategic Imperatives and Western Responses in the South and Southwest Pacific* (Honolulu: Pacific Forum, 1986), 85–86; a representative collection of authors and materials of this genre can be found in Peace Movement Aotearoa, *Beyond ANZUS:*

Alternatives for Australia, New Zealand and the Pacific (Auckland: Benton Ross Publishers, 1985).

12. *Defence and Security: Annex*, 18 and 37.
13. For an analysis of the growth of the Soviet naval fleet in the Pacific, see Paul Dibb, *The Soviet Union as a Pacific Military Power* (Canberra: Strategic and Defence Studies Centre, Australian National University, 1984), 9–12.
14. New Zealand Ministry of Defence, *Briefing Papers Prepared For The Ministry of Defence* (Wellington: Ministry of Defence, 1984), 5–6; Merwyn Norrish, "The Prospect for New Zealand," *New Zealand Foreign Policy: Choices, Challenges, and Opportunities* (Wellington: New Zealand Institute of International Affairs, 1984), 94–95.
15. New Zealand, Institute of International Affairs, *The Defence Question: A Discussion Paper* (Wellington: Government Printer, 1985).
16. New Zealand Department of Statistics, *Report and Analysis of External Trade 1972–84* (Wellington: Government Printer, 1985). For good surveys of the trading relationship, see Barry Gustafson, "New Zealand and the Soviet Union," in E. Olssen, ed., *New Zealand Foreign Policy and Defence* (Dunedin: University of Otago, 1977), 107–19 and "New Zealand Trade With the Soviet Union," in John Henderson, ed., *Beyond New Zealand: The Foreign Policy of a Small State* (Auckland: Methuen, 1980), 87–92.
17. New Zealand Department of Statistics, *New Zealand Transport Statistics 1972–83* (Wellington: Government Printer, 1984); J. M. Lane, "Mutual Advantage: Relations between New Zealand and the Union of Soviet Socialist Republics 1972–1985," unpublished M.A. thesis, University of Auckland, 1986.
18. "Soviet Fishing in NZ Struggling to Expand," *Christchurch Press*, 6 September 1987.
19. P. Lewis Young, "Soviets Seek to Exploit US Pacific Insensitivities," *Pacific Defence Reporter* (June 1985): 7–8; Scott Allen, "The South Pacific: Setting Priorities," *Proceedings, U.S. Naval Institute*, 113, no. 7 (July 1987): 50–56
20. Barry Gustafson, "New Zealand and the Soviet Union," in *Strategic Imperatives*, 87.
21. Kim Small, "Nakhodka: Discussing the Pacific," *New Zealand International Review* 11, no. 6 (November–December 1986): 15–16.
22. Richard Long, "Big Powers Eyeing Pacific, Says PM," *The Dominion*, 31 July 1987. On the reasons for denying Adamov a visa, see *New Zealand Herald*, 26 November 1986.
23. *New Zealand Herald*, 26 March 1986.
24. "Nuclear Blasts Should Be Banned," a *Pravda* editorial in *Evening Post*, 23 December 1986; criticisms of the Opposition National Party in *Dominion*, 1 October 1986, and *Evening Post*, 1 November 1986.
25. Ramesh Thakur, *In Defence of New Zealand: Foreign Policy Choices in the Nuclear Age* (Wellington: New Zealand Institute of International Affairs, 1984), 137–38; Greg Fry, "Australia, New Zealand and Arms Control in the Pacific Region," in Desmond Ball, ed., *The ANZAC Connection* (Sydney: Allen & Unwin, 1985), 91–118.
26. *New Zealand Herald*, 27 August 1986.

27. *New Zealand Herald*, 28 August 1986; *Dominion*, 27 August 1986; Ian Templeton, "Lange Brushes Soviet Move Into ANZUS Void," *Bulletin* 180/5535 (9 September 1986), 129–30.
28. Vsevolod Ovchinnikov interview, *New Zealand Herald*, 9 March 1987, p. 3.
29. Dalton A. West, "Perspectives on Russia in the Pacific," in E. Olssen and W. Webb, eds., *New Zealand Foreign Policy and Defence* (Dunedin: University of Otago, 1977), 90–106, and "The Soviet Union's Relations with New Zealand," *The Round Table: Journal of Commonwealth Affairs*, no. 278 (April 1980): 195–209.
30. Dalton A. West, "Soviet Union and the Pacific," in John Henderson, ed., *Beyond New Zealand: The Foreign Policy of a Small State* (Auckland: Methuen, 1980), 173–78.

15

Pacific Island Perceptions of Soviet Security and Economic Interests in the Region

Pamela Takiora Ingram Pryor

SOVIET INVOLVEMENT AND POLICY IN THE ISLAND REGION

Historical Background

Until recently Soviet relations with the Pacific islands have been minimal; their involvement has been limited to a keen interest in oceanographic research for scientific purposes. Although their interest could previously be labeled purely scientific, it is clear that knowledge of seabed contours, ocean currents, and water salinity and temperature are all vital for tracking submarines. The Soviets have been collecting these data in the Pacific for over twenty years. Western security analysts are well aware that submarine warfare will more than likely be the deciding factor in any future conflict between the superpowers using conventional forces.

Although Soviet presence in the Pacific islands has recently increased, they have been in the Pacific for many years, initially with trawlers and scientific vessels plying Pacific waters. As early as 1976 the Soviets had established diplomatic relations with the Tongan and Western Samoan governments, and the Soviet ambassador reportedly offered Tonga economic assistance in exchange for port facilities for the Soviet fishing fleet. By 1978 Soviet representatives were negotiating a fisheries treaty with the Cook Islands (these negotiations were ultimately unsuccessful).

The Australia and New Zealand governments reacted to these Soviet overtures by increasing aid to the region and offering other assistance. They recognized that the lines of communication with

Australia's major trading partner (Japan) and with its major ally (the United States) run through the region and could be put at risk.[1]

Fisheries Agreements

In August 1985 the Soviet Union concluded a fisheries agreement with Kiribati that lasted for twelve months. Despite the outcry from the United States and others in the Western alliance, President Ieremiah Tabai insisted that the fishing agreement was "simply a commercial deal," much the same as the Americans selling wheat to the Russians.

The agreement was terminated by Kiribati in 1986 when the Soviet Union claimed that it was not catching sufficient fish to justify the fee and refused to renew at the same price as the first agreement. Some observers see this as evidence that the Soviet Union was interested only in fishing, "that its intentions and motives in the South Pacific are benign, and that those who speak differently are alarmist. They point out that, in refusing to pay an extra half million dollars in fees for the fish, the Soviets obviously had no great strategic stake or interest" in Kiribati.[2]

The Soviet fishing agreement with Vanuatu, signed in January 1987, provided for one year's access to that country's fishing grounds for eight Soviet vessels for a payment of US$1.5 million, and "shore access for provisioning, rest and relaxation and for transhipment of the catch."[3] This is the first agreement to give the Soviets shore access.

The outcry from the United States and its Pacific partners, Australia and New Zealand, was vociferous and in some ways patronizing. In response, some Pacific islanders argue that most island nations understand Soviet motives and have the administrative capability of dealing with the Soviet Union. They maintain that the island nations have the same right to negotiate fisheries agreements with the Soviets as do Australia, New Zealand, and the United States.

New Policies and Diplomatic Initiatives

In addition to the Soviets' seeking fishing agreements with Pacific island countries, they have also demonstrated a new, more aggressive foreign policy toward the islands. In his July 1986 Vladivostok speech Gorbachev referred to the island nations specifically, expressing interest in promoting relations with them.

This was the first time in over a decade that the Soviet Union had focused specifically on the island states.[4] Official and semiofficial statements from Moscow since then have reiterated five themes: (1)

criticism of U.S. policy in Micronesia; (2) support for New Caledonia's independence (with an attempt to link Micronesia and New Caledonia in UN debates); (3) support for the South Pacific Nuclear-Free Zone (SPNFZ), and the New Zealand government's antinuclear policy; (4) condemnation of the ANZUS alliance; and (5) promotion of the Soviet notion of "equal security."[5]

Although Moscow has no embassy in the Pacific islands, the level of diplomatic activity has increased. The Soviet missions in Canberra and Wellington are holding fisheries talks with Papua New Guinea, the Solomon Islands, and Fiji.

Accompanying increased diplomatic efforts, there has been a restructuring of the Soviet bureaucracy to buttress this increased interest in the Pacific. In June 1986 the Kremlin created a new bureau within the Foreign Ministry, the Pacific Ocean Department, and began dispatching high-level trade and goodwill delegations throughout the region.

The Soviets have expressed opposition to the Compacts of Free Association negotiated by the United States with the Federated States of Micronesia, the Marshall Islands, and Palau and the terms of the Commonwealth of the Northern Marianas. The Soviets view Micronesia as a strategic trust of the United Nations, not of the United States. In an interview, Soviet UN delegate Valentin Berezovsky stated that Micronesia is a "strategic territory for the preservation of international peace and security, but not for the unilateral interest of the U.S., or for making it a strategic territory of the U.S."[6] The Soviet Union supports the nuclear-free constitution of Palau, stating that it is in favor of the creation of denuclearized zones in any part of the world.

It is clear the Soviet Union is trying to develop a greater degree of political influence in the region and is claiming rights of access to all parts of the globe as a superpower. Pacific island observers note that the new Soviet foreign policy uses economic diplomacy to complement political diplomacy. On his visit to Australia in March 1987 Foreign Minister Shevardnadze stated that he expected political influence to follow the establishment of commercial ties, but he ruled out any attempts to establish a military base. According to one analyst, "the Soviet Union's prime interest appears to be in establishing constituencies, reducing western influence and in detaching the islands from a commitment to the West."[7]

Island Views of the Soviet Initiatives

It is important to look at the issues from the islanders' point of view. It can be argued that until recently, Pacific islanders have viewed the

Soviets through the eyes of others—as ruthless enemies who should be feared and kept at a distance. This is the traditional view of the United States and its allies and probably also is a perception of some of the educated elite in the islands. However, this is changing, especially among those Pacific islanders who are members of the Non-aligned Movement (mostly the Melanesian countries). Even some of the more conservative countries now have dealings with the Soviets. Tonga, which is one of the most conservative island countries and usually takes pro-Western positions on issues, recently made arrangements for its crown prince to visit the Soviet Union.

The average citizen in the islands, however, would be unlikely to have any definite perception of the Soviets. Until recently Pacific islanders had no direct experience with the Soviets, and, unlike some Asian countries, have had no real negative experience. Now that fisheries agreements have been established, there is more understanding of the Soviets. These agreements have caused great concern on the part of the United States and others who question the ability of Pacific islanders to negotiate with the Soviets. While it is clear that much remains to be learned in dealing with the Soviets, this criticism is seen by some islanders as a form of intellectual arrogance on the part of the United States, Australia, and New Zealand, and it has caused some problems in the Pacific island countries' relationships with these nations.

The image of the Soviet Union in the Pacific islands under the Gorbachev administration is more positive than it was a decade ago. Obvious economic benefits have accrued from the fisheries agreements, and the Kiribati agreement was adhered to quite stringently by the Soviets. In addition, the Soviet Union signed the protocols to the South Pacific Nuclear Free Zone Treaty (commonly known as the Treaty of Rarotonga) in late 1986. Although there were some qualifications in the Soviet accession, this improved their relations with the Pacific island countries, who had asked all world nuclear powers to sign the protocols. To the dismay of island leaders, Britain, France, and the United States stated their refusal to sign the treaty early in 1987.

Thus, the Soviet Union appears to be taking positive steps to support the Pacific islanders' economic and political objectives in the region.

RELATIONS OF THE WESTERN ALLIANCE WITH THE PACIFIC ISLANDS

The United States

Several factors shape U.S. interests in the Pacific islands region. First, the United States has a national presence in the region with its territories of Guam and American Samoa, the Commonwealth of the Northern Marianas, and its close ties with the emerging entities of the Republic of the Marshall Islands, the Federated States of Micronesia, and the Republic of Palau. In addition, the state of Hawaii is the site of the largest U.S. military base in the region.

The United States also has vital security interests in Australia and New Zealand and has other mutual security treaties with individual Southeast Asian countries. The Pacific islands region is strategic to the United States because the lines of communication with the Western Pacific and Asia pass through the region.

According to the State Department, U.S. policy in the region provides for (1) denying the region to the Soviet Union; (2) ensuring the United States' operational ability and access to the region in times of crisis; (3) securing the support of dependable allies in the region through assured port access; and (4) encouraging friendly democratic governments and a harmonious environment for Western interests in the region.[8]

The tenor of policy of the United States toward the Pacific islands region has been one of indifference since the Second World War. Aid to the region (excluding the U.S. territories and colonies) is minimal and efforts at lobbying within Congress and the administration have been virtually nonexistent. Yet the region represents "the rear flank of American maritime strategy in the North Pacific, and so would be of importance to the U.S. in the event of a crisis."[9] Pacific islanders are also aware that the United States has 41,000 soldiers defending the demilitarized zone in South Korea. South Korea has long served as a key link in a pro-Western defensive chain that includes Japan, Taiwan, the Philippines, Australia, and New Zealand. Because of the Soviet Union's demonstrated intention of expanding its military and diplomatic presence in the Pacific, the United States has increasingly recognized that chain's importance.

There is growing resentment toward the United States in the Pacific islands. Initially this was a result of the refusal of the United States to recognize coastal jurisdiction within states' 200–mile Exclusive Economic Zones (EEZs) over highly migratory species of fish. As tuna is a major resource for many of the resource-poor islands, the illegal fishing of island nations' waters by U.S. fishing fleets caused much resentment. The 1987 Fisheries Agreement between the Forum Fisheries Agency member states and the United States (which took four years to negotiate) will help in improving relationships. However, the agreement has not yet been ratified by the U.S. Congress and U.S. fishing boats continue to fish illegally.

The refusal of the United States to sign the protocols to the Treaty of Rarotonga has also increased the dissatisfaction of the Pacific island nations. In a statement explaining the refusal to sign, the U.S. State Department declared that "in view of the United States' global security interests and responsibilities, we are not, under current circumstances, in a position to sign the SPNFZ Protocols." Apparently the United States perceives its strategy of nuclear deterrence to be threatened by nuclear-free zones. Many Pacific islanders interpret this refusal to sign simply as U.S. support for the French presence in the Pacific and particularly of unpopular French nuclear testing at Moruroa Atoll.

Some island countries also resent the alleged "bullying" by the United States of New Zealand over the rift in the ANZUS Treaty. These nations (especially the Melanesians) feel that the United States is punishing New Zealand for its antinuclear stance, which is very popular in New Zealand and in the region generally.

Soviet policies contrast favorably with these U.S. positions, causing the USSR to be perceived in a more positive light.

France

French policies in their territories in the Pacific are causing major problems both for France and for its allies. As noted previously, U.S. support for France's nuclear testing program is adding to anti-U.S. sentiment. This nuclear testing has been unpopular with the Pacific island countries since they gained their independence. France has tried to justify its testing program, stating it is necessary in order to provide an independent nuclear deterrent. These arguments carry little weight in the region, as it is well known that the United States has offered nuclear testing facilities in the Nevada desert to the French. The French have refused these offers.

A real crisis in the region that has polarized most of the island countries against the French is the issue of France's refusal to grant independence to the indigenous Melanesians (Kanaks) of New Caledonia. The South Pacific Forum supports the Kanaks in their struggle for independence. As a result of the Forum's request, in December 1986 the General Assembly voted to reinscribe New Caledonia on the UN list of nonself-governing territories through the Committee on Decolonization.

Since the resolution was adopted, however, France has chosen to ignore it and in September 1987 held a referendum on the independence issue. The Kanaks boycotted the referendum, and the majority of the non-Kanak population (58 percent) voted to maintain the status quo, whereby New Caledonia would remain part of France.

France has stepped up its diplomatic efforts by distributing aid more generously throughout the region. Offers of aid and disaster relief assistance were made to the Cook Islands and the Solomon Islands. These increased diplomatic efforts and aid have contributed to division and tension within the region. To add to its troubles there, the independence movement in French Polynesia, while still nascent, is gaining strength and is also seeking Forum assistance.

Japan

Since the Second World War, Japan's role in the Pacific islands had also been minimal. However, that too is changing rapidly. The Japanese are becoming concerned about the growing anti-U.S. sentiment and increased Soviet interest and activity in the region. It is significant that Japan's Foreign Minister Tadashi Kuranari visited Fiji in January 1987; Fiji has courted Japan to become its second major economic benefactor (after the European Economic Community). Japan is also the second largest donor of bilateral aid to Tonga and Kiribati.

While on his trip, Kuranari pledged an expanded aid program in technical training, support for regional initiatives and arrangements, and efforts to preserve regional peace and stability in the region. The new policy represents a significant shift in emphasis in Japan's attitude toward the region.

Kuranari stated in Suva: "However much one may wish it otherwise, peace and stability cannot be maintained without adequate thought being given to global security considerations. This principle does not allow any exception for the Pacific region."[10] Japan is alarmed by growing Soviet influence in the region, but there may also be a link between these recent shifts in policy and efforts by Japan to establish a space tracking and launching platform in Kiribati for security purposes.

Australia

Australian policy in the Pacific islands region is concerned mostly with the southwest Pacific. The Australian government has stated: "We share a common concern with these countries to strengthen regional stability and to limit the potential for external powers to introduce tension or conflict."[11]

Australia has special defense arrangements with Papua New Guinea, which are formalized by an agreement that commits them to consultation and cooperation on the full range of defense issues.

Papua New Guinea's geographic location makes its security a major factor in Australia's strategic policies.

Although Australia's policy focuses on the southwest, the Pacific islands region as a whole contains important trade routes and approaches to Australia's east coast, where most of the major population centers are located. Thus, according to an Australian government statement, "an unfriendly maritime power in the area could inhibit our freedom of movement through these approaches and could place in doubt the security of Australia's supply of military equipment and other strategic material from the United States."[12]

Australia has extensive aid, trade, commercial, and diplomatic relations with Pacific island countries. It maintains diplomatic missions in all independent countries except Tuvalu and has a consulate in Noumea. Although relations with most of the countries in the region are good, there are some problems. Vanuatu recently suspended Australia's defense contacts following Australian criticism of Port Vila's Libyan connection and subsequent allegations by Vanuatu that Australia was conducting intelligence activities in the region.[13]

After the 14 May 1987 military coup in Fiji, Australia strongly criticized that action and the Fijian Alliance Party leadership. Australia suspended its defense cooperation program with Fiji. Pacific islanders were concerned that some form of intervention in Fiji was contemplated by New Zealand and by Australia, which had a naval vessel standing off the coast of Suva. The Australian prime minister caused further strains in the relationship with the island Forum countries at the Apia Forum in May 1987 when he proposed that he lead a high-level Forum delegation to Fiji to offer assistance to the governor general. Other Forum countries refused to participate, and the whole plan was dropped.

Although Australia has been contributing the most aid to the islands (A$261 million in 1987), a reduction in aid is expected in the future. Australian defense initiatives in the region include upgrading of surveillance systems; deployment of RAAF long-range maritime patrol aircraft; increased Australian Navy ship visits; and an expansion of the Defence Cooperation Program to give the islands as high a priority as the ASEAN nations.[14]

New Zealand

The rupture of the ANZUS Treaty has caused a degree of uncertainty in the Pacific islands. When the New Zealand Labour government came into power in 1984, it adopted a ships-visit policy that banned nuclear-capable ships from entering New Zealand ports. Subsequently the U.S. government refused to compromise its "neither confirm nor deny" policy, whereby U.S. officials will neither confirm nor deny the presence of nuclear weapons on board ships entering foreign ports. This has caused a split between the former allies. The island countries had looked to the alliance for protection from superpower rivalry; now that security no longer exists.

The collapse of the ANZUS Treaty in August 1986 has been called the "most serious blow to any U.S. alliance in 20 years."[15] U.S. Secretary of State George Shultz declared that the United States no longer had defense obligations toward New Zealand. The alliance between New Zealand and the United States is now inoperable, but that between Australia and the United States remains. The Pacific islands are finding they must diversify their foreign policies to cope with these changes. New Zealand has also modified its defense policy, giving priority to the security of its immediate neighbors in the region.

PACIFIC ISLAND FOREIGN POLICIES

Until recently most Pacific island countries had maintained strong strategic and security ties to the Western alliance, especially to the United States, Australia, and New Zealand. Now several island countries are diversifying their foreign policies. As they form their own policies, this sometimes brings them into direct conflict with former colonial masters.

As a result of the changes that have taken place in relationships between the Pacific island nations and the metropolitan powers, island leaders are reviewing previous security arrangements. In addition to the security problems caused by the breaking up of the ANZUS alliance, Soviet penetration, and other tensions, some changes within the islands themselves have contributed to this new outlook.

First, the majority of the island countries have acquired some form of independence or self-government over the past two decades, including Western Samoa, Papua New Guinea, Vanuatu, Solomon Islands, Nauru, Fiji, Tonga, Tuvalu, and Kiribati. These nine countries are fully independent. There are also two self-governing countries in association with New Zealand (Cook Islands and Niue) and three self-governing countries in association with the United States (Republic of the Marshall Islands, Palau, and the Federated States of Micronesia). There are still four colonial powers in the Pacific: the United States (with the territories of American Samoa and Guam and the Commonwealth of the Northern Marianas); France (with its territories of New Caledonia, Wallis and Futuna, and French Polynesia); Chile (with its territory, Easter Island); and New Zealand (with its protectorate, the Tokelau Islands).

With independence a new generation of young leaders has arisen, an educated elite that lacks the prewar, colonial mentality. These leaders are looking at the world and the solutions to their development problems unhindered by colonial ties.

An outstanding example of this is Vanuatu, which under Prime Minister Walter Lini has joined and become an active member of the Nonaligned Movement. Vanuatu and the Kanaks of New Caledonia have also established links with Libya, much to the distress of the metropolitan powers.

Other Pacific island countries do not agree with Vanuatu's establishment of a diplomatic relationship with Libya. For example, the Cook Islands' foreign minister recently protested this action, saying that Vanuatu is flirting with terrorism, "and that kind of thing we don't need in the Pacific."[16] These Libyan ties may create a potential for terrorism, and based on previous experiences elsewhere in the world, countries dealing with Libya may have difficulty in breaking these links. This situation also raises the surveillance costs of the Western powers.

In Fiji the short-lived Labour coalition government had declared its intention to join the Nonaligned Movement before it was ousted by a military coup in May 1987. Since the second coup in September 1987, no clear foreign policy has emerged.

Kiribati has made its mark by establishing an unprecedented fishing agreement with the Soviet Union.

With the breakdown of the ANZUS Treaty the former prime minister of the Cook Islands felt the security of the Cook Islands was in jeopardy and proposed a policy of neutrality. The present Cook Islands government, however, appears to be committed to the earlier policy, which is based on New Zealand's foreign policy.

Papua New Guinea concluded an important Treaty of Friendship with Indonesia in 1986 and is strengthening its relationship with the ASEAN states. The treaty is important to Papua New Guinea because of strained relationships with Indonesia over the Irian Jaya problem.

In contrast to the foreign policy activism of these island states, Tonga has taken the most conservative position of any of the island states, especially in its policies toward the Western alliance. The King of Tonga recently flew to Mururoa Atoll at the invitation of the French to inspect the nuclear test site. He declared afterward that he had observed no detrimental effects on the environment.

A NEW ERA IN THE PACIFIC ISLANDS

This is a dynamic period in Pacific island–Soviet relations. What cannot be ignored or overlooked is that the rift in U.S.–Pacific islands relations will continue to be exploited by the Soviet Union, which has been carefully watching political developments in the region and seeking opportunities.

Several factors contribute to the creation of opportunities for new relationships with the Soviet Union. The first is the increased presence of the Soviets and their new policy toward the region. The second factor is the willingness of Pacific island leaders to negotiate fishing agreements with the Soviets. This willingness often grows out of the islanders' frustration with Western countries who are not supporting them fully in their development goals. Third, the younger, more liberal leaders now emerging do not have the strong colonial ties of the earlier leaders, and their thinking is more expansive. The "Spearhead Group," made up of the Melanesian bloc countries, is charting innovative courses in foreign policy and will continue to put pressure for changes on the other Forum countries.

NOTES

1. Iosefa Maiava, "Australia and the South Pacific: Politics and Defense," *Pacific Perspective* 11, no. 1, 1983.
2. David Hegarty, "International Relations and Security in the South Pacific: A Background Paper." Presented at the Conference on ASEAN and the Pacific Islands, East-West Center, Honolulu, September 1987, 6.
3. Hegarty 1987, 6.
4. Hegarty 1987, 6.
5. Hegarty 1987, 6.
6. E. Rampell, "Soviets Speak on Micronesia," *Pacific 86*, Northern Marianas Islands, March 1986.
7. Hegarty 1987, 6.
8. Hegarty 1987, 6.
9. Hegarty 1987, 6.
10. Robert Keith-Reid, "Tokyo Unveils New Initiatives," *Islands Business*, February 1987.
11. Government of Australia, Department of Defense, "The Defence of Australia," policy information paper, 1987, 6.
12. Government of Australia 1987, 17.
13. Hegarty 1987, 6.
14. Hegarty 1987, 6.
15. *Time*, 17 November 1986.
16. *Cook Islands News*, 11 May 1987.

"Fishing for More than Fish":
Soviet Fisheries Initiatives in the Pacific Islands Region

David J. Doulman

Although the Soviet Union has attempted to strengthen its economic and political ties with Pacific island countries over the past decade, its attempts to achieve this goal have been generally unsuccessful.[1] Nevertheless, in 1984 the Soviet Union increased its efforts to strengthen relations with island countries by proposing fisheries access arrangements for its tuna fleet. As a result of this fisheries initiative, the Soviet Union concluded an access agreement with Kiribati in 1985 and, subsequently, an agreement with Vanuatu in 1987.

To consolidate their position in the Pacific, the Soviets established a Pacific Ocean bureau in the Ministry of Foreign Affairs in 1986.[2] Moreover, General Secretary Mikhail Gorbachev's speech in Vladivostok in July 1986 made it clear that the Soviet Union considers itself part of the Asian-Pacific region. Gorbachev indicated that the Soviet Union would expand ties with Pacific island countries and would consider turning Vladivostok into a major commercial center for the western Pacific.[3] What is clear from these moves is that the Soviet Union is shifting attention toward the Pacific, that it intends to have a higher profile in the Pacific islands region, and that fisheries will be a major focus of attention.

This chapter discusses the background to the Kiribati and Vanuatu agreements, reviews the terms and conditions of access and the reasons for the termination of the Kiribati agreement, outlines responses from other island countries approached by the Soviets, examines Soviet motives for the agreements, and evaluates prospects for long-term fisheries cooperation between the Soviet Union and Pacific island states.

BACKGROUND

The conclusion of the Kiribati-Soviet fishing agreement was directly linked to the collapse of the multilateral fisheries agreement between the American Tunaboat Association (ATA) and three Micronesian countries, Federated States of Micronesia, Kiribati, and Palau. The two-year ATA agreement expired in December 1984, and it was not renewed in 1985 because the ATA refused to pay higher access fee payments. Increased fees would have brought ATA payments into line with payments by other distant-water fishing nations (DWFNs) operating in the region. U.S. industry argued that it could not afford to pay higher access fees. Furthermore, U.S. fishermen knew that they could operate unlicensed throughout the Pacific islands because they had the protection of U.S. fisheries legislation. If U.S. tuna fishermen are apprehended for unlicensed tuna fishing in a coastal state's 200–mile zone, the fishermen are compensated by the U.S. government under the Fishermen's Protective Act.[4]

While domestic economic considerations in Kiribati were primarily responsible for the conclusion of the Soviet agreement, the arrogant and inflexible attitude of U.S. industry toward island countries and the persistent illegal fishing by U.S. vessels also played a part.[5] According to a U.S. Department of State official, the tuna problem caused by the U.S. industry has "cast [the United States] as the bully beating up on the small defenseless countries that had only one thing [tuna] in the world . . . [U.S. tuna] boats had moved from poachers to pirates . . It was a terrible political problem."[6]

Economic necessity, a lucrative offer, and the smooth running of the Kiribati agreement induced Vanuatu to sign a fisheries agreement with the Soviet Union in January 1987. As early as 1984, Vanuatu had indicated an interest in a Soviet agreement, but it opted to reserve its decision on concluding an agreement until the operation of Kiribati's agreement had been observed and assessed.

The origins of the Soviet agreements with Kiribati and Vanuatu were therefore slightly different. In the case of Kiribati, U.S. tuna policy, events surrounding the collapse of the ATA agreement, and the loss of access fee revenue figured significantly in Kiribati's decision to enter into a commercial arrangement with the Soviet Union. Since Vanuatu had no prior fisheries contact with U.S. industry and no recorded cases of illegal fishing by U.S. vessels, it was primarily motivated by the attractive financial package offered. Ideological considerations played little or no part for Kiribati and Vanuatu in their decisions to conclude fisheries agreements with the Soviet Union.

SCOPE AND EXTENT OF AGREEMENTS

Kiribati-Soviet Agreement

The conclusion of the Kiribati-Soviet fisheries agreement happened after several rounds of negotiations that started in Sydney in February 1985 and finished in Manila in August 1985.[7] The agreement was styled after other DWFN access agreements in force in the Pacific islands region. It contained no special or discriminatory provisions and complied with the minimum terms and conditions of fisheries access that member countries of the South Pacific Forum Fisheries Agency have agreed to incorporate in all of their arrangements with DWFNs.

Kiribati concluded the agreement with Sovrybflot, the Soviet fishing agency. A total of sixteen purse-seine and longline vessels and one processing/factory ship were individually specified in the agreement as being eligible for license. As with other DWFN vessels operating in Kiribati's exclusive economic zone (EEZ), the Soviet vessels were required to report as they entered and exited the country's EEZ, to regularly notify their locations within the zone, and to periodically report the quantities of fish harvested.

The one-year agreement came into force on 15 October 1985. Extension of the agreement was to be subject to review and renegotiation. The Soviet fleet did not have port privileges nor was it permitted to fish within Kiribati's territorial waters. These restrictions apply to all DWFN vessels operating within the country's zone; they were not specific to the Soviet fleet. The negotiated access fee for the agreement period was US$1.5 million.

According to U.S. industry sources, the Soviets encountered considerable fishing difficulties in Kiribati waters, and the fleet landed less than 2,000 tons of fish over the agreement period. According to one report, the Soviets harvested 2,300 tons of tuna, which at April 1987 American Samoan prices was valued at US$1.7 million.[8] Tuna caught by the fleet was reportedly sold on the international market through a Soviet joint venture company in Singapore. Most of the tuna was probably sold to Thai canners, with some of the processed product finding its way to the U.S. market, the world's largest canned tuna market.

The poor fishing performance by the Soviet fleet in Kiribati was primarily due to the fleet's lack of familiarity with tropical fishing conditions, though the Soviets maintained that it was due to fishing in unknown waters.[9] Although the Soviets are one of the world's five leading DWFNs, they are poor purse-seine tuna fishermen, particularly in the central and western tropical Pacific Ocean where fishing conditions are significantly different from conditions in other parts of the world.

The Kiribati agreement was a commercial failure for Sovrybflot. Sales of fish harvested by the fleet did not cover the cost of access and other transaction costs associated with finalizing the agreement. This prompted Sovrybflot to try to rationalize fishing operations and to seek a less costly agreement with Kiribati. Soviet negotiators therefore proposed to Kiribati that their fleet be reduced in size by 50 percent and that fees be reduced by a corresponding amount. Kiribati found these revised terms unacceptable and decided against extending the agreement. This led to the formal termination of the agreement on 14 October 1986. However, industry sources believe that Kiribati remains committed to an agreement with the Soviet Union should the Soviets be willing to meet its terms for access.

Although Sovrybflot is required to pursue broader political objectives in the execution of its economic mandate, the company is also under pressure to operate profitably to minimize subsidies to the fishing industry from more efficient sectors of the Soviet Union's economy.[10] Consequently, the proposal to eliminate poorly performing vessels and to reduce access fee payments was a genuine attempt to improve the company's financial performance under the agreement. Nonetheless, it is also recognized that the Soviets pursued the renewal of the agreement less vigorously than might have been expected because Sovrybflot was aware that it was likely to conclude an agreement with Vanuatu. An agreement with Vanuatu would enable Sovrybflot to redeploy its fleet while simultaneously enhancing its profile in the region.

Vanuatu-Soviet Agreement

Vanuatu observed the operation of Kiribati's agreement and was satisfied that an agreement with Sovrybflot would serve the country's financial and fishing interests. The Soviets had complied fully with the terms and conditions of the Kiribati agreement and the impending closure of Vanuatu's tuna base at Palikula due to the withdrawal of its Japanese operator induced the government to agree in principle to a Soviet agreement. Several rounds of negotiations were held in Sydney and Canberra, with agreement being reached in January 1987.

Details of Vanuatu's agreement with Sovrybflot have been less publicized than those of Kiribati's agreement. In comparison, Vanuatu's agreement has not received the same degree of international press coverage. This is attributed principally to two factors. First, Vanuatu's agreement was not the first Soviet agreement in the region, and therefore it was less newsworthy. Second, the October 1986 agreement between the United States and Pacific island countries to conclude a tuna treaty removed the precipitating factor that encouraged the Soviet fisheries penetration in the Pacific islands. The U.S. Department of State was confident that its financially lucrative treaty and other fisheries aid programs would counteract the Soviet gains.

Like Kiribati, Vanuatu concluded a one-year agreement with Sovrybflot. It is understood that the agreement is modeled on the Kiribati agreement and is therefore similar to other DWFN agreements in force in the Pacific islands. Vanuatu's agreement provides fisheries access for eight vessels. However, it is significantly different from the Kiribati agreement in that the agreement gives the Soviet fleet port access. Vessels are permitted to use Vanuatu's ports to transship fish and to take on fuel and provisions. Kiribati's refusal to grant port access to the Soviets was a keenly negotiated issue; but throughout its negotiations with Sovrybflot, Kiribati would not yield on this point.

In return for fishing and port access, the Soviets paid Vanuatu a fee of US$1.5 million. Renewal of the agreement will be subject to review and depend on the terms and conditions offered by Sovrybflot.

Some commentators believe that Vanuatu could have driven a harder bargain with the Soviets and extracted a higher financial return for fisheries and port access. Although deploying fewer vessels in Vanuatu than in Kiribati, the Soviets gained shore access in a more strategically advantageous location yet paid the same fee as it did to Kiribati.

The conclusion of the Soviet agreement was well timed for Vanuatu because of the closure of its longline fishing base in December 1986.[11] The base had been operated by Mitsui since the 1950s. However, Mitsui (a trading company rather than a fishing company) decided, as a matter of corporate policy, to disinvest in primary production worldwide and, as a result, withdrew from Vanuatu. In concluding an agreement with the Soviets, it was perhaps in the minds of Vanuatu officials that the Soviets might reactivate the fishing base, thereby restoring an important industry. Vanuatu's exports of tuna during the 1970s and early 1980s accounted for up to 40 percent of the country's export income. Moreover, domestic purchases by the longline fleet generated substantial commercial activity. The government wanted to minimize the adverse economic impact of the loss of its tuna base, and the Soviet agreement was seen as a possible means of achieving this objective.

Other Soviet Initiatives

Most Pacific island countries were approached by the Soviets in 1984 seeking fisheries access; but apart from Kiribati and Vanuatu, only Fiji and Papua New Guinea indicated an interest. Initially, in 1985 Fiji was critical of Kiribati for concluding its agreement with Sovrybflot; but in 1986 Fiji's prime minister indicated a willingness to license Soviet vessels if "the price is right."

Soviet officials visited Fiji several times during 1986 to discuss trade opportunities, and the possibility of a fisheries agreement was raised.[12] However, a decision by Fiji to license DWFN fleets would have required a change in licensing policy because the country does not license tuna vessels unless they offload their catches at the country's Levuka cannery. Commentators believed that Fiji's interest in concluding an agreement with the Soviets reflected its dissatisfaction with the United States on its posture toward the Pacific island region rather than Fiji's desire to conclude an agreement per se. Furthermore, Fiji was reportedly dissatisfied with the size of its U.S. sugar quota, and its stated interest in a Soviet fisheries agreement was a reaction to the quota.

The Soviets were anxious to conclude an agreement with Fiji because it is the most pro-United States country in the Pacific islands. An agreement with Fiji would have effectively legitimized the Soviet fisheries presence in the region and paved the way for agreements with other island countries. It is a matter of conjecture, but despite statements to the contrary, it seems that Fiji would not have concluded a fisheries agreement with the Soviets even if extremely favorable terms had been offered.

Papua New Guinea and Vanuatu were the only two Pacific island countries that openly supported Kiribati when it concluded its 1985 Soviet agreement. But in 1986 when a Soviet fisheries agreement was seriously debated for the first time in Papua New Guinea (following a series of representations by an Australian company acting on Sovrybflot's behalf), the government was undecided. The minister for primary industry was opposed to an agreement, but more influential ministers favored the development of commercial fisheries ties for financial reasons and as a means of furthering Papua New Guinea's emerging independent political stance. When it became clear in late 1986 that fisheries relations with Japan were likely to be terminated because of Japan's refusal to consider increased fee payments, there were renewed moves in Papua New Guinea to seek a fisheries agreement with the Soviet Union. However, when the Papua New Guinea–Japan agreement was formally terminated in March 1987, preparations for general elections were underway in Papua New

Guinea, and the Soviet initiative was put on hold. If elections had not been called, it is likely that the minister for fisheries and marine resources (who replaced the minister for primary industry following a reorganization of ministries) would have actively pursued a fisheries agreement with the Soviets.

Solomon Islands rejected the 1984 Soviet approach to conclude a fisheries agreement, and successive governments there have maintained a "no-deal" position. Although having extensive and rich tuna fishing grounds and despite being eager to license certain types of DWFN tuna vessels as a means of generating public revenue, Solomon Islands maintains a conservative foreign policy and does not want to take on controversial arrangements with the Soviets.

Similarly, Tuvalu (one of the smallest countries in the Pacific islands region) turned down a Soviet request for a fisheries agreement. The precise reasons for the refusal are not known; but like Solomon Islands, it is believed that Tuvalu did not want to become embroiled in a controversial fisheries agreement. Western Samoa, with a small EEZ and limited tuna resources, also refused to cooperate with the Soviets and to conclude an access agreement. This refusal primarily resulted from Western Samoa's strong pro-Western position.

SOVIET MOTIVES

The motives of the Soviets in the Pacific islands region are mixed. Having been unsuccessful in the region politically and unable to establish a single diplomatic mission, they sought to strengthen economic ties with island countries through the region's principal natural resource—tuna. To a greater or lesser degree, all Pacific island countries have a desire to commercially develop their tuna resources. Aware of this desire, the Soviets seized this issue as a means of trying to enhance economic and political relations.

At the same time, the impact of extended jurisdiction throughout the world has had a profound impact on the Soviet fishing industry.[13] The Soviets are heavily dependent on the EEZs of other countries for the deployment of fleets, and the implementation of coastal state management regimes since the mid-1970s has forced Soviet fleets to start harvesting pelagic fish stocks (including tuna) and deep-water fisheries resources, often on the high seas. As a result of these management measures, the Soviet fleets have been excluded from some coastal zones or have had their catches restricted. Strategic and political considerations aside, changing conditions of access to coastal states' EEZs, where Soviet fleets have traditionally fished, have required the Soviets to seek new fishing grounds to productively deploy fleets. Their fisheries initiatives in the Pacific islands region are part of that ongoing policy to secure fisheries access for displaced fleets.

The Soviets also saw an opportunity to win influence in the region as a result of deteriorating relations between the United States and Pacific island countries. In the period between 1983 and 1986 relations reached an all-time low. This was due to a combination of "benign neglect," the U.S. position on tuna, and the "boorish behavior of U.S. tuna fishermen."[14] To put the United States on the defensive, the Soviets sought to increase their visibility in the region.

The Soviet interest in the "tuna war" between island countries and the United States provoked discord among groups in the United States. The U.S. military blamed the U.S. tuna industry for the loss of U.S. confidence in the region and the growth of widespread anti-U.S. sentiment. The military also claimed that U.S. tuna policy and the attitude of the U.S. industry had given the Soviets a strategic advantage in the Pacific islands. The U.S. military's criticism was persuasive, and the U.S. Department of State took steps to improve the country's image and standing in the region. A U.S. Department of State official summed up the situation: "What the Soviets see here is an almost irresistible target of opportunity to penetrate an area where the U.S. has always been able to operate without impediment."[15]

As a first step toward improving relations, a special U.S. fisheries aid program was announced in 1986, and efforts to conclude a tuna treaty that would protect the jurisdictional rights of island countries were increased. These efforts paid off and led to the signing of a five-year tuna treaty in March 1987 between the United States and Pacific island countries. Without the increased Soviet presence in the region, it is unlikely that the United States would have so keenly sought to conclude a fisheries agreement with island countries nor would the financial package negotiated under the agreement have been so generous.

The Soviets maintained that they were not deterred by the U.S. tuna treaty.[16] They claimed that the treaty would not affect their ability to conclude fisheries agreements with Pacific island countries. Furthermore, the Soviets say that they are not interested in being drawn into competition with the United States for influence or advantage in the region.

DOMESTIC REACTIONS

In Kiribati, the conclusion of the Soviet agreement caused intense political debate, lobbying by the Catholic and Protestant churches, street demonstrations, and the formation of a new political party, the Christian Democratic Party (CDP). Indeed, the agreement remained an issue after its termination and became a major issue in Kiribati's general elections in mid-1987. Undaunted by the CDP's charges of the spreading "red peril," the Kiribati electorate returned the country's president and main proponent of the Soviet agreement to office for a fourth term.[17]

There was political opposition to the Soviet agreement in Vanuatu, but it was not on the same scale as in Kiribati. Two new political parties, the New People's Party and the National Democratic Party, opposed the fisheries deal.[18] The Union of Moderate Parties (UMP), the parliamentary opposition, also opposed the Soviet agreement. The UMP argued that most Vanuatu citizens were opposed to it and predicted that there would be a public campaign against it. This campaign did not develop.

Little public debate was evident in Fiji, Papua New Guinea, Tuvalu, or Western Samoa concerning the proposed Soviet agreements because of popular indifference or because it seemed evident that agreements would not be concluded.

PROSPECTS FOR LONG-TERM COOPERATION

The Soviet Union has clearly indicated that it wants to strengthen political and economic ties with Pacific island countries. However, the Soviet enthusiasm for closer relations is generally not shared by island states. This lack of enthusiasm primarily stems from the conservative foreign policies that island countries have pursued since achieving political independence in the 1960s and 1970s and a preference to align themselves with the interests of traditional allies. Consequently, to gain a firm foothold in the islands region, the Soviets will have to rely on a radicalization of domestic politics in some countries and the adoption of more independent foreign policies.

In concluding fisheries agreements with Kiribati and Vanuatu, the Soviets were able to capitalize on a number of factors of a domestic and international nature. The collapse of the ATA agreement and the loss of license revenue, a desire to reduce the country's dependence on foreign aid and an attempt to lessen the impact of impending aid cuts induced Kiribati to conclude an agreement with the Soviet Union. Similarly, deteriorating economic conditions within Vanuatu and the closure of its tuna base were the motivating factors that led to the conclusion of its agreement with the Soviets. The Soviet Union was also able to take advantage of the strained relations between the United States and Pacific island countries, particularly the buccaneering attitude of the U.S. tuna industry and the failure of the U.S. government to control tuna poaching by the U.S. fleet.

The inroads made by the Soviet Union with its fisheries agreements in the Pacific islands region did not result from an intrinsic desire by Kiribati and Vanuatu to foster closer ties with the Soviets nor from well-conceived Soviet policy. Rather the Soviet Union was "in the right place at the right time," and it was able to offer attractive financial packages in return for fisheries access.

On balance, it seems that the Soviet Union will not be able to establish stable and long-term commercial relations with Pacific island countries. Except for access fees, the Soviets have little to offer island countries. The Soviet Union gives virtually no aid to the region, and the fisheries technology that they have available is dated and generally unsuitable for deployment in the tropical Pacific. Therefore, unless the Soviet Union is prepared to continue its policy of making highly attractive payments for fisheries access, it appears unlikely that it will maintain its current profile in the Pacific islands.

NOTES

"Fishing for More than Fish" is part of a statement made by Admiral Hays, commander in chief of the U.S. Pacific Command, while in Apia, Western Samoa, *Sydney Morning Herald*, 6 April 1987.

The author is grateful to Philip M. Chapman, Sydney, Australia, who provided research assistance for this chapter.

1. The Soviet Union has diplomatic missions in Australia and New Zealand but none in the Pacific islands region. However, the Soviet Union has diplomatic relations with Fiji, Kiribati, Papua New Guinea, Tonga, and Vanuatu.
2. "Russians Push Fleet into South Pacific," *Fishing News International*, October 1986, p. 86.
3. "The Soviets Look South," *Sydney Morning Herald*, 30 October 1986.
4. The existence of this legislation encourages U.S. tuna fishermen to violate the rights of coastal states that claim jurisdiction over tuna resources within their exclusive economic zones. See Jon Van Dyke and Carolyn Nicol, "U.S. Tuna Policy: A Reluctant Acceptance of the International Norm," in David J. Doulman, ed., *Tuna Issues and Perspectives in the Pacific Islands Region* (Honolulu: East-West Center, 1987), 105–32.
5. "Shultz Trip Signals Pacific Concerns," *Honolulu Sunday Star-Bulletin and Advertiser*, 22 June 1986.
6. "U.S. Turns Attention to Long Neglected Islands of the South Pacific, "*Washington Post*, 13 June 1986, A28.
7. For a more detailed analysis of the Kiribati-Soviet fisheries agreement, see David J. Doulman, "The Soviet Union–Kiribati Fishing Agreement," *Pacific Viewpoint* 28, no. 1 (1987): 20–39.
8. "Pictures Tell the Story of Increased Soviet Power," *Pacific Islands Monthly*, April 1987, p. 25.
9. "Soviets Hook a Deal," *Islands Business*, January 1987, pp. 33–34.

10. Vladimir Kaczynski, "The Economics of the Eastern Bloc Ocean Policy," *American Economic Review* 69, no. 2 (1979): 261–65.
11. Vanuatu has also been hard hit economically by the slump in copra prices and in its tourist industry. See "Soviets Hook a Deal," *Islands Business*, January 1987, p. 34. The country is also heavily reliant on aid, primarily from Australia, Britain, New Zealand, France, and the European Economic Community.
12. "Fishing Talks on Agenda for Soviet Mission to Fiji," *Sydney Morning Herald*, 13 September 1986.
13. See Kaczynski. Extended jurisdiction has affected all DWFNs in a similar way. Gulland has estimated that 99 percent of the world's commercial fisheries fall within coastal states' EEZs. See John Gulland, "Developing Countries and the New Law of the Sea," *Oceanus* 22 (1979): 36–42.
14. "Pacific Overtures: Moscow's Moves in the Far East Worry Washington," *Time*, 17 November 1986, pp. 58–60.
15. "Soviets Take Advantage of U.S. Indifference to South Pacific," *Christian Science Monitor*, 4 June 1986, p. 7.
16. "Moscow in Search of Tuna Deals," *Sydney Morning Herald*, 29 October 1986, 13.
17. *Pacific Islands Monthly*, May 1987, p. 25.
18. "Soviets Hook a Deal," *Islands Business*, January 1987, pp. 33–34.

Selected
Bibliography

Albinski, Henry S., and L. Vasey, eds. *Strategic Imperatives and Western Responses in the South and Southwest Pacific*. Honolulu: Pacific Forum, 1986.

Ball, Desmond, ed. *The ANZAC Connection*. Sydney: Allen & Unwin, 1985.

Bialer, Seweryn. *The Soviet Paradox*. New York: Alfred A. Knopf, 1986.

————,and Michael Mandelbaum, eds. *Gorbachev's Russia and American Foreign Policy*. Boulder, Colo.: Westview Press, 1988.

Buszynski, Leszek. *Soviet Foreign Policy and Southeast Asia*. London & Sydney: Croom Helm, 1986.

Caldwell, Dan, ed. *Soviet International Behavior and U.S. Policy Options*. Lexington, Mass. and Toronto: Lexington Books, 1985.

Cassen, Robert, ed. *Soviet Interests in the Third World*. London, Beverly Hills, and New Delhi: Sage Publications, 1985.

Chawla, Sudershan, and R. R. Sardesai. eds. *Changing Patterns of Security and Stability in Asia*. New York: Praeger, 1980.

Cline, Ray S., James Arnold Miller, and Roger E. Kanet. *Asia in Soviet Global Strategy*. Boulder, Colo.: Westview Press, 1987.

Colton, Timothy J. *The Dilemma of Reform in the Soviet Union*. New York: Council on Foreign Relations Books, 1987.

Dibb, Paul. *Soviet Strategy Towards Australia, New Zealand and Oceania*. Canberra: Strategic and Defence Studies Centre, Australian National University, 1984.

————. *The Soviet Union as a Pacific Military Power*. Canberra: Strategic and Defence Studies Centre, Australian National University, 1984.

Ellison, Herbert J., ed. *Japan and the Pacific Quadrille: The Major Powers in East Asia*. Boulder, Colo.: Westview Press, 1987.

Feshbach, Murray, ed. *National Security Issues of the USSR*. Dordrecht: Martinus Nijhoff Publishers, 1987.

Gorbachev, Mikhail. *Perestroika: New Thinking for Our Country and the World*. New York: Harper & Row, 1987.

Han, Sungjoo, ed. *Soviet Policy in Asia: Expansion or Accommodation?* Seoul: Panmun Book Co., 1980.

Harries, Owen, ed. *The Red Orchestra*. Stanford, Calif.: Hoover Institution, 1988.

Hart, Thomas G. *Sino-Soviet Relations: The Prospects for Normalization*. Aldershot, England: Gower, 1987.

Heller, Mikhail, and Alexandr M. Nekrich. *Utopia in Power: The History of the Soviet Union from 1917 to the Present*. New York: Summit Books, 1986.

Hough, Jerry F. *The Struggle for the Third World*. Washington, D.C.: Brookings Institution, 1986.

Kim, Hakjoon. *Korea in Soviet East Asian Policy*. Seoul: Institute of International Peace Studies, 1987.

Kim, Roy, and Hilary Conroy, eds. *New Tides in the Pacific: Pacific Basin Cooperation and the Big Four (Japan, PRC, USA, USSR)*. Westport, Conn.: Greenwood Press, 1987.

Korbonski, Andrzej, and Francis Fukuyama, eds. *The Soviet Union and the Third World. The Last Three Decades*. Ithaca, N. Y.: Cornell University Press for the Rand/UCLA Center for the Study of Soviet International Behavior, 1987.

Laird, Robbin F., ed. *Soviet Foreign Policy*. New York: The Academy of Political Science, 1987.

Low, Alfred D. *The Sino-Soviet Confrontation Since Mao Zedong: Dispute, Détente, or Conflict?* Boulder, Colo.: Social Science Monographs, distributed by Columbia University Press, New York, 1987.

McLane, Charles B. *Soviet Strategies in Southeast Asia: An Exploration of Eastern Policy Under Lenin and Stalin*. Princeton, N. J.: Princeton University Press, 1966.

Mediansky, F. A., and Dianne Court. *The Soviet Union in Southeast Asia*. Canberra: Strategic and Defence Studies Centre, Australian National University, 1984.

Morrison, Charles E., and Pushpa Thambipillai, eds. *Soviet Studies in the Asia-Pacific Region*. Honolulu: East-West Center, 1986.

Nathan, K. S. *Détente and Soviet Policy in Southeast Asia*. Kuala Lumpur: Gateway Publishing House, 1984.

Niiseki, Kinya, and Seweryn Bialer. *The Soviet Union in Transition*. Boulder, Colo.: Westview Press, 1987.

Pike, Douglas. *Vietnam and the Soviet Union*. Boulder, Colo.: Westview Press, 1987.

Rozman, Gilbert. *A Mirror for Socialism: Soviet Criticisms of China*. Princeton, N. J.: Princeton University Press, 1985.

Scalapino, Robert A. *Major Power Relations in Northeast Asia*. Lanham, Md.: University Press of America, 1987.

Segal, Gerald, ed. *The Soviet Union in East Asia: Predicaments of Power*. Boulder, Colo.: Westview Press, 1983.

Solomon, Richard H. *Asian Security in the 1980s*. Cambridge, Mass.: Oelgeschlager, Gunn and Hain, 1982.

Stephan, John J., and V. P. Chichkanov. *Soviet-American Horizons on the Pacific*. Honolulu: University of Hawaii Press, 1986.

Swearingen, Rodger, ed. *Siberia and the Soviet Far East*. Stanford, Calif.: Hoover University Press, 1987.

Thakur, Ramesh, and Carlyle A. Thayer, eds. *The Soviet Union as an Asian Pacific Power*. Boulder, Colo.: Westview Press, 1987.

Turley, William S., ed. *Vietnamese Communism in Comparative Perspective*. Boulder, Colo.: Westview Press, 1980.

————, ed. *Confrontation or Coexistence: The Future of ASEAN-Vietnam Relations*. Bangkok: The Institute of Security and International Studies, Chulalongkorn University, 1985.

Zagoria, Donald S., ed. *Soviet Policy in East Asia*. New Haven, Conn., and London: Yale University Press, 1982.

Contributors

J. SOEDJATI DJIWANDONO has a Ph.D. in international relations from the London School of Economics and Political Science, University of London. He is a member of the board of directors, Centre for Strategic and International Studies (CSIS), Jakarta, and editor of *Analisa*, a monthly publication of the CSIS.

DAVID J. DOULMAN is deputy director of the South Pacific Forum Fisheries Agency in Honiara, Solomon Islands. He was formerly chief fisheries economist in Papua New Guinea and director of the East-West Center's tuna project. He is internationally known for his economic and political commentaries on fisheries development in the Pacific island region.

GRAEME GILL is a senior lecturer in government at the University of Sydney. He is the author of three books and numerous articles on Soviet affairs. His most recent book is *The Rules of the Communist Party of the Soviet Union* (1988).

TSUYOSHI HASEGAWA is professor of Soviet history and politics at the Slavic Research Center of Hokkaido University, Japan. He received his Ph.D. in history from the University of Washington in 1969. His publications include *The February Revolution: Petrograd, 1917* (1981), "Soviets on Nuclear-War-Fighting," *Problems of Communism*, July-August 1986, and other articles both in English and in Japanese.

ROBERT C. HORN is professor of political science at California State University, Northridge, and a consultant to the RAND-UCLA Center for the Study of Soviet International Behavior. He has published extensively on Soviet policy in Southeast and South Asia in various journals and edited collections. His latest monograph is *Alliance Politics Between Comrades: The Dynamics of Soviet-Vietnamese Relations* (1987).

HAKJOON KIM is associate professor at the Seoul National University. He received his Ph.D. from the University of Pittsburgh in 1972. His publications (in both English and Korean) include *Unification Policies of South and North Korea, A Comparative Study* (2d ed. 1986).

STEVEN I. LEVINE, a student of Chinese politics and East Asian international relations, has taught at Columbia, American, and Duke universities. He is the author of *Anvil of Victory: The Communist Revolution in Manchuria, 1945-1948*, and has written extensively on Chinese foreign policy, Sino-American relations, Sino-Soviet relations, and related subjects.

DANIEL C. MATUSZEWSKI is director of Soviet programs at the International Research and Exchanges Board, Princeton, New Jersey. He received his Ph.D. in Russian and Turkic history from the University of Washington in 1972, and is the author of studies on modernization and nationality trends in inner Asia, as well as Soviet international affairs analysis and policy in Asia.

NI XIAOQUAN is a lecturer in strategic policy analysis at the Institute of Soviet and East European Studies, Chinese Academy of Social Sciences, Beijing. He has written on Soviet foreign policy, especially on Soviet-U.S. relations. One of his latest articles is "The Third US-Soviet Summit Meeting and the Prospects for US-Soviet Relations," in the Chinese People's Institute of Foreign Affairs' *Journal* March 1988.

CHANTIMA ONGSURAGZ is assistant professor at the Faculty of Political Science, Thammasat University, Bangkok. He also lectures at various Thai military institutions. His interests cover communism and Soviet affairs.

PAMELA TAKIORA INGRAM PRYOR is the executive director of the Pacific Islands Association. She is interested in the international affairs of the Pacific islands and has contributed to several publications, including *Pacific* magazine.

BILVEER SINGH is presently a lecturer at the Department of Political Science, National University of Singapore. He received his doctorate from the Australian National University, and his research has mainly focused on Soviet foreign policy in the Asia-Pacific region, especially vis-á-vis Southeast Asia.

PUSHPA THAMBIPILLAI is research fellow in international relations at the Resource Systems Institute, East-West Center. Her interests include regional cooperation (ASEAN) and international relations in the Asia-Pacific region. She is the coeditor of *Soviet Studies in the Asia-Pacific Region* (East-West Center, 1986).

CARLYLE A. THAYER is senior lecturer in the Department of Politics, University College, Australian Defence Force Academy. His main interests are in Southeast Asian comparative politics and international relations, especially on contemporary Vietnam.

WILFRIDO V. VILLACORTA is professor of international relations and assistant vice-president for external relations of De La Salle University in Manila, Philippines. He was a member of the 1986 Constitutional Commission. He is presently a trustee of the Philippine Council for Foreign Relations and a fellow of the Academy of ASEAN Law and Jurisprudence.

DALTON A. WEST is currently a senior fellow and director of research (Pacific Basin) for the U.S. Global Strategy Council, Washington, D.C. He lectured at Massey University in New Zealand, 1972-1986, and subsequently became a fellow at the Center for Strategic and International Studies (Washington).

Index